Understanding your past helps you in the present to guide you into your future.

S.J. Cole

Two Years

Stuart J. Cole

authorHOUSE®

AuthorHouse™ UK Ltd.
500 Avebury Boulevard
Central Milton Keynes, MK9 2BE
www.authorhouse.co.uk
Phone: 08001974150

First published by AuthorHouse 10/6/2009

ISBN: 978-1-4343-7120-1 (sc)

Printed in the United States of America
Bloomington, Indiana

This book is printed on acid-free paper.

Another day has started the same way.

A loud bang on some sort of gong at about 6 am.

A roll and a cup of tea for breakfast and about four hours in the yard.

There have been arguments in my cell, which I share with three other inmates, one of whom happen to be gay, which other inmates seem to dislike even more than the murderers here. No fight but quite heated. Most of the prisoners have taken to me but one or two seem to have a problem with me. Anyway, I stay away from them the best I can (strange I should say that because it is lock down and one of the dons' has just passed by my cell to offer me a piece of coconut).

Few more days have passed.

Same ole ritual, but I have started to exercise now. No gym here so it is back to the basics, my water bottles double for dumbbells and the iron bars of the cell gate for whatever I can think of i.e., push ups, sit ups, leg raises, etc. It is March the fourteenth, I know this because an inmate has been bringing me books of prayer in the morning, each with a prayer or verse for the day but I kind of stopped this because one of the books had the date right across the top of the page in bold writing. Date and time at the moment; not interested.

I heard from my son yesterday, funny thing though; I have spent the last six weeks trying to get in touch with him. When as soon as I start a letter to Kayana, I get four lines into the letter, there is a banging on the cell door, letters from my son arrive. I have read the first two lines and the last two lines two days ago and I know all is well, but I keep putting the rest off. It's as if I am waiting to be depressed, so that the letter can cheer me up.

The drink, or the lack of it goes well and I am off the medication...I am beginning to realize just how much I could have achieved if I had not let drink take control.

It's another day and while I peacefully try to study Othello amongst the usual banging of dominoes and arguments over who is going to use the phone next (big brother with one hundred inmates), in comes a group of school children with teachers and a guard. At this time it is the best I have seen the prisoners behave. The children were free to mix with the prisoners without supervision and ask questions of how, and for what reason, they committed their crime. There are no paedophiles in here (unless you count the lad who killed his pregnant girlfriend), but the change in behaviour was such a storm before calm. Although looking back, St Lucia's population is about 180,000 and being the only prison on the island it was more like a family and friends reunion, of course with my exception. I stopped going to the zoo because I thought it unfair to keep animals in cages. I committed a crime so I deserve to be locked up, but I will still never go to a zoo again.

Another day, a little different.

An apparently well known band did a performance for the inmates. It wasn't bad, and for the fist time I saw the female inmates, albeit from behind a fence. I would have thought I would have felt different but I did not really care. I still only have one woman on my mind.

It's funny in different situations. The other three in my cell did not go to the concert but prefer to stay in the cell, although now that the concert is finished, they are totally bemused by the roadies clearing the stage, as they look on through the two inch by four foot slit in the wall of the cell. Except for sleep they have never been so quiet.

3 days since the band has been here.

We were watching TV and a broadcast came on saying "this one is for our friends at Borderlais, thank you for your hospitality, see you again soon". The movie we were watching was "*Escape from Alcatraz*". There was a roar of appreciation but fifteen mins into the movie, "Roll Check!" At first nobody wanted to move but after testing the warden's patience and being threatened with punishment, we returned to our cells.

Another few days pass peacefully.

Although today we have tuc shop (the first I have seen). They sell cigarettes, biscuits and toiletries. It is now pay back time for the ciggs, lots of arguments but it all seems in jest, they are just so happy to be paid, or just to get a piece of one. Today I was also informed of a gang who are planning to hurt, or worse, a fellow inmate who up until now has been quite cold to me (I wonder why?). It's got me on edge a bit because in here you never know when or how. Although people have been giving me pieces of ciggs today and it's been quite okay.

Yet another day.

The guy in my cell, who has been threatened, is now being extra nice and so are the others. Where they used to just turn off the lights when I was reading or writing, now they ask. And where they used to speak Creole they now speak English. I even get extra food now. It is also weird because the other two are not speaking to him, so they try to out do each other by being extra nice to me.

Yesterday I found a small insect in my food, along with a strand of hair. With all this talk about voodoo and black magic I began to think about it a bit more than I probably should have. Of course, I did not eat the food and was happier going to bed hungry. At bedtime while I was reading Roots the lad above me burst out laughing: "English look", and he showed me a few words from a passage from a religious pamphlet. It said: "what a joyful life". I could not help but laugh.

All things during the day: a small fight breaks out over a bread roll. I think Chelsea and Fulham played today. I thought Jamaicans were bad when it came to football. One tackle that may or may not have been a foul, gets disputed over until the next foul. And this takes place at unbearable shouting levels. I swear they make more noise than the crowd itself.

I keep getting people asking me for advice about every thing from leprosy to going about finding work on an oil rig and, of course, the easiest, safest airports for trafficking; it's the English in me I suppose. So, I have a certain position now, call it what you will.

Most amusing thing happened today; A guy got caught in the shower masturbating while the rest of the lads were all turned towards the Kung Fu movie on TV (it and football being the only time the lads are altogether), but one man coming out of his cell spotted him and that was it. Screams and shouts as if it was a fight and then bursts of laughter as the whole block began jeering at him. In the end there was thumbs up and fists against fists in approval with pats on his back as he came out of the shower.

Another day starts.

Been here about 7or 8 weeks, still not sure if J got my letter, I would love to hear from him, Kayana, Nicky and Emilie. I was half watching TV today, the day I promised to post her letter, when an actor said (in answer to question) "my name is Kayana", it is the first time I have heard of anybody else with that name. I am also at a part in 'Roots' where Kunta is naming his child. He was stating the importance of naming your child. I am glad Emilie named her. Boy, I hope she is still there for me when I have finished with this messy part of my life.

As I sit down to write, my mind drifts upon Andy and the good times… Well, I guess I am getting used to prison life. Some days it seems like two years is a long time (when I think about the family after not hearing from them in such along time), other days I can feel the time slipping by.

The American/Lucian whom I talk to quite a lot, asked me if I also had strange dreams (I have woken up twice screaming because of nightmares, to me it would seem like my spirit and others spirits in here are not getting on) because his cell mates and he were. It made me feel better in some ways and perplexed in others. I wish they had a better variety of books. I could look for something under dreams. So much time and so little to do.

A female warden addressed the prisoners this morning about school kids coming in for a visit and we should be on our 'best behaviour'. It bothered me her saying that because the last time they came, they acted different but they behaved. Then I learnt why she said it; the time came for the trip to arrive and there was about 7 or 8 boys along with about 15-20 girls, thirteen or so years old. It was so ridiculously funny watching the inmates change from there usual "I am bad man" attitude to "I am even badder": those who used to walk and dip, dipped lower; those who screwed their faces screwed harder; the shorts came down even further (in a style observed by the younger generation in London today) and shirts off showing their muscles, (which everyone under the age of about 60 has). Hardly had the group got into the centre of the room the inmates started their football racket. All at once but not together, they were shouting that the teachers should let them mingle or they would learn nothing of the day. Anyway after the children got over the initial fright, they all mixed and explored the way we live. After that, back to normal. A fight to end the day about someone who said something to someone else that happened two years ago.

The weekend comes again, same shit different day. The dinner is taking unusually long today and there is a strange silence in the air. Ah! I just realised Chelsea are playing today and apart from the workers, all the inmates are locked up and have to listen to it on their radios. Oh, and I have just finished 'Roots'. I tried to make it last till Tuesday but it was so good I could hardly put it down.

Well, its Tuesday again, (library). I have decided to read the classics. So I went for "Kidnapped" but the librarian thought it too small, so I ended up with "The Tip Toe Boys" ("Who dares wins"); I will let you know. The norm has been taking place and I begin to look at the inmates' actions in a different manner now. It seems that most of the inmates are serving terms of 7-28 years, (I will get back to this). An inmate just wanted to know what I was writing. I started to explain and we got onto the subject of sticking together and trying to make this place more liveable, (he was one of the guys I thought to have an aggressive look) but talking to him (although his expression did not change), he seemed more passive. I even enjoyed talking to him. Now the cell, which was full, has emptied, most of them gone. I think it is because the man I was talking to had been pulled away but they were playing on the fact that one of my cell mates had just lit a spliff. As most human beings do need some kind of routine in their life and a sense of purpose, for example, the inmate who screams and shouts at the ref's decision (more so than the others) maybe wants to be a singer, because as soon as it gets quiet at night he screams out Rod Stuart songs (which nobody objects to).

The dominoes are played consistently through our free time. The banging of the domino is to break it and then the broken pieces are shaped into small balls by rubbing the domino against the concrete which in turn is used for sexual aid of some sort. Check this out: they slice the skin of their penis, blood flowing, and insert the ball (no, we are not in a hospital), wrap it up so the wounds will heal (if they are lucky). The balls move about under the skin to allow the muscles to grow around it or them (some guys have up to nine balls). When all is well, it looks like the man has a serious case of leprosy on his organ. It is not for men to men, but apparently gives the multiple orgasms that they, the women, yearn for.

For those who cannot take the time, they try to escape, which is not all that difficult being as once you are in the rec yard, all you have to do is climb three fifteen foot barbed razor fences, then all you have to deal with is the bush and the snakes. And because St Lucia's population is about 180,000, hiding on the outside is not that easy.

Another day in paradise.

First, the tuc shop. They give you all you order except for the cigarettes, then, they call 'Roll check!' so you have to wait another three hours, which is a long and noisy three hours. I am preparing for an onslaught because I owe quite a few guys.

Funny thing happened to me the other day: a tall slim inmate came into my cell while I was reading and asked me if I was a 'bad man', because (now get this), someone said to him (he told me) I said that I was going to pray for him. So he (the tall man) has been watching me for the last three weeks because he had to check me out. He told me pretty much all of my movements over the last three weeks. It actually gave me quite a chill because there are over one hundred inmates on this block and I did not even know he existed until he walked into my cell, telling me what books I had read, who I had spoken to, and where I sat for dinner. I told him I did not have a clue what he was on about and that I do not really speak to many people in here, I just read my book and write. "I know" he said, "They just want you to be in their gang". So I sat up (in a defensive mode, I am on the top bunk) and asked him what he was going to do if he did not believe me. "Don't worry English" was all he said and walked out. Weird, huh?

Two guys were caught together last night.

Guess what? A guard came to my cell last night and an inmate said to a guard, "I need some weed". "I can see that, I'll see what I can do"... Oh well, no show.

I have been busy with cigarettes. What a palaver. The bad boys I thought would rush me didn't. The few people I do owe cigarettes to are casual and I got to them first, but the people who I owe pieces or a piece to (which is how they do it - oh, by the way you double what you take.) were on me like flies to shit. At one time a few of the guys who I paid my debt to came running to me because they thought I was in trouble. I was in trouble but I said it was okay because "nobody ain't getting nothing until I am ready and it don't make sense, all the noise". But three guys who never gave me anything bugged me for three days: The one foot man, who chain smokes everyone's' butts (you have never seen a man move so fast on crutches when some one lights up, big fella, got shot in the leg by police so he would stop running; I lost my temper with him and he actually congratulated me, as if to say 'it's about time') and the other two, who I shared a cell with when I just came here, and who conspired against me by stealing another mate's skin oil and pointing the finger towards me (which actually caused quite a stir but I came out okay). They came with the lame excuse that one allowed me the space under his bunk on the concrete ground. I got angry with them too, and have not seen them since, except for when they just stand outside their cell, watching.

The post came today. I was thinking it was J, as he is the only one who knows I am here (or so I thought) but the return address was from Sweden, God, I am thinking Emilie must be there with Kayana on holiday. I did not open it for hours; when I finally did, it was from a group called "Prisoners Abroad".

I knew these prisoners must have some talent. I was getting ready for the usual 6.30 lights out, when one of the fellas started shaving different colour soaps, which he moulded into some kind of sphere with little balls attached to it to go beside a photo frame also made of soap.

Well, another day and I have spent a phone card trying to get through to Emilie, J, Kayana, and Nicole but to no avail. That alone is getting to me. I have written three different letters but no reply or though the officer has told me that it could take up to six-seven weeks for a reply. I am not sure how Emilie is going to take this or how I am going to take the way she takes it, but I have a knack for survival, and this time in life I promise to be a better father, given the chance.

Well, this package from "Prisoners Abroad" has been quite helpful already. It contains news letters about other prisoners in different countries, puzzles, and booklets on how to help you cope with your new way of life, etc.

Well, I have been as good as possible but it seems I am still resented by one or two, possibly all three. One of the shelves that I was using has been taken back by the said person who gave it to me and they insist on talking about me in their own language. They definitely suffer from B.B.S (Big Brother Syndrome.)

New day, new prisoners, more fights, same ole same ole. One of the fights, the management showed their true colours. I told an inmate to watch, I knew what to expect.

During the time of writing this, I have finished another book. It's at night I have the most profound thoughts I think, but I cannot remember them when I start to write. Bummer, most of my thoughts are on the kids and Em, things I did and should not have done. Must get in touch.

Another week has passed, same routine. A few scuffles, the biggest of which was a few nights ago; a new prisoner was put into cell 5. During the late of the night, I was woken up to sound of screaming "officer in charge! help! help!" I looked through the cell bars towards cell 5 to see the new inmate being beaten by the other inmates rather badly. *It reminded of me of growing up in Kingston, raising chickens for a living. From time to time I would bring in new chicks and there would be times when all the chicks would turn on one in particular. I never understood why then, I begin to now. I saved one once and we called him "Thumper", after years of friendship, hard times came along and Thumper was Sunday dinner.* A guard went to his aid but was scared to open the cell gates so they just carried on beating him. It was bad. I think it is something to do with him being gay. Another brawl had the head warden involved.

My goods keep going missing (which my cellmates have assured of me it has nothing to do with them. Ha!).

I have nearly finished another book which is based in Portland.

I find myself on a roller coaster of emotions. A smile, a frown, a silent laugh, apprehension and more, can all come within minutes, seconds, from each other. It all depends on the different things surrounding me e.g. the sound of silence (which is very rare in here), the rain fall at night, a word or phrase on TV, a bird singing (also rare), or the constant bickering between inmates, etc. Each sound sends my mind on a collision course with some part of my history: the ups and downs, a place of work, girlfriends, wives, acquaintances, enemies, frightening times, happy times, times of love and times of hate. It's all there now. Maybe if I took the time to see it all then, I would not be here now. But if I did, would I have met or been apart of other beautiful peoples lives? Wow, I wonder if they wish they had never met me. It would be sad if so, but if they look into their children's eyes I do not think they could wish that. Or say such a thing.

Well, it's another 4/5 days that have passed since I have not written because it seems like same ole same ole. The exception is it is Easter now and we had Salt Fish Fritters for dinner. Not much, but a welcome change.

The big thing is: I finally got in touch with my son. He spoke of minor situations, but I, knowing him, feel he is not telling me the full story, because I would worry too much (he is probably right). When I asked him if Emilie was talking to me, he said, "I don't know". This got me worrying and writing and hoping that it has not all gone completely fucked up. Then this morning the phone got put on early and because the other three in my cell work, they get let out earlier than the other inmates, which gave me the opportunity to call him again. He sounded much better and asked if I needed money. I said no, but settled for ten pounds. I wished him a happy Easter and told him to tell the rest of the family. He said he would. He said Emilie had missed my call, after I told him I thought she was in France. Then I asked if she was talking to me and he said yes: at first she thought I was vex ,and on a suicide mission but after she heard my voice she felt better. It is a good state of mind to be in now. I can do some time in my own peace of mind, oblivious to the other blue suits and the pale cream wall that surround me. It is the most medicinal news I think in my life, but I must not go into obsession, for this is one of the reasons I am here. Now to make the circle complete, I must get in contact with Nicole.

Well, roller coaster kicks in again. It's Wednesday evening. I have not written for a few days but not for any other reason than I just thought of giving up. All in one day, I go from the top of life's tree to the bottom. I phoned Emilie and she told me that she and Kayana were doing better without me and was glad I was gone and that I had also done a few thing she did not like: I went into Kayana's money box to get money for a beer, and I left her (Kayana) at home to run to the shop.

I was also told that I could do nothing about her not letting me speak to her. Hearing this, I of course, wanted a drink and to hang up the phone. But I did not want to give Emilie anymore excuses for us not to be in touch. I listened with tears in my eyes with about 80 inmates tuning in. It took less than I thought to get over (two days), because I told myself I was going to get better no matter what, and this was just a trying obstacle.

So, back again to now. Everybody in the cell is pissed off with me because I talked to another inmate about them stealing my stuff. Of course, I should let them just take my goods. I don't think they can remember all of them not talking to me at once before. So it really does not make any difference. Actually, it's quite amusing watching them talk amongst themselves in English, pleading their innocence in English and wondering what, if anything, I am going to do next .

It's the first time I have written in the morning. No one in the cell says good morning (contrast to Jamaica). The workers go to work in the kitchen or the field (yesterday they found and killed a Boa snake). In the usual regularity of the guys in the cell, two of them go about the arduous task of shaving, sweeping and cleaning, and "the spreading of the bed", immaculately as though they were in a hospital or the army. At this time, I start to read a book. The other lad sleeps as long as he can, after staying up all night winging about something or the other. So now let's see what happens today.

After breakfast I watched Jerry and Maurine on the TV but my mind is far away, with the exception of the occasional glance over my shoulder, for obvious reasons.

Why am I here? I had everything and lost it. But for what? I ask myself, "is this part of the torture, or more of the cure?" I am sure I can do the time but what will become of me? The beginning has come. I can feel my mind reversing to what it once was. I have had joy and happiness in my life but did not respect it. Big mistake. Will I get another chance?

I am now amongst inmates who do not seem to be there. In the dinning room area, the rec yard, or the cell, it all seems like a dream where I am the only reality. It could all disappear as if I was on the holo deck of the Enterprise and it would not surprise me one bit. Maybe one day it will. Maybe I will be happy again and hold on to it.

Half an hour till lunch. Tin tuna and rice, not as good as Junior's, but edible none the less.

Bang! One of the officers has just opened the cell to let the workers out. I have to wait another ten minutes or so.

He has just come back to lock me in. At least I get my food before time. I think this guard is waiting for me to be out of the line. For some reason, it does not bother me though, I just read, write and think. Boy do I think. I never thought of how hard it is to try to think rather than to just think, although trying to think usually ends up as thinking (Ah, must remember to draw a picture of the goblet and the woman. The woman reminds me of Vj and the goblet reminds me of a beer, but both have nothing to do with why I am going to draw it). And now, lunch.

Well, I have watched a movie, (Just friends) and slept for an hour. And now, tea, a roll and a cup of chocolate, alas! I think a guard is late for work so I will have to sit here and listen to the noise of the inmates getting louder and louder, so I will just read some more.

Had the roll, one fight broke out, I think because one inmate ratted on another about something. Anyway, no one died. Shower time and "Roll Check!" Everyone back to their cell. One starts on his soaps and the other two will talk for hours, and I will read and think some more and then sleep. Well, that is what a day in my life has come to.

More days have past.

Thoughts come and go. I can remember again why I am here; to escape from life, for a while, to take a break, have a holiday, what better place than St Lucia? Full bed and board for two years for the price of one week. Sure there's the inconvenience of others having to share my room but now I have got used to it. There's the racket that goes on when the TV is on, which is always, but with the movies that are shown you really do not have to hear the sound.

I have acquired a bucket from an English inmate so I can now store my water and wash whenever I want to (freedom!). It can also double as a multi-gym. Amazing. I used to have free access to the "Queen mum sports centre" but only used it occasionally (thanks Jana!), probably because I always had something to do (yeah, right). Now, I have just one bucket and I work out for longer than when I was in the gym. Must sort that out and remember to enjoy the world for what it is.

Someone just entered the cell and wanted to see what I was doing. I showed it to him. I wonder if it is going to be a mistake.

It's Tuesday and I have already read the book for the week. The editions of 3 public eye magazines turn up. I was really looking forward to another book but the library did not turn up. Now, that's a downer. (Never thought I would use those words in that context but, c'est la vie).

It is tuck shop on Thursday; I guess the cigs will have to do.

Things were okay until the day before tuc shop; I was watching a movie. At the same time, one of the guys decided to have an argument about a gay issue (I think). I heard some of the lads shouting, "Salope!" I turned and looked up towards the shower and an inmate had his hand on another inmate's throat and brandishing a razor blade fixed to a short rod of some sort, he held him up against the wall and started to slice him up calmly as he spoke to him (something about some thing he should not do). There was blood pouring everywhere.

The other lad would not even put up his hands in defence. One lad, having a shower at the time, somehow found himself between them, and not wanting to get involved, was trying to get out of the way. With the two circling around him, it took the rest of the lads (who were watching from downstairs but would not get physically involved), shouting at the one who was cut, to "Run!" Otherwise, I have no doubt he would have willingly died today. He more walked than ran around the landing, holding onto his forearm as blood poured from his wrist, spurting up like a little fountain, and flowing from his face and neck while trying to get away from his assailant, who was following him at what looked like a much slower pace but was gaining on him like one of those bad dreams. Wow. I wonder what it felt like from is point of view.

On the other side of the landing he found refuge in a cell which he tried to lock himself into. While all this was happening, the guard on duty has made no attempt to stop it and the other prisoners do not seem to be in a rush to see the end of it. This is not nice... This, is not nice. The officer finally gets the wounded man in a cell and locks him in. And now another inmate who is also gay tries to get to the assailant with a keg full of water, but the guard stops him. The men in black arrive and grab the assailant very unceremoniously and take him out of the block. As he passed me, he glared at me cold. It was the same guy who came into my cell to ask me if I was a bad man. Well, they took him to seg and the other went of in a Bordelais vehicle. What got me the most about the whole scenario was, I just disconnected myself from the whole situation, something I would not do on the outside. I think about how the human mind can change under different circumstances, I am becoming accustomed to prison, I am adapting.

Cleaning the blood took some time but was eventually done by the cleaner inmates very thoroughly. It was an awful sight to see. They used a fire hose to wash down the block and from my cell, you look directly at the stairs from the gate and it looked like -and was- a waterfall of blood. The next day, I hear through the grape vine that the injured party lost the use of *his* arm and had over two hundred stitches.

I had my first smoke on tuc shop day. Not the best idea around a bout of paranoia.

I am thinking what's happening to J, Nicky and Ky. With all this technology in the world today, I feel so out of touch. Prison life is not for me. However, I am here for a reason. I am going to make sure I will not fail myself or my children again.

After a game of mini cricket, it's tin mackerel for lunch again. And so time goes on.

If I were in here for ten, twenty years I would die in here, not seeing the kids again. Not good. I am glad I had a son first I am sure he will be a better dad than me though my failure is not through lack of love but through the lack of turning it into something I now begin to see but did not see then.

Ah ha! Something to do: I am going to write my CV. The numerous hotels and restaurants I have worked in, I have got through word of mouth. I was actually head hunted before the booze overtook and good friends were lost.

Tried to phone J again today. No luck. I am trying to get used to not worrying too much, he is a big young lad, and can take care of the experiences coming his way.

Something happened in the rec yard the other day which got my attention. A show of stupidity and authority: The inmates transport things from one block to another by means of air. Usually the guards pay no attention, but today a mate who should have been on lock up, was caught throwing. All he had to do was wait until the guard had turned his back. But because there was a crowd growing, he had to play tough and of course the guard had to show who the boss is. So the boy threw it. I am sitting alone watching the outcome, voicing my opinion to the guard without talking, or movement of my limbs. The boy turned to the crowd and grinned and said "I don't care". So the guard took him to his cell. When the guard came back out he walked towards me, stopped about 6-7 yards and proceeded to talk to himself in English, as if to say it to himself that he gave the guy four weeks, and the boy laughed. So he gave him six, then repeated it in Kreole, with most of the inmates nodding in approval. I did not let him know what I was thinking. I just let him hang there. I like this game. I have learnt that you can do a lot more damage with silence (or you can achieve more) than you can with threats.

I started to exercise today only to sprain my ankle. It was the first time I got the guts to exercise where the others could see me (in the rec yard). I need to sweat more but I don't look bad for forty four. The time is passing not too slow. I await the embassy, mainly for my glasses, as my eyes, I fear, are getting worse. J's phone is off again. I think I know why. I want to call Emilie but I can't take her tongue when I am in this sensitive mood.

The other day an inmate passed me with a cup of dirt; he said it was for his plants. A few days later, he passed me on the stairs with 5 sucklings in different containers. I asked him what they were. "The tree of life", he said.

Well, I really should wait for my glasses, but writing is a part of my program and I would like to keep it up.

The cell is strange now.

One of the guys in the cell was telling me about something that happened last night but I could not understand a word he was saying. Someone else translated it the next day. A few days ago my free toothpaste and soap went missing. I was told who did it, but it is hard to retaliate, because I don't trust any one in here. And then if I do fight, is it one or all of them? Not worth it for a free soap, but I have my ways. We will see how it works.

Went to the chapel today.

I have told the cell mates about the theft and the atmosphere in the cell changed for the better from last night till this morning. They also put back my soap and tooth paste.

The telephone is not working (again a piss off) and no embassy visit, so I'll read "silence of the lambs".

My writing book is falling apart. Must get another one and put this in my case.

The phone is back in order, and I have spoken to J. He did not send things with the embassy. Little does he know how much this means to me. If sent through the post some of the items may get withheld at the gate. I may not receive my French lessons, which means longer hours of boredom and my goal of learning French put back. And my glasses will take longer to get here. Oh, well...

The kleptomaniac has changed cell for the good of every one. The new cell mate talks a lot but seems okay. But I would still like to leave this cell now. If you have never been locked up with someone who talks to himself obsessively, I do not recommend you try it. Outside the cell has been relatively calm. One or two minor scuffles. And the library did not show up again.

Britain has just signed an agreement with St Lucia to allow inmates to finish their time back in Britain. I do not know when it will be up and running, or if I would apply. As much as I would like to see the family, and get better meals, books, conditions, I am sure I would see a lot of people I know and do not wish to see. And the main reason I do not wish to go back to England yet is that my mind is not as stable as it can be, and besides, I am getting a lovely tan at the moment. I must stick with the program.

Something weird, something nice; I was watching TV today (terrible film) and I started looking at some of the inmates. I was so glad I was not on any mind altering drugs because the prisoners around me, all bar English, looked dead. Literally, walking dead. It was though I was in a horror movie and was surrounded by the living dead. A lot of it has to do with the water. Too much chlorine with the heat combined seems to draw on the natural elements of the body. Black skin, if not oiled after a shower, becomes a pasty grey/ black. Brown skin highlights blotches and blood shot eyes. Personally, I have not seen a proper mirror for three months, so I do not know what I look like, although others say it's a vast improvement from when I first came here.

Nice; I was sitting on a bar in the rec yard with English, looking out through the three fifteen foot high barbed wire fences that surround this place. Across the thick green hills over looking the Atlantic sea towards the horizon (apart from the fence, a lovely view), English spotted a whale, flashing in and out of the water. It was quite some way out, but you could clearly see the blue and white of its body as it went in and out of the water. To be quite honest, I could more feel it than see it. "Oh to be free" I thought, as I navigated and plotted an imaginary line as to where it would come up again. "ROLL CHECK!" "Oh, to be locked up"...

For some reason, an inmate has taken a liking to me. He keeps giving me stuff his mum sends him. They say no one gives anything for nothing in prison. But being as the gay thing here is under raps, I'll play along for now, see where we go...

Another few days have passed and still no embassy. Don't too much care about it anymore. Cricket is on but the noise is too much for me, so I'll just sit on my bunk and read and write.

The tuc shop came, no incident. Some prisoners seem to understand that if they give me when they have I give them when I have. But I make no promises now, as yesterday, I promised a neighbour I would give him a piece of cig when it was quieter, and he woke the whole block in the early hours of the morning to remind me.

The cell is better now that the other one has left, but I am still alone. I really don't mind because when I do talk to them, the conversation always ends up about shooting or some form of violence.

I got one magazine from "Prisoners Abroad" via English, but that will only last a night. Still, got to be thankful. Some nights can be so long in here. For anyone who might read this, think and care about what you do have in life, instead of what you do not have; Because if it gets taken away from you, you will think of why you did not.

A few days ago I heard news that my new cell mate got 37 years. Woe!!! Stop press. In here I could cope with ten years but thirty seven...couldn't do it. No purpose. That would be it for me. It gave me mixed feelings about my time. Two years... not so much a piece of cake, but manageable. And my reason for being here is to eradicate the half of me that does not belong and deep inside of me, I know 2 years seems reasonable for me to achieve this. If I was offered an early release now, I honestly would not take it. Not that I like it here, it's just that I am better off here. For my future depends on me being here, so I may become and be, who I am capable of being.

The sun is treating me well. My friend upstairs said I am looking better. He said I needed the rest from all the stress in my life and I should stop thinking about other peoples' problems. I have not told him my stories, but I like to hear him talk.

Sometimes I wonder if Emilie has found a boyfriend yet. Good for her if she has, but I would really like Kayana to have a full brother or sister. Well, they say nothing is impossible. Time will tell. "Roll check!" Pig for dinner.

The past two days have gone by peacefully, apart from the odd argument at the telephone. It's been only three days since tuc shop, so they are still calm with their cigs.

I have started Creole classes today again; I hope it lasts longer this time. This class was better organised than the last one. It was a welcome change to my daily schedule. Still no library. I told one of the guards and some inmates that I saw a whale, and I was told to seek medication. I was rather disappointed with the guard because he looked quite intelligent and over the time spent here, we could probably have conversed but, alas. I suppose it is also impossible to see a whale in the Thames outside Big Ben and the houses of parliament than in the middle of the Atlantic Ocean, off the coast of St Lucia.

It's night now; It's the first time without any one in the cell calling "lights off!" while I am reading. The usual sound of dominoes and shouting in the background, but the cell is quiet. Then, all of a sudden, a voice shouts out ringing through the whole block, "Praise the Lord, in Jesus name, praise Him, praise the Lord!" The whole prison perimeter was strung up like a sound system in a park and the preacher was preaching. At first the inmates were shouting things like "Fire bun!" and "hypocrites!" above the sound of the microphone and they carried on until the music started. Then the inmates changed their tune and started singing and clapping their hands praising the Lord. And the rain came down. But it went on for good three/four hours. For me, it was a welcome change in the evening schedule. The next day, I asked one of the guys why the abuse. He said "because they have condemned us and they are free!" Selassie is the one they bow down to as the second coming of Christ, they seem to believe, so I go no further.

The library came today while I was at Kweyol class. English picked up some books because he had heard that the embassy was not coming until next week, so it's Kweyol class and a book, not bad for in here.

A strange feeling; coming down the stairs to my cell from class today at Roll Check, when I saw the cells, all the other prisoners were already locked up and I was watching them behind bars. Only I and the two teachers remained out. It was eerie; it was like this was the first time I was going to get locked up in a cell. I don't like that feeling.

I have not been with them all their lives but I really do miss the young ones, each for different reasons. Nicky is turning into a woman now, J's smile and Kayana chasing pigeons, spring through my mind. God I hope I did the right thing. I know I did. I saw the future and changed it in the way. I knew how.

Lunch time; I am in my cell reading. There is a commotion outside; I pay no attention to it. An inmate shouts "new arrivals!" so get up to have a look. All the cells have four inmates, some, more and are over crowded. When I look out I see two big new lads. All is okay. Then, as if for a show, a fight breaks out between two other inmates, so I go back and sit down. A few minutes later, more commotion. The biggest of the two new inmates, who seriously looks like King Kong in all shape and form, is shouting at a woman officer about him not wanting to share a cell with anyone (he was by far the biggest person I have seen in here and easily the most frightening).

You could see and feel the fear in all the other inmates, as they worried about whose cell they were going to put him in. Even one of the so called bad boys came to me after and told me that he was a 'coke' man and they should not put him in here with normal people. He was jumping and raving about what he was going to do to anybody who came near him. To the relief of all, the special squad came and took him away.

So that Tuesday (it's now Friday) was the busiest day since I have been here: the library, and Kong's entertainment, the Kweyol class (if only for half an hour) and finishing with the preaching of the gospel. And I do believe that it is my third anniversary: three months to the day. Woe! I hardly ever remember anniversaries.

Well, the news from the outside is that Bush has warned Americans about coming to St Lucia because of the growing violence. Apparently they are not safe in the hotels or the beaches. I fear it will get worse, if my recollection of Jamaica has anything to do with it, especially with the up coming election. The bad part of that for us is that the prison is already over crowded. There is only one prison on the island. It's tough enough with four in a cell, different moods, length of patience, mental stability and, sexual gender, let alone six.

The weekend is drawing near and the tempers are beginning to flare up again. I was sitting in Abs's cell, talking about nothing in particular (for what ever subject I choose with him, it always ends up with religion). And a fight breaks out between a short pit bull cross Tyson type fella and a large-headed-not-all-there type fella; because one of them, the cleaner, would not hand over some cigs he was given while out cleaning. It looked quite comical actually, because some disinfectant was thrown on the floor and was making the fighters slip, as if they were on ice. After the fight was over, it was found out that the disinfectant was actually concrete cleaner and the bull dog had thrown it in the others face (eyes). Ouch! They took him to the doc to see the extent of the damage. I'll know in the morning. Meanwhile, I have managed to drag English into the Kweyol class, which I have been trying to do since I started. But him being the known pessimist always has a silly excuse not to attend. The Rasta teacher snubbed him for a while because last year he had been telling inmates that the language was useless to him and he would have no need for it. But it passed. I felt like I was in school again, learning something, keeping my brain oiled. While we were learning some words, Teach, turned to me and said "Do you know what "jawi" means, Collins?" "No", I said. "Many of them are in here on it," he said. "Crime" I answered half innocently. "No! To kill!" He said guiltily in a raised voice. The other inmates turned to me and laughed. I now often forget that the majority of these prisoners are murderers, sex offenders and, of course, drug offenders and thieves. But I am usually reminded of that in a split second of a good or bad day.

SATURDAY MORNING 20 MAY 2006, 6.30 AM.

There is a radio on that has been playing all night.

I have decided not to exercise this morning, give my muscles a rest.

I am bored. Can't get up and turn the TV on, or pop out to the shop for a newspaper or to the kitchen to make breakfast, or make love, better still, have me some plain old fashion sex. Nope. The cell door is locked until 8 o'clock for the workers. I will have to wait the extra 30 mins before I get to enjoy my roll, cup of tea and walkabout with the other 90 or so inmates. Then, at about 10 am gates open for the rec yard, so, I thought I would jot down a running weekend at Bordelais; before the cell doors open, the cell mates on the bottom bunk arise to begin their daily routine, which we must see or hear. Starting with the making of the bed, brushing of the teeth, shaving of the head and cleaning of the cell. So I'm up to date. My next entry will be after breakfast. Let's see what happens this weekend, if I make it.

Morning has passed well in terms of violence; noise at the phone as usual, but with a difference. The West Indies are playing cricket and losing to India. 'I cry' has given me a radio and English has given me some batteries, but now there is no reception, so I will wait until an inmate is outside cleaning and ask him to throw an antenna (that I have put together with wire and dead batteries that I acquired) up on the roof.

Dreading it to be pork today, which I will not eat, I was kindly reminded that we get served the snout and ears, and if we are lucky, the tail, the alternative being dumplings and kidney beans. I now remember another reason as to why I did not exercise this morning.

A very quiet lunch (comparatively). Shock, surprise. It *was* dumplings, but they were in some kind of curry soup. It was not terrible. After lunch, I wash the bowl in my cell.

English pops in more often now, to smoke a piece or shoot the breeze, but as soon as he does, three or four others turn up, hoping to get a piece or even a drag from the butt. I give it to them with the understanding that they must leave the cell. We chatted for a while and then I went into the rec yard to look for my whale. No luck, so I decided to take my bucket and have a shower during which, "Roll Check!" cut me short, and voila! I am here in my cell. It's eleven thirty, most people take this opportunity to sleep or play games.

Three forty five, gates close. Gates open again at five. Days like this seem to take longer than the rest and I get this low feeling that I usually get rid of with a nights sleep. Although the old saying "a calm before the storm" crosses my mind. The evening passes quietly and that's another Saturday come and gone.

Sunday I am first up again. This time I decide to exercise for about forty mins (will do bits and pieces through the day).

A corned beef roll has been served and it is noticeably noisier, so I have gone back to bed to read the book.

Finally finished it. So, I listen to the radio for a while. Well, the weekend passed no incident. For the gaps in time I either read or slept. It's 5.45. I look forward to next week (if I can say that):

I have Kweyol, a possible embassy visit, the library and maybe my glasses, and books, and even a letter might turn my week into something nice.

Two days to go. It's getting hot in here. One man, who has been locked in his cell for a couple of days, has been let out. Some of the other prisoners went to his old cell for revenge but the guard then locked up the guilty party, amidst the shouting of who's going to kill who.

No Kweyol today because of the cricket, but at least the embassy is coming. I still fail to see why they give out razors every week especially when temperatures are still running high.

Yeaaah! Forget Friday, its T, G, I, T. Its tuc shop day and I have also heard that the embassy is coming today. I have resumed my morning workout to ensure that I feel good for the best part of the day. If embassy and tuc shop do show up, that will take care of rest of things .

There are new officers working in admin now because of the foul ups. So after a request for my missing phones, I was taken to the admin for more information. Upon reaching there, I was stood in front of three soldier like men. One of them sitting down bluntly told me if he saw me there again with my hair uncombed he would cut it off. He said this pointing to a pair of clippers in another small room. After going through my suitcase for the phones for a second time, I was questioned about days and dates of when certain things had happened. After hand cuffing me and herding me back to my cell, I was told further investigations would be made. That evening, the only guard I talk to on a somewhat personal level, came to my cell to enquire about why I was taken out of the block today (when the special squad come for you, they do not have to give a reason to anyone, they just hand cuff you and take you away). After telling her my story, she told me, with her experience, that I should forget about the phones. I should write home for any numbers I might need and she would personally post them on the outside so that they do not get "lost". That's just great I am in here for a crime and the people who represent the body that put me here are stealing from me. Oh well, c'est la vie...Which reminds me: while I was going through my suitcase, the officer saw a bracelet that Ky gave me for a present. I wanted to bring it back to the cell, but it was considered a possible weapon. Kind of made me think of the razor blades they issued two days ago.

I am beginning to get a bit irritable now. I had not banked on being out of touch with Ky for so long. The time would be easier with a picture, a few scribbled words. Emilie can only guess what this feels like. I have been told that when I leave here, I will be searched and if this diary is found it will be taken away. That would be a bummer. Oh well, shit happens. Anyway, the embassy sent some stuff for us (5 in all from around the prison) and some money. There was one girl, quite chirpy, a London accent. We only get to see the girls on rare occasions.

Word is she is pregnant; she is rather short and blond, gossip's say "An inmate had five mins with her in the area of admin when one of the guards was using the toilet and. Bam! That's all he needed". I see the girls miss sex as much as the guys: I wonder what it is like for the female guards to watch us shower twice a day, because even though there are a lot of scars, the bodies are... Well, let's just say that there is not much to do in here but exercise.

The Rasta man is furious; it would seem 'an informer' wrote to the guards, telling them of a suspected breakout by the lifers, which obviously upset them. They seem a decent trio; I guess circumstances happened to them also.

In my cell, they have been arguing, about one shouting when another one is praying, although I know there is more to it than that.

I have been trying to get writing paper for Nicole for some time now, but to no avail (even though I am not sure what I would write). If I do not write something, she will, I am sure, think the wrong thing.

As we enter the second week, (tuc shop) the tension on the block is rising again.

News from the outside is: someone has shot a former inmate in the head (this guy demanded my shoes on my first day here. He did not get them. He is, or was, a problem guy).

When these guys get together, to play cricket or football or so, it really is quite pleasant. I think a lack of programs is leading to a lot of frustration. I would like to try to set something up, but I need more togetherness and optimism for it to work,

I can read and write kweyol now, but I still do not understand it.

The batteries in the radio are on their last legs, so I have to wait for tuc shop. At night I find myself listening to the young and restless, the news, the countdown to the football world cup, and a movie, all on a TV channel I have found.

The guys in my cell, who are constantly trying to make me their boy, are now making wine in here, which means I could drink for the rest of my time, for free, but I have not even been tempted. That makes me feel good. Now if J sends the tablets, I can kill the cigs.

The hurricane season has officially started, and while I wish for no loss of life, I am hoping to witness nature erupt.

It is depressing now. Most people look forward to the weekend, but in here, it's not nice. Nothing to look forward to, even if it does not come. Everything, except the church on Sundays, stops. It may not seem a lot, but even the anticipation of a letter can eat up a few hours of a day.

I was playing dominoes earlier. For a while, I was away as a teenager in Jamaica, playing in the yard of Aunties' dancehall, over looking the sea. Not inside here, where the continuous noise and arguments make you lose your concentration because you have to be sure it is not aimed at you and coming your way. And then "Roll check!" It's a strange feeling when you learn to block out the time zone. You're in a happier place and time, only to be bought back to reality by two words, people who have taken coke or crack before would refer to it as 'a bad come down.' It's depressing. It is times like this when I start to think of the months ahead, and they look further away. Oh well, as long as I am not a veg when I get out, it would have worked out okay. I bet Emilie will be pregnant. I wish she would have waited.

Tension still high due to lack of cigs. On the block, fights are breaking out for what would have been forgotten in the first week of tuc shop.

I pay my washer a pack of cigs every fortnight and if the meat is good, I pay one cig for an extra piece.

I have decided to stop smoking (not that I really smoked on the outside) but because this is the biggest hassle on the block, I often go into seclusion (on top of my bunk) just to get away, just to have a smoke, in peace, alone.

Another English man is in, he reminds me of cousin junior. He and the other English are getting on, so I will leave them to it.

They (the Special Forces) have raided the cell at six thirty this morning, looking for weapons and drugs etc. They took the wine but there is another batch bubbling already. I can see the difference now to when an alcoholic is sober and then drunk. Most of the people I hung out with were always inebriated, so I did not see the other side. I must have let a lot of people down, me included.

Well, it's that date: 666. I phoned J; got an answer machine, not worried though, try again later.

New man on the block.

It is impossible to smoke even a piece of a cig without the hassle of constant beggars, but that's good.

I am getting fed up with Kweyol class now because I am not learning the meaning of the words, just the grammar and pronunciation, but the teacher keeps coming, so I keep going.

I think about what might have been with Emilie and Ky, but I also know, that the way I was, I would have been no good to anyone.

J's birthday has passed. I interrupted a dinner date and could detect the timing was wrong, but what can I do, I phone when I can, not when I want.

The tuc shop is going to be a day late because of a public holiday three days ago. Tempers are not as bad as I thought they would be and I managed to save a piece of cigg, simply because I did not get the chance to smoke it.

So I lay here reading another book by Wilbur Smith ("A time to die"). It makes me reminisce about how much I have left out my family, in such a long, short period of time, so unintentionally but wrongly. I have tried to make it up to J, which, if not for his acceptance or understanding could not have been done, and little Ky. I have chosen consciously to give up a few years of my life, to heal my diseases' and wounds so I can, in time, be a good father. If only her mother could see this, even if we do not get back together. I hope she does not do anything silly, off the cuff. As for Nicky, I just cannot find the words.

I woke up on Friday morning, to hear that a man has raped a twelve month old baby in England. I go to sleep listening to the, A.B.C. account of the American situation in Bagdad, earthquakes and volcanoes erupting. I wonder to myself, what would I be like if I had no children, or what I would be like if I had stayed with one of them? Which would be hard as they are all from different mothers. As it happens, J and Nicky's mothers chose me. It was I who chose Emilie. It would appear that I am safer in here than the outside world, anyway, food for thought.

Time for my roll and cup of muck.
   Oh, tuc shop day and I don't feel like smoking. Yeahhh!! Twelve o'clock, tuc shop has arrived. I spend the morning in my cell in silent protest because I still have not received any paper or envelopes. But of course no one gives a shit, so, I will try another angle. In the mean time, I will enjoy the festival biscuits, the new batteries and the baby oil I have received. No cigs just yet as we have to wait until the next roll check (two hours) because no smoking in the cells (HA!). They sell us cigarettes, but no lights and if you are found with a light, they take it from you and you can be punished. But for a price, you can get a guard to bring one in from the outside world.
   It seems that the foreigner, the new English lad (he changes his accent all the time, so I'm not sure where he comes from), is fitting in quite well and my feelings towards the prisoners at

the moment is that they all, bar one or two of them, actually deserve or need to be in here, because of the lack of life for them out there. Most of them scorn coming back in one breath and in the next, scream out who they are going to kill when they get out. I think if the government here wish to change attitudes, they should carry out the programs that they report to the press as ' up and running at this time' and teach these lads who wish to change, that life 'is' worth living.

I was thinking today, if I really wanted to get out, I could phone Bro. Once he'd finished with the screaming and the shouting I think he would sort it out. But I know I need longer and it would be such a waste of time done so far.

The World cup has started, there are three matches a day, but we can only watch parts of two, because of roll check (that's another downer). It's been up and down this week, so I listen to it in my cell on my radio, not the same but better than nout. Brazil is playing, yea, Brazil! The noise is the same as if it were a premiership match, but more so, especially when Trinidad played Sweden.

A girl called the radio station last night from Canada, exposing the mistreatment of the prisoners and how she, 'Tamara' had found love in here and how they communicated with each other even though they were blocks apart. Her boyfriend has been on remand for four years without charge (here, unlike England, remand time does not get taken off your sentence if found guilty). It was hot, but made good listening to the delight of the inmates here. My cell mate and I were discussing if we could fall for a woman in here. The answer was decisively no (I personally don't think I could fall for anyone anymore anyway). I have had my chances and they have come and gone now, but I had a good innings, pity, just as I was getting ready to declare, I was bowled out.

Two days later, an embassy visit. An English girl, who I had seen twice before, showed up in another room and came across to where a window separated us. We got talking. To take nothing away from the girl, she is not my type. However, after discussing things with the Embassy (phones, etc), I went back to my cell and strange things were happening inside my head. I actually kept thinking of this girl in flash thoughts, long blond hair, blue eyes, nice smile, a bit on the chubby side but there you go. They were not sexual thoughts, but pleasant ones. Sometimes, no thoughts, her face just popped into my head and it made me smile. The lady on the radio show commented, 'If you can fall in love at Bordelais, you can fall in love anywhere'. At first I disagreed, although I fear I will never fall in love again. I have seen how very easily it can happen, when in the right or wrong circumstances, especially after months or years of being surrounded by men. Heteros' would find a new level of love and appreciation for the opposite sex. I now, at this moment, enjoy the different level of emotion, but I know it will not last.

Well, England played T&T and they lost 2-1 and I have an extremely bad headache.

I have finally written to Nicky. I hope I chose the right words. As for Emilie, I have a gut feeling that it is finally all over. There has been no letter from her in five months but I still need contact with her to find out how my kids are doing.

I was told my release date is one year from today.

I have not written for three days now. It's like I have that giving up feeling, like, 'what's the fucking point'. Emilie has not been in contact, even for the sake of Kayana. She, I suppose has told Mrs Bond, who in turn, wrote me a wonderfully condemning letter about how much she is against drugs and booze and how disappointed she is. I don't think any body gets it. This was done so I could be a better father and live. The state let me down, chain reaction! What I want now is my tablets and a fucking phone. I have an uneasy feeling about my temper at the moment, I really hope nobody in here pisses me off, you know like a blind man's hearing; such is a prisoner's senses. If a person says something or nothing, it's analyzed for sometimes days, because there is nothing else to do. It is (dare I say it), criminal. So now I spend more of my jail time thinking Emilie could do better.

England is through to the K.O phase. No cigs, the prisoners are making it easy for me to stop smoking.

Wednesday, I have written to Mrs Bond after finally getting paper and I hope she understands.

I have kinda given up watching football because the good games coincide with the lock up.

I called J today, he told me he was 'dreaming about pretty girls'. I told him I also dream of pretty girls, but when I wake up and look around, it's not the same.

Something strange; I very rarely have an erection in here, I begin to wonder why. I know of course the main reason: I am surrounded by men. But I still think about women, albeit mostly Emilie. I guess I don't think much about her sexually anymore. I wonder what I or it will be like in bed. I think I will caress girls more and have more appreciation for a woman's body. I thought I did but with all this time to think about it, I guess I did not.

I am quite sad. I still have that giving up feeling.

Its tuc shop; I bought the wrong batteries and the person I bought two packs for does not need them. No problem.

I still feel empty inside, like, nothing, but it has to be worth it. It just has to be. Even a fight at the telephone did not deter me from gazing at the football, even though I was not really paying attention. The constant shouting and arguing about guns and killing; they really are like a bunch of kids in a play ground on a non stop lunch brake. In this respect I do not belong here at all and I still think I deserve a scribble or photo from Kayana, and I hope nobody pushes me while I am in this mood, though to be fair to them, they have left me alone. It would seem they have noticed something is wrong with me and they understand and follow their instincts not to mess with me.

Tempo is getting up in the cell. One of the guys, who thinks he is Mister Big, tries to provoke, making unnecessary noise to wake everyone up. I have tried to stay out of the way of everything in and out of the cell but with the whole block being about the size of a football field, well, you can imagine.

My new neighbour came to me yesterday with a smile on his face. (He is the phantom writer). He showed me five pages of writing paper and told me he was going to write his life story. "It's about all the people I have shot, stabbed and chopped up, blood everywhere but I haven't reach the part where I kill nuff people, it's gonna make millions".

If you like football, don't get caught up in a place like this during a world cup; I am sitting on my bunk listening to England v Uruguay, on a radio with very poor reception. The guy in my cell, who is a worker, has closed the cell gate, which is usually left open by the guards so that I can get a good view of the match. But I'll let it ride, we will see for how long. Otherwise it's dandy.

I have been listening to a Rasta on TV and I would really like to meet him. I am thinking of ordering some of his book recommendations.

I am not bad with the French so far, and get help from across the way.

Still at the French. I am tempted to write Ky in French, but I think I will leave it for a surprise.

If I did this crime for other reasons, I would like to do the time back home. I don't like it here. It's the Kayana part of it. If she (Emilie) is doing this to hurt me, then she has succeeded. I would like to phone, but worry about conflict. I want to ask Junior to talk to her but I feel 'I' have to. I do not want to become more of a problem, but I have to have some contact while I am here. You can't just take a child away completely. I guess you can. It happened to me. And Kayana is as innocent as I was.

I spoke to Kay on the phone. She is in England now, seems to be okay. I still have not heard from Nicky. I don't know what to expect. Maybe I do deserve all this, but I still do not think so. Maybe I have been too kind to the wrong people in my life. Maybe I neglected myself too much; maybe I could have taken the right path instead of the left. Maybe, maybe, maybe. It's just not adding up. Yes, I'm in prison because of cocaine, but does this cancel out all the good I have done in my past years? Maybe it is only good at the time, and now all gone. Maybe this is only bad now and soon all gone. What does one live for? Is money really all that important or have I been trapped in a society, where it is made to be that important? I think the latter. I wonder if I could just go off alone where money would not be the prime in life. I wonder...

Well, here I am again on top of the old bunk. It's pretty nearly a week since I last wrote anything. Things are getting silly in the cell. Two grown men acting like silly children trying to goud us, but they always speak in tongue, so I don't care what they are saying. Although I'm pretty sure one of them stole my packet of cigarettes from my box along with some weed, so I told him to stop washing for me, hence no more ciggs. Then, he purposely left my bucket outside my cell, so now he cannot use my other bucket to wash his clothes. I think he is slowly realizing that the more he fucks with me, the worse off he is. I could just ask for a request to leave, but what the hell? It made me give up smoking.

And England is out as deserved...

I took the flak and went to church this morning. I did not like it, just could not agree with what preach was saying. I am however enjoying my French although I do not know how bad I am. It seems I am in business, but we will see.

I keep having horrible thoughts about how I will behave if Emilie keeps this charade up. God, give me strength.

Good conversation with a guard who used to talk to me about psychology. She's okay.

The news on the BBC sucks. All I hear about is America and Iraq and I have to wait for hours to listen to it.

Well, I have finally had enough of this bull shit in this cell. I woke up three nights ago to find a broom stick (that we use to collect cherries (rolled up lit pieces of tissue) that have fallen short outside the cell door) deliberately broken in half to form two sharp points and put back together, as if it was not broken. It was only because it was the stick that I use for exercise that I found out. I handed it to the guards, upon which followed a very heated argument in the cell. The following night (these things always happen at night when the guards go walk about); all the free desinfectant was removed from the shelves and put to one side of the cell by the guy who thinks his the boss. During the screaming and shouting amongst themselves in Kweyol, I heard one of them say he was going to break my legs if I touch the bottles (they do speak English well). I confronted them to speak English, but they would not, so after another sleepless night, I reported the growing tension. The guard immediately put me in another cell. Credit to him on his swift action. I am only sorry that I have to leave 'I cry' in the cell, but he has assured me that the treatment I was getting was simply because I am English and he will be okay.

So, I am here relaxed in my new cell, number 19, with three men who seem humble like me, so I am more relaxed. Funny, though. Now I have more time to think about how much I have fucked up, if I could turn back the hands of time, but c'est la vie. One year to go. Let's see what happens next.

I finally called Emilie. I had to hear Kayana's voice. It was good and bad, but I am happy that I spoke to her and if this had to happen in her life time, I am glad it is now because I cannot remember when I was four.

"Happy birthday to me". I suppose the new cell was my birthday present.

Breakfast; I saved two eggs and a roll from yesterday. I got a corned beef roll today (strange).

The guys in my cell only smoke weed, so that's good. Still waiting for my pills, but I am much more relaxed.

Another good night's sleep;

Early morning and one of the workers came with a message for me 'anything to wash?' (I have a new washer who wants to wash for me every day and does a better job at the same price, and, makes my bunk. No, no, he is not gay, believe me. Anything to do for something to do is done. He has been locked up since '1979, think about it).

Although my new cell is just upstairs, there is a 'similar difference' as between uptown and downtown. Larger room, less noise and a calmer atmosphere, although I hasten to add the worst attack I have witnessed took place up here.

The foreigner who came in recently is lying so much about ridiculous things. More over, he is trying to borrow one hundred dollars from me for some T&T thing, when he, is supposed to be a millionaire. I even gave the millionaire a phone card. But we do not talk anymore. He has been telling everyone all sorts of stories and getting caught out. Anyway, he is only staying four months.

Meanwhile; I have been staying in my cell, simply reading and writing more. It's funny how quiet a cell can get when you get used to the constant shouting, dominoes, TV, radio. You can sleep during the day with the cell door open, and still be alert. If anyone enters, you adjust the period of time on who enters to how you react. For example, if it's someone you had words with, you wake fully; if it's a cell mate, you remain semiconscious. It's good finding these senses I had lost.

Well, I am learning chess now. I have just beaten the guy who taught me and drew against English, who keeps reminding me his time is nearly up. The playing of chess outside lock up time differs a lot from the way of passing time. With dominoes, inmates surround the players and constantly tell you what you should and should not have done. It's quite irritating. Whereas in chess, I visit another person's cell and we usually play alone. Once again, I am not in prison until... "Roll check!"

Two nights ago; we had the ambulance in again for the same man who was involved in the disinfectant incident. Only this time, he was faking it: on the way to the hospital, he escaped but was found later. He had only three months left, now he has 3years plus loss of remission. As I and a female officer were saying, 'some of these people have nothing on the outside, or it's just plain ole 'stir crazy'.

Finished another book (by Ken Goddard). Well, would you believe this shit! France playing Italy in the world cup final. Bets for ciggs are being taken. A few inmates are from Martinique, a lot of them neutral. More noise than I have ever heard since I have been here. Five mins to go to half time. The score is one all. "Roll check!" The inmates try to stage a sit in, in front of the TV. The guards turn it off and we are on a complete lock down.

Well, world cup is over. Have to find something else to pass the time.

Strange thing: Inside here, the days go by quickly; Wake up at six, roll and tea at 8.30, the shower is on for half an hour, rec yard until 11.45, 'Roll check!' dinner at 12.30, rec yard again until 3 o' clock, 'Roll check!' (Sleep or read). 5 o'clock, a roll and tea. 5.45 shower again, 'Roll check' back to the cell for the night. The weekends and the months seem to take for ever, but tuc shop seems to come quite quickly, even though it's fortnightly.

Two of the three lads in my cell exercise in the morning, which is good for me. They leave respectfully two weeks and three months from now, which leaves me apprehensive about who will take their place. Although you sometimes may have a say in the matter, you don't know their true character until they settle down.

There have been minor scuffles in the past weeks. I tend to stay in my cell, it's much more tranquil and my mind is as relaxed as, I'm sure, it will ever get in here.

Last week, the BBC decided to do a four part program about sleep and dreams, and so I decided to jot down some of my dreams.

As I look up from my bunk, I look through the slit window across the open yard with the barbed fences, towards the green hills. St Lucia, and it's raining, St Lucia. Caribbean prison, I still say 'I needed this,' but I should have got proper help back home, especially if 'England is meant to be the fourth richest country in the world.'

'English' wants to put a tattoo on his skin for some sick reason. They do it here by burning rubber from bands or so into liquid for ink and use the wire inside of a dead battery as a needle. I tried to talk him out of it but he has 'dominoes', so what's a tattoo?

Its Thursday morn just after dawn; (ah, a song).

I have just finished exercising with my trusty buckets and I feel okay. I am beginning to see signs of the middle part of my journey though life. My joints pain me at times during the day (that would be lack of sleeping space). Either side of my stomach muscles, are showing what I think are dead cells (that could be all the reaching I had been doing prior to here) and I am growing grey hair (that must be stress). Oh well, whatever it is, it does not seem that bad and it's not as bad as it looks. Thing is though, now I have to be in a hurry to leave things for my kids, but first I got to get out of here.

In here, every so often, the routine breaks. Sometimes you see it coming, sometimes you don't, but when it's over, it's like a breaking news story; Last evening just before 'Roll Check!' I was on my bunk when I heard a commotion. I know it's a fight, but I grow tired of them, so I relax. Then, I hear the word 'telephone'. Now, I know quite a handful of people seem to think that the phone here is in their living room, but a lot of other inmates including myself do not agree. So I think the time has come. I get up to have a look over the rail and it's a full house. The fight was under the landing, so I drift aside to check it out. It's the head bull and the neighbour (the one who likes lock ups and writing degrading letters). As he told me, he did not want to go to seg until he had done something 'seriously great'. Meagre attempts were made to break it up but no one wanted to get hurt. Then, all of a sudden, the bull rushes to his cell and returns brandishing what looks like a sock, with rocks in it. A few swings at the head, a few punches thrown. Later, they are still fighting on the other side of the block. It was all even to me but then the bull was getting the upper hand. The other lad tripped and then 3 or 4 other inmates jumped in to help the bull (not that he needs it). The other two lifers joined in also. So now all the keepers of the block and some guys looking for points are battering the one man. Somehow, he manages to get back across to the other side of the block and into his cell, but it is locked open and has to hold it shut with his hands. By this time the bull appears with a cricket bat and starts to bang his hands off of the cell bars so he can enter and finish him off. In the meantime, as usual, the guards are at the other end of the block as if nothing is happening. 'Roll check!' It took a few minutes extra but amongst all the shouting we all returned to our cells. Then, the reports start; apparently there was a commotion at the phone booth while Kali was passing by, so he grabbed the phone and smashed it against the wall. The fighting started outside. Bull was getting the better, so Kali ran inside to his cell for a weapon which he concealed in his shirt. He attacked again and when he went down, people saw the sharp tool (foosh) and joined in. Now, apparently he has problems on all of the blocks so there will be danger where ever he goes. He has beaten up three other prisoners on this block and cannot go back to his home town, where he is wanted. He happens to be prisons 'most hated inmate' (I personally thought he was all right). Through the night stories go on; what happened, what's happening, and what's going to happen. Through the night he was shouting apologies to the head bull but the response was, 'It's not finished yet!' Nobody doubts the 'Head Bull'.

My thoughts were interrupted by the 'Bull' at 7 o'clock this morning, at my cell gate, explaining to me (whilst showing me what I thought was a carving knife but turned out to be a one foot long, sharpened piece of steel iron), that 'it was not finished yet'. Then he walks away mumbling something in patois.

After breakfast (I have mine in my cell now), I hear some commotion. 'Bull' is working, serving food. He has secured a bat. Bang! Over the head. Bang! Again and again. Blood! It's all over the floor, blood, pouring from his head. I go back to my cell, 'he had it coming' say all 'he has beaten up weak people for being weak.' Time to exercise.

Morning again;

I dreamt of cowboys. Yesterday's fight is the Topic of the day. I'm not with it. Early night.

I am very bored and tired of this, but it's still not time. I can't help to wonder 'when' or 'if' I have to show what I 'can' or 'cannot' do. Not too much time to be tired now. The atmosphere changes in a split second in here. Earlier on, someone came up behind me and pushed his finger in my waist. He laughed and said, he was "joking". I told him not to do it again because 'somebody might get hurt'. He said "Okay". What a waste of life for some people in here.

They really should make it easier to get help in England.

I missed school yesterday, sick, back today. The French is kicking in slowly. I still wait for my letter or pills.

If people really knew what it is like; as I sit down on my bunk and reflect the day, looking out of this slit window from the bunk in my cell. I can't see any stars, because of the perimeter lights. I wonder what the crime rate would be like if this was the standard punishment in England, and people really knew what 'this' actually feels like. (Memo to self must look at stars with or without someone, preferably with).

One of the lads in a so called 'gang' had disappeared for a few days. I personally did not notice him gone and when he returned, I thought he was a new inmate. I had seen him walking around rather subdued, with plaster covering half of his face, but it was not until he passed me, going to play football, that I recognised it was him. Some of the lads got fed up with him acting 'bad' because of his gang and decided to teach him a lesson. There are only three untouchables in here and they are doing life. Show the unwritten law. 'Respect' if not, you end up like Kali. I heard through the grape vine there was a reception in the other block for him. I'm not sure how bad, but he is in seg now. There is no punishment for lifers in this prison. I don't see them taking advantage of this but if they slip up and a new guard gives them a warning, another guard may shout 'what are you going to do with him', smiles all around and it's forgotten about. It feels good to have them on my side. One thing with these guys, they don't have to pretend to 'get on' with you or deceive you. In this manner, they are sincere. Time to play dominoes. Bonne nuit.

Fresh morning:

It would be so easy not to try and contact Emilie, if not for Kayana. It's hard to use the phone in here and my letters go unanswered, but I can't have Kayana think I just disappeared and I have no way of knowing what her mother has told her. If she thinks keeping her out of my life for a year and a half is bad, she should feel what happens after a life time. It's more than likely the real reason why I am here.

Another few days pass.

It seems there are no ciggs on the unit. I have not smoked for two days and have exercised more intensely.

I keep being indecisive about a once a month phone call to Kayana. I think now, I should be able to call her when I can, if she is available. Nicole I must call, even if I am not sure what to say. What ever she thinks of me, somewhere inside, she will know I made an effort (I know... if you can call it that).

I broke one of my rules yesterday; I played dominoes with one of the guards. It was alright, I got to beat and mock them outrageously (if you have ever seen me winning in a game you will understand), still with keeping my distance though.

Today I thought they added a thick slice of cheese to our diet, but later realised that our Monday egg had been replaced by it.

I missed chapel on Wednesday. The pastor asked for me, so I will go this week.

It's a pity; I have had to cancel my dream writing because of the lack of paper, I will have to get a book somehow.

No tuc shop Thursday because of a holiday on Monday.

I phoned J, he is working. Good. He said he phoned Nicole and that she received the letter and Kayana was okay. He said Emilie has written a three pages letter for me. I want it to get here but I don't want to read it. I will defiantly wait for the ciggs before I do. Well, all the kids are fine, I'm fine. It's one of those days that I don't mind being locked up. I think when I get home I will have a room for myself alone.

The head warden (kindly, I think,) enquired how I and my family were doing and complimented me on my 'looking good'. I thanked him saying that "The establishment is working wonders". As I was leaving, I heard him telling other inmates, that I was a 'good prisoner' and that he has a lot of 'time' for people like me. Interesting: oh, who to trust and to walk home. Lucians?

Well, a few more days have passed and the coming week represents the end of another month. As soon as the phone is free, I can phone Ky. Strange, now it's here, it seems to have flown passed. 'I no tired' I keep hearing her say in my head at different times of the day or night, and I smile, it's when I miss her the most and of course the memories of her running after pigeons.

The Lord works in mysterious ways; one of the lads who were messing with me in the other cell has had his head busted. For him, I hope he has learnt his lesson.

Well, everyone is awake now and although it has been going on for some time I have only really just heard the noise. So breakfast will be served soon. I was hoping for a fry up but....

Tuesday morn.

I am seeing what English said I would see; prisoners are returning a few weeks after being set free. It makes me realize how much of my life I have wasted and how sad their life must be, to want to live here after tasting the water. Upon their return they are put in cell five, which now I know is the 'Fresh Cell'. First entrance, you get treated like a door mat but nothing physical. Re-offenders get beaten up pretty bad as a lesson. All is forgotten soon but to this once again the guards turn a blind eye. It's the prisoners' law.

I have now begun to read the bible, the gospel at present and I go to meetings on Mondays. It's intriguing and I will keep going.

At the moment I am in a mood of resignation for this place. If you try to occupy your mind with things that challenge you, you feel (or at least I do) that time here is not being wasted. Yes, I realize what I could be doing with life out there and I pray that I will not mess up a second chance, by making use of what I have (which for the first few months I thought was nothing). I am now better at chess and draughts, which helps the concentration. I read whatever I can find. I even found myself reading four pages of adds from a South African magazine that someone lent me. I first scorned it thinking, 'why on earth would I be reading this?' until boredom kicked in and I found them quite, er..., I don't know, but I read them and the reading has been good. These pages that I write, hopefully, I will be able to leave with them, they speak for themselves.

I am not at all sure about the Bible yet. And of course, there is exercising. Actually, even though I remember why I am here, I feel (at the moment that is) that this is like a recreational time in my life, for recharging and reorganising. A time to sit back and check it out, without the interrupting stress of the outside world. Oh yes, I can feel myself becoming ready for the outside world again, but it's not time yet. A seed has been planted, that now needs to grow, before being transplanted.

In a few days time, a cell mate will leave. I still wonder about his replacement, but now, they meet me here. It's my turn to make the rules (another unwritten law, if you can handle the job).

I am still apprehensive about Emilie's letter, every time I think about her I get butterflies, jeez I really do care about this girl (careful guys, watching a woman give birth to your child sure can do things to you). I wonder 'Is it better to have loved and lost than to never have loved at all?'... 'Yeah.' It is better. Even if it's just to know of all the crazy things you say and do but did not think you were capable of. And of course the feeling inside that hits you when you realise that you miss him or her. It's like a sudden come down, a bummer.

Thursday night, like most nights, consist of draughts and radio (which has been fixed by some talented inmate upstairs).

'English' quit his job through pressure (he was serving drinks in the servry).

I phoned J today. I also phoned Kay. Bug in stomach. Cannot get through to Emilie and Ky.

02.08.06, Saturday Night.

Things in the cell were at their quietest. A cell mate leaves tomorrow and instead of rejoicing for him, it was more like, 'mourning'. It was quite a lull...So now the cell has a free bunk and it appears that the boss will not just put anyone in here and that's good.

Pen ran out again. I had to wait for a few days to borrow one 'Tall Man' and a new comer, ('I cry's' friend) had a fight at the phone. Then, the phone was broken for a while so I could not talk to Kayana. I called a while ago but she was with her Grand'Mere. I spoke to Emilie but it did not feel good. No doubt the one-sided story has gone out again. I have said to say hello to her parents. I would like to explain my side (or maybe I should get to understand I don't have a side). And although I think they are wonderful people, maybe this is too much. I wonder how everyone would have felt, or said about me if I just carried on the way I was, and died early. Maybe; 'he could have found another way' or 'we should not have given up', Ha! Maybe some would even say 'he could have locked himself away for a while, it would have been better' I don't know what to do. I guess it really is over but I still have the chance to see Kayana grow up. She is four years old. I can remember as far back as five properly. Do not all humans do things that are considered wrong? Do we all suffer like this? I read about Oprah and King in the 'Voice'. (Something to do with their supposed gay relationship). It's no one's business, what her relationship with her is. I always thought Oprah was happily married (she maybe, I don't know) but if something went wrong, does it have to be the end of everything that was beautiful (if it was). My biggest problem was alcohol (just like Mel Gibson at the moment). What I did, I did to rid myself of the problem, after seeking help everywhere else. Seems to me, people who used to know me, would prefer me to be in the gutter, well, I hate to disappoint you lot, but, 'I ain't finished yet'.

I guess I will leave the phone calls. It's too depressing and being depressed in here brings a whole new meaning to the word. I can understand the high rates of suicide in prisons and I would bet most of them are because of outside influences and not inside. It's night time, the cell is locked and Sketa Davis plays on the radio 'I had something special'. Now ain't that a bitch? And it's in the other cell, so I cannot turn it off, maybe you get my drift about depression now. Good. Depressing music, no ciggs, pork yesterday, (which means I did not eat) I'm locked up, the phone call was lousy. And I can get a hold of a gallon bottle of prison booze, guaranteed to perk me up or put me in a coma, either way, forget life for a while; and I refuse it with no effort. So I guess I am getting better, but at what price. I don't think I shall ever be completely happy in my life now, but I will still be around to help my kids in anyway I can ... 'Roll check!'

FRIDAY;

It's been a few days since I have not written, simply because I could not find a pen that worked. Pens are not on the tuc shop list.

Well, we have a newcomer in the cell, and so, we are back to four. He is Chi Chi, from Venezuela. He was next door, but their where five in the cell and he is of our like (out of trouble, no friction). So we will have to get used to his habits and he, ours. Just like the 'Taxi man' in the cell who flosses his teeth for 15 minutes and hair tweaser plucks. He would give any woman a run for their money in the bathroom.

The phone has been free. But no ciggs, in case the call upsets me. That's bad, I know, but when you have bad feelings in here, you don't just 'see a friend' or 'go for a walk in the park' by yourself. If you can take the noise, and hassle, you can mix with everyone, but if you are like me and prefer some solitude, then it's difficult, and that, becomes frustrating, so although it's only short term, it is, sometimes, all you need to get into another frame of mind.

I have seen guys in here, who are addicted to cigarettes, but when they have none and have to wait for tuc shop, they get by. If it were alcohol, they would not, so my conclusion is; although death from cancer maybe worse than that of alcohol, I think alcohol is physically harder to stop, but, I think I did it. So congratulations to me.

Six months now.

I have still stuck to my program, apart from the Kweyol (which the teacher will start when he feels like). The French is comming on, but I lack conversation with another. It would be nice if someone who spoke french shared the cell.

You know what? I did not have a bad build. But now, I understand the term; 'prison cell body'. If everyone had to do a year in this place, there would not be so many gyms on the outside. The improvisation is good and the bodies in here, on average, out do the gym users. I have not got the most muscular body, but I hold my own in the shower, and if anyone thinks it's a rumour, forget it. Some of these guys are like tripods and you don't have to look (I am still hundred % hetero) but you can't, not see them.

The fighting has chilled. I am now going with some inner self stuff, see how that works, see if I can find something deep and meaningful about me. Actually, being here in prison, in this world, it has to be more than just a string of mishaps, tragedies and coincidence, yeah, what is, the meaning of life? It's a pity that's not original. I wonder what it would be like, to meet a real Buddhist monk, and live in their life for a while (memo to self, challenge).

I still hope I have not paid too much a price being here, but to be honest, I still think it is worth it.

Dinner was dinner. I am in my cell alone at the moment. Everyone is downstairs, in a mob, for the tuc shop, but I am broke. No problem. I have quite a few guys that give me cigarettes, which is good, and another up is that they can all see I did not shop, so their is nothing to beg. It's a good day, not getting paid this time.

Weekend comes to a close. First time for a complete lockdown for me (all day). The staff are having a family day, food, booze, music, a fashion show ect, and so to keep us out of harms way, we spend the day in our cells. It was not so bad, we have a few games. Even so, I slept a while and dreamt well. The women of the families pass by our block and get the obvious wolf whistles. For this, we do not get let out for tea.

SUNDAY 03-08.

Just had a cheese roll for breakfast, and caught myself with my eyes closed, mulling over it, as though it were an advert. Shocking. Anyway it's been along time since I have had one.

I guess I have been at my lowest since my arrival. With no letters from Nicole or Emilie, no arrival of vitamins from J, no embassy visit. And my radio batteries are low. It's taking its toll. The other day, the Indian (my x washer) from the cell I was in, entered this cell, to talk to my cell mate. I explained very coolly (after he left) to my cell mate, that if he has business with him, he should take care of it outside of the cell, and if he (the Indian) sets foot in this cell again, I would beat him up badly. I have been here for six months. I have put up with all of his shit and more when I was in his cell. I had this feeling that I am not really accustomed to, I think it's called rage and I know I would have messed him up, but life has been good to me and as luck would have it, my cell mate understands my rules.

I called Junior. We had a long chat. He told me, 'Jamaica knows' and want to know if, 'everything is okay'. Not counting Mrs Ivy, I didn't think they really cared.

I received a letter and pictures of Ky from Emilie, telling me about Kayana and how they had been to the Caribbean, and about school etc, and that we would never get back together again. Pity, the real me does not deserve this, but the sick me did not deserve her in the first place. The feeling I have at this time is also new, I am really sorry, and I do love her. We have a beautiful child (who looks just like her sister) together, and we have had some good times, but I was letting her down in the end. So I kind of feel happy for her to get away from me, and relieved that I won't be the blame of screwing up someone else's life. Thing about that is, when I am better (and I am getting there), when I leave here, how will I feel and behave then? Time will tell.

Meanwhile, outside of my head, we have had some new arrivals, most noticeable, a little white guy from Dublin. He has left his cell just once, and that was for a shower. What a palaver, as soon as he came on the block, shouting came from every cell; 'put him in here!' Poor lad maybe thought he was going to get raped. Little did he know they wanted everything but, his arse. As luck would have it for some people, they put him in the same cell as our friend the liar. The warden has had to threaten the guys to leave him alone. I only got in a quick, quiet 'are you okay.' He looked shaken, not stirred, so I leave it to the other English on the committee to welcome him. Hell! I just promoted myself to mayor, I like that.

The phone is not working again, and although I have finally got the code for Ireland I have no card. Priority: next week, phone Nicky. Well, I feel better now. Back to normal, back to writing, and back to french. I wonder what's around the next bend on this ride.

TUE. 15TH

The letter I have received from Emilie has been having strange effects on me. I wrote a reply that I was happy with, and then decided to read it, which I never do. (If I did, I recon I would still be on the first letter I ever wrote). I found mistakes that would suggest my thinking was not all there. e.g. first sentence ' I got received your letter letter', so, I decided to rewrite, but with the strange mood I am in now (I think, because I still do not want to lose her, I also don't want anyone I begged for), it would not be becoming of me, and I would never be allowed to be myself again.

I spent all day on my bunk, hardly moving, except for picking up and putting down the book I was reading. I did not even have dinner, I just lay there. You know, most of my thoughts were about what I hated about other guys in the cell, who are not really all that bad, it's just that, when you want to be alone and can't, it's their idiosyncrasies that are torture:

the pluck, pluck, bloody plucking noise of dental floss after every meal is incessant (guys make a silent one, it will sell, trust me), the brushing of the teeth, 15 minute's a day 3 times a day. I'm all for hygiene but 15mins 3times a day! At a time when the cell is locked up, come on. When all is finally quiet (a rare thing in here), that humming over the ear phones. You know how it drives you crazy on public transport? Unless the culprit is 'Tyress' (the coca cola add). Imagine being locked up with it, and you can't tell a man to stop, because these are his rights, and for all I know, I could be getting on his nerves just by staying in the cell all day reading and writing. It becomes a lesson of tolerance, hence another new bloody feeling intensified by the..? Of it all.

A guard came into my cell today to ask my name. He wrote it down, I enquired what it was about 'don't worry about it, trust me'. This is a place where I don't trust anybody, not even the Embassy at present.

AUG 17TH.

'Balbo' has this knack of digging himself holes and stepping in, just to see if he can get out and look at the damage he has caused to land that needed no hole in the first place. The hole is filled, but the ground upon which it lay, will never be the same again. I hope I will never be the same again after this experience. I also hope I will not be stripped of the qualities in me that made me a vibrant, energetic, lovable and caring human being. Because in here, all of those feelings are either disguised or diminished.

I have written a reply to Emilie's letter 3 times but I don't know whether to send it or give it to English when he leaves on the 18 sept.

I have lent my french book to 'Icry' but I think about it a lot, because I believe the other lot in the cell (my former cell) will try anything to get to me. I trust 'Icry', let's see what happens.

I have just come back from watching a movie. Here's some advice if you have a love on the outside while you are in prison. Don't watch 'Notting Hill.'

The usual start to the day;

I have started to go into the rec yard more now, and every so often, I see new faces. One of the new guys was warned by my cell mate, to 'have a bath.' He grumbled and walked away. Later we heard thumping and screaming coming from his cell, the reason for this: he has been here for about two weeks. He uses the toilet, maybe three four times a day and the boys in the cell had enough of the smell. He was warned.

The next day seemed normal but during "Roll check!" while we were relaxing, 'you disrespect my mother!?' So, as usual, we go to the cell door. To see the head warden spraying an inmate with his pepper spray, kicking and punching him. The inmate cannot retaliate, for fear of 'the injection'. The next day, after a lot of mumbling and half hearted voiced condemnments of the wardens actions, (with the exception of 'Blaze' who once starts, is like a town crier, and does not stop.) I have returned to my cell, the young Irish man tells me he witnessed the same inmate getting beaten up by another guard, and it really scared him. He is about five foot six, slim frame and the only white man on the block. I can understand him being 'terrified' as he told me he was. I tried to put him at ease, by letting him know that it's not all that bad, 'just don't go out of your way to make trouble'. Anyway he phoned home and his parents are paying the fine and flying over for his release, he leaves tomorrow. I wonder if he knew his parents would do that, would he have got into trouble in the first place? I fear, some kids do not know how much their parents would go through or do for them, because maybe, the way they perceived being brought up was not how it was 'supposed' to be i.e. getting punished for what the child perceived to be acceptable behaviour, or not being able to live up to the smiths, or a basic lack of communication.

Which is only found again when the child finds him or her self knee deep, because then, it's time for the safety net to pop up; a telephone call. Hands up to all you guys an gals without safety nets. Stay strong and do your kids a favour: stick by them. You know what it's like.

One of my cell mates shocked me the other night; while we were playing dominoes, Chi Chi declared that he had ' had sex' with a donkey before. The other guys in the cell thought it was hilarious. What, with him describing it and me trying to ascertain whether he was joking or not I guess it must have looked funny but as the night went on it became increasingly clear it was true (he speaks little English). I began to think how easy to sway the human mind into behaving morally wrong. I grew up in Jamaica and the morale code is high, you do hear of such things happening but it is by no means funny and if you decided to tell the town you would more than likely receive a severe beating. In here, however, the cell mates saw it as a joke and wanted more descriptive images of the process. What it would seem to me, if you told a select group of people (kids) who have been brought up 'properly' act out this manner in this way it is quite likely that the disgusting aspect of the scenario begins to cease, being exchanged for or to a more experimental point of view. When saying this, as long as there are some sensible adults around to bring back and enforce the correct morals, I think the Mary Whitehouse's of today are still going a bit too far, but still.

Now it's Monday. 21st; and I got my creatin although I missed my vitamins, to me this is more important. Sometimes I think my son is hiding something from me because he forgets things like my slippers or vitamins. Sometimes I think he is doing this because... no! I was not always there for him, but on my good days, I think it's just hereditary. Program starts today. I have decided to give up smoking but it seems to have come from within rather than something I just decided (another weird feeling I do not recall having, it's hard to describe but I just don't want to smoke) I have however put a few in my box just in case.

'I cry' is having problems in the cell with the same assholes I was, I think something will happen soon.

THURS.24TH;

'I cry's' cigarettes have gone missing from inside the office, he is not happy.

It's the third day of taking creatin, and no cigarettes. It's a big difference (memo to self: maybe I should get on an add like the lion bar). I can see and feel the change, more energy and strength and I feel generally good all over. Problem is, I felt aggressive for about ten minutes yesterday morning and I had to go to my cell to 'get over it.' I hope once again, when this feeling comes about, nobody pushes me.

Last night 'Taxi' and I had an argument over a game of dominoes. I think he was just letting off steam. A few things I do were niggling him and he used the dominoes (not the socks, Oprah) to release it from his system. Anyway, by the end of the night we were talking again, not that I really cared.

The so called 'Jamaican', has been filling up Irish with extraordinary amounts of bullshit. He has told him that he will pay his fine of eighty thousand dollars. The Irish man believes him.

AUG 28TH.

First phase of creatin is over, and I feel fine. I have much more energy, and have asked my English mate to send me over some more. Not that J will not, but I think he is too busy and probably has enough on his plate. And English, well... I know he wants to do me a favour. He also knows exactly what it's like in here, waiting for letters and packages from abroad and all the rest of it. I reckon it will be one of the first things he does. Must check up on him; see if he keeps his promises to himself.

Meanwhile, the so-called Jamaican (amongst the lies that he tells to anyone who happens to be around) is building the biggest hotel in St. Vincent. He has two condos in Barbados, two containers of high powered bikes on the docks here, waiting for business. He has a bike shop on Kingsway, in London (and get this, he needs a map to show me where Kingsway is). He is in here for money laundering 5000 U.S dollars and he has 20 false passports. He is also transporting one ton of coke to the U.K (which, according to him, he has done already). He has now told me that he has given 40K of coke to a man in the unit next to us. I know this man, and it's not true. He has given a guard 200 U.S dollars to smuggle in weed, and the guard, who basically went to school with, or knew these inmates from childhood, did not have a clue about it. He also apparently spent 5 years on 'Ryckers Island' and knows the head warden in here, from over there (not true, I spoke to the warden). Then, he is arranging $22000e.c, to pay the Irish man's fine and get him out. He also told 'English', that he has sent the two girls they met in the visiting room to America, and all he wants is the plane fare.

31ST

𝒮𝒾𝓃𝒸𝑒 𝓉𝒶𝓀𝒾𝓃𝑔 𝓉𝒽𝑒 creatin and not smoking, I have become somewhat recluse, spending more time in my cell reading. 'A question of up bringing' and four other books. I have also been exercising more, but because of a lack of mirrors, I am not sure about the results, though I am getting encouraging comments from other inmates.

I am not mood swinging now. I am just in a constant state of suppression, hoping it will pass without an explosion. Example: I was in the cell playing draughts last night. Kenny, my cell mate, took four of my players in one move, and before

I could stop myself, I messed up the entire board. If it was not for the creatin I would have felt bad, but even though it was a reaction, I had no time to stop it. I must try to control it, think about making love, (I look around)... Naaa.

English leaves in 17days; my reading is constantly interrupted by him, because he spends most of the time in this cell. He has hinted that he has problems in his cell (he is with the lifers), so I give him a break, and play big brother. I have also given him a verbal message to give to Emilie. I know she is getting on with her life, but I feel she has to know what I cannot write or say on the phone.

The circus for the phone has started again, but now the warden takes names before the cells are open. The only problem with this is that the workers, who are out first, put their names, and the names of their mates down, so the list is full. Of course a few ciggs will sort that out (if you have). I have a stronger urge to call Nicky, but with this and the other problems, it is difficult.

A routine unit search, cell by cell, including a body search. Basically, four special squads come into the cell, and wreck it. They bin the odd piece of sharpened metal (foosh) and doctored razors and weed. There is no charge or punishment; they just throw it all away (yeah right). We had breakfast locked up, but as soon as we were allowed out, I think it is the most smoking of weed in here, on a single day. One guy told me they found 16 five dollar bags (not a lot) because he threw it through the slit window in the cell, but, with a smile on his face he told me they did not get the four ounces (quite a lot). So, 'business as usual'. He reminds me of Kennington and the drug scene there. I am pretty sure governments and police agencies can do more to deal with drugs on the street than they are. They know most of the buyers, sellers, and takers, but the police I speak to, and the news I hear on the box, such as 'Kilroy', seem to be saying that the police's hands are tied. I can remember being arrested in Lewisham, in my college days, for a three pound draw. I asked the officer how he knew, he told me they had been 'surveying the place for days,' and I was 'not the only one.' Funnily enough, there were a few more, but no sign of the man who sold it to us. 'Turn off the tap, nobody drinks water.'

Tue 4ᵀᴴ

It's hot very hot. It's about 3 o'clock, I am lying on my bunk face down, and I can hardly breathe for the humidity and stillness.

Yesterday, I wrote Emilie a letter. I think it will be the last one. Ah! Old boy returns, shouts of 'salope!' (fucker) echoes around the block in anticipation of a beating...

Wed 6ᵀᴴ

I was going to go to a special chapel meeting today, but after showering and grooming, putting on socks and trainers, and waiting at the gate, the officer told me he had forgotten to put my name down. So no go. No problem, back to reading.

Sept7ᵀᴴ good exercise;

I have a lid that fits my cup now, so I have my creatin, 'shaken not stirred.' You know, there is a big difference (thank you Mr. Bond). It seems to reach my system quicker and in larger dosages I can see and feel a difference.

This morning I interrupted my exercise to watch a 'slap down'. One of the lifers (the softer one), after some verbal confrontation, told 'sound boy' he was going to 'slap him' and he did, hard, knocking him of his feet. 'Sound boy' did not retaliate but other inmates took it upon themselves to show disapproval and so I resume my work out.

English is slacking. The closer it gets to him going home, the more he seems worried about something.

I finally have a new pen. 12th sept.

Embassy came. A change from the norm. It was funny in some ways. When I was called into our little room, I said to Jerry (embassy official), that, I know she comes from Shepherd's Bush, in London, in England. The look on her face was of panic and disbelief; I was not expecting it to be that intense. She looked at her partner and then at me (I was standing at the time). There was I with a sly grin on my face but I could not keep it up. I felt sorry for her and burst out laughing. I went to sit down while explaining to her how I knew, but, I missed the chair, which made a racket, as I fumbled for it. So, there's me on my backside, in this tiny room laughing my head off, when two guards come running in ready for combat duty, and the embassy staff staring at each other in disbelief. Then they turn to the guards explaining all is well. I told her how I knew; when she came three months ago I gave the post code of Emilie to her, she told me it was the incorrect code and I just put two and two together, she was relieved.

While we were waiting for the embassy officials, I saw Candy. We had a laugh about sex and stuff; it was nice to talk to a female again.

I did not receive my tomato ketchup but I got my ciggs. Its two days for the shop. I am the only one on the block with cigarettes. It's not funny. 'English' did not get his because he is leaving next week; it is to be arranged that I pay his bills, should be fun.

SUN 16TH

Something has just come across my mind, as I lay on my bunk, not thinking about anything in particular. The sum of my children's age (26, 16, 4) almost add up to my age. It just made me think of the paranormal, coincidences, destiny, and the things that have intrigued man. From, I guess, when time or man began, I wonder if life is mapped out. Is there an over all being? Is life just one long chain of coincidences? I personally don't believe 'it all just happened'. Although my brain is not apt enough to comprehend, that once upon a time, 'there was nothing,' and if an overall being created us, what created it? Itself? Okay, out of what? I do not believe we, as life forms, can be completely destroyed; as a solid can become liquid, and liquid, gas, I believe we have other stages of being (e.g. liquid (sperm), solid (human form). For gas: disintegration (after death)). And if aliens do exist (I believe they do), I really hope they are beyond the traits of human beings, in terms of jealousy, lust, greed and hate, etc... The sort of things that would describe us humans, to other planetary beings (if, they could comprehend such traits,) as we might describe people and, their ways, from different parts of the world, e.g. most of us condemn suicide bombers and extremists, for the belief in something they have no fundamental proof of existence (not that I say it does not exist) but aliens, higher or lower on our I.Q level, might think how strange it is, that we not only strive to destroy our home, but we also rely on our for mentioned traits (greed) to evolve our solid form when it will be of no use to us in our gaseous form (spiritual). I wonder if there are aliens out there making sure we cannot contact them, least we try to impose on them; democracy, Islam, Christianity etc. I think if we do make contact, we will know if God exists, because I am sure he would have told them, as he has appeared, to have told us.

Well, English leaves tomorrow. I guess I'll miss him a bit, but I hope I have helped him somehow. I have sent my final message to Emilie with him. I hope he delivers it properly.

I received a letter from Mrs. Bond. She seems to think I could have stopped destiny. She also seems to have forgotten that I did ask for help. 'As clear as I could'. It would seem to me no one takes a fairly good looking, okay built, 6"4, male with dreadlocks seriously, when he cries for help. I wonder if that's how movie stars feel; 'oh, he/ she has money, fame, and fortune, who are they kidding? They, need help'. Here's a secret: I bet the aliens would not think that. Well, as if to be reminded of my hate for certain human beings, the lad on the bunk above me, has started his ritual gospel singing, not loud, just very, very out of tune and repetitive, continuous, and irritating. Apart from that, Kenny is ok, unlike the other inmate, 'Taxi'; who irritates me just by the way he walks. He is everything I hope I am not. Wow! That's quite strong. I wonder how many people could say that about me. Unless it's been jealousy, I do not recall people hating me for being who I am.

I'm trying to figure out, how to smuggle a 'learning french' cassette to my cell, from my luggage in admin. I have already 'acquired' a machine (no recording devices allowed). I must get this french sorted, can't let my french daughter grow up and I can't speak to her in french. Not good form at all.

There has been more new admissions, more small fights, nothing to scream about, although one was because a mischievous lad, who can no longer hold his liquor, decided to beat someone up in the shower (I was in the shower at the time). So bang! goes my old theory about no fights in the shower. But remember, he was drunk, and as I know, in that state, you really don't know what you are doing.

TUES. 19TH.

I really do not feel good mood wise, so I have not exercised for three days. 'Taxi man', who I can't stand, has decided to get up at five in the morning to exercise, at the same time I do. I think he was expecting me to join him but...Anyway 'Chi chi' is with him, and especially in this cell, three *is* a crowd. I am still taking creatin, I wonder if this boosts the intensity of my moods.

I am thinking of Nicky a lot. I suppose I will not be forgiven, for not being able to get her on the phone, which has been down for three days, and, I still have to wait for another phone card from shop.

I really don't feel like writing, but I got to keep it up, even if just to say 'I feel like shit'.

THURSDAY. 21ST.

Still feel moody. To add to it, I have a rotten cold.

An insight into a particular inmate: He asks me if I could write him a letter to a pen pal, that someone introduced him to over the phone. "No problem" I say, "give me a few days" (I was writing for other people at the time). A few days later he comes to my cell, he hands me two pages of A4 paper and a pen, and says 'can we deal with it now.' 'No problem' I say, and with that, he turns and walks away, leaving me with unspoken questions like; what's her name and address? And most of all, as far as I am concerned, what the fuck do you want me to write? Anyway, at the other end of the mental stick, the Rasta teacher came into my cell with another inmate, Lincoln lord, and a two page document about, why all inmates must suffer, when one breaks the rules, (applying to the recent stopping of batteries, cereal ect, that family were allowed to bring in on visits). It was drafted as if by a lawyer. I signed it, even though it does not affect me, but for some strange reason, I do not think it will reach the intended ear, and even if it does, it didn't. They do fall short of a lot of the human rights act, namely, the minimum dose of vitamins, minerals and supplements for a healthy diet. I should check out the doctor. To be honest, I am quite worried about this cold. I would use home remedies in England. In here there is nothing, and it appears to me, that every time someone goes to the hospital, one of three things happen; one, they come back with massive bandages, saying they had an 'operation' (the average prisoner is about 33). Two, 'the injection' which is given to 'calm' an inmate down(an inmate, who already had one, was merely warned about getting another and his whole system reacted as if he had already had it again). And three, they escape. So I think no hospital (I hope).

THUR 12TH;

Still got the cold, but not as bad. I feel quite low, and try to cheer myself up, by believing, there has to be a purpose for all this.

According to human nature, I am about half way through this journey of life. I have done many things and have had multiple experiences; I can't help thinking that just around the corner, is an up.

MON 24TH;

I have done no exercise for days. I have let this joker and his side kick (although that's a bit harsh on the side kick) carry on with their monotonous routine. I think, my friend the 'Bird Man' (the guy who said taxi was leaving in two weeks) got it wrong. Someone else told him it was the following month. I was not going to exercise until he left. It's kind of thrown me.

I think I will have to continue my stomach exercise on my bunk, as my stomach seems to be reluctant to develop in my old age (middle age). I realize again how old I am. What really went wrong? Did anything actually go wrong? Remembering that my time here is only a snap of the finger, compared to universal time, but also consider, cause and effect. My time here will soon be over. I have three wonderful kids, so the effect of me being here, has a chance of going on for many more generations, and maybe, some time in the near or far future, that mere snap of a fingers existence will turn into the clapping of hands, so, maybe I have overlooked the simple reason for being here: To take my part in the survival of the human race. Naaa, if that were so, I'd be dead already. There has to be something in that summary, but what is it? Do I have to die first to see it? My chain of thought has been interrupted by a message from a guard by the gate asking me to see him. He spoke about being serious, about making connections in England. Now surely you see the predicament. Here I am, locked up for possession of drugs and the guard, quite seriously, would like me as a connection. So, I make a few enquiries, and I find out he brings grass in. So he is straight (if you get my drift). Now, I'm not saying 'all the guards are corrupted' because, the other day I over heard a certain female guard would, 'not do anything,' to 'chance' her career, 'even for an inmate' she new on the 'outside'. Funny thing though, the guard who sent the message, just happens to be her man. Wow, news, Flash! I was going to write about, 'what a man will do for a woman' and then slag women off for being, whatever. But I have just realized: Women in the past have done pretty much anything I have asked, and more (I wonder why?) and I don't think I really appreciated it, so I guess where're even now.

TUE, 6 O'CLOCK.

Up early as usual. We played draught with 'Chi chi' last night. We taught him how to play, and now he is almost as good as us (we're not that brilliant). He was playing okay, and then he went to phone his family. When he came back, I gave him 6-0. Of course, he was jeered. He complained that his mind was not there. I back him on that. Let's say, if I spoke to one of my kids today, I would probably have lost 12-0. Thinking about it though, if I spoke to Nicole I would be so happy I would probably lose for a week. Two more days for a phone card, I'll try again then.

Wrote Cousin Angela, she's cool.

What I could do with is a pen pal, but no one seems to have the time. It would be nice just to write Emilie, and tell her things, other things that I have done, other feelings I have felt, not about us, about me, and other things about her, like what she does from day to day. It would be something to look forward to, receiving a letter, lying on my bunk, and losing myself in a world of my imagination, but alas...

It seems the Queen has something to say; we are going into the euro money thing. Hmm, I bet she wasn't amused. Another one of those strange feelings coming on, I think I am sad to be out of England while this is happening. Maybe it's because it's a new era for Britain, and I am not there to witness it. I was there in the seventies when shillings turned to pence, I could not understand why, and never questioned it. To be honest, I didn't really care. But this euro thing, I have always thought was a good idea, but instead of being leaders, they're 'bringing up the back lot'.

And breakfast has been served, and they have run short of bread (which is breakfast), so we have our first excuse of the day for unnecessary commotion. So, I'm standing on the first floor landing, watching the scene, the smokers, who always have and continuously beg, are smoking on the day before tuc shop, when nobody usually has any, and there are a very few people who smoke in public around this time, because no one wants to be seen asking them for a puff. One guy takes his usual position; on the rails opposite my cell, lying sideways, with his legs and arms threaded around the bar, looking somewhat like an 'ape in a zoo.' He reminds me of when I was in Jamaica and tourists would drive by and snap pictures of us just 'hanging out' and we would curse them. I remember when I first asked "why curse them?" 'Because they go back to foreign and tell their friends we live in trees like monkeys'. (I think they should see this guy).

I was interrupted earlier by a few things: a guard came to see me and asked if I was interested in school.

"What subject?" I asked.

'Just school.'

"Okay." I went along to the class room, and a man from somewhere was interviewing inmates, to see what subjects they would like, and, if they could write their own name. I asked him if we could get 'the TV and video that is on the premises, locked up, as it would help with the Kweyol class we have already started'. He will see what he can do. Then later during "Roll Check!" shouting in the next cell to me. A fight has broken out between one of the older inmates, and a new one. Blood was drawn, the head guard came and broke it up and moved the younger one out of the block (about four new lads have been behaving wrongly). Apparently, the youngest urinated in the others drinking can. I said, 'he was taking the piss' it didn't go down to well. Later, another member of the gang had a row with one of the bad boys, it didn't get too far. The big bull laughingly broke it up (I think it reminded him of his youth). Then the water: after filling a keg, the water was musky brown. I wanted to complain about it to the head warden, but he left early. Ah yes! He said of the fight: 'I told you to ignore him'. 'Ignore him?' I thought. Ignore a man who has just pissed in your water bottle! Could you? I couldn't. Remembering, by the way, the average night temp here is 82 degrees. It's late afternoon, and the pipes do not come on until 10am, and the water is bad enough anyway.

I'm on my bunk again, the night draws in, I will settle down with a book until lights out at ten, and then listen to the BBC on my little radio, with the diminishing batteries. Goodnight.

THURS 28TH

Emilie's birthday; I wonder how she is feeling. I hope she had a good one.

A guard has just passed by the cell for head count before they open up the gate it's a sombre morning ,a lot of male touching going on, as if bonding. One inmate (one who had a fight yesterday) picked up a small guy and ran up the stairs with him smiling and took him into his cell, a few minutes later they came out arms around each others shoulder, grinning. Others are feigning fighting matches. Me? I just observe. The other day while I was observing, an inmate slaps my ribs (not too hard) I told him not to do that again, I don't like being touched, he said 'No problem'. So no bonding for me even though I know today is special in here; Tuc shop, cigarettes.

Chi chi is depressed because he has no smoke. I tell him cool, just a few more hours. He says "No, I need now, too many problems, need to relax". So I thought I'd tell him it's a good thing he really does not need them. "Suppose" I said "you were an alcoholic and you needed a drink? You wake up in the morning knowing you will soon start shaking involuntary. You start thinking what you can do to stop the inevitable, except to have a drink... but their isn't any. You brush your teeth just to throw up and watch the yellow bile flow from your mouth, it's finished but you still try to throw up some more. Why? Because you think it will relieve you of the craving, but it doesn't. You wash your face and look in the mirror, it's not you but it doesn't matter. The only thing that matters, and I mean the only thing, is to get a drink. Even if you get it to watch it for a while until it becomes too unbearable or until you know where the next one is comming from. For the first is only temporary relief and you know this. You stretch out your arms and fingers to see how much they are shaking-not a lot now- but there's worse to come. You have a bit of time now to think. How did you, of all people get into a mess like this? You start to pace; where? Where? Where! Can I get a drink from now? You go down a few steps, only to find that your legs are shaking now. Huh, you can walk but only just. Must avoid steps and obstacles that make you lift your feet to high, otherwise the shaking moves through out your body. Your hot your cold, your sweating you're shivering. That is when you need a friend" I told him all that. What I did not tell him is that I was describing myself.

My past helps me and my kids know who or what I am about... (Yeah, good idea).

FRI 30TH

I have received my tuc shop: 5 sweeties, small Vaseline, small baby oil, four batteries, 2 telephone cards, 10 packs of ciggs, total, $120. I receive $375 every 3or4 months, from P.A, depending on when the Embassy shows up. My bills are: 8 packs of cigs (for washing, extra food, and what I borrowed, 2 for1). Next, I have my name down for the phone. Who first? Junior is most logical, because he will deal with everything, but he has a small problem of his own. Nicky next because, I really feel it could be damaging for what relation we do have, if I do not speak to her on the phone, I fear, no excuse, no matter how true, will do. Kayana; because I promised once a month, and I don't want to let her down, (now that rings a bell). A few weeks ago, I received a letter from Mrs. Bond. Stating how 'disappointed' she was with me, (I'm still not sure who told her, but it can only be one of two people) and how 'I know people have let you down.'

Mrs. Bond was the head of a children's home I was in since the age of five (prior to which, I was in a nursery, the only recollection I have are from photos) until the age of twelve.

Oakfield 7 Sunset Avenue. Woodford Green, Essex. Tel, 5047270. It was grilled into us as early as possible, in case we got lost (which is funny because at that time I think I was already lost). It was a large house, and there were approximately fourteen children, all in for different reasons, but all to do with parents, somehow, not being able to 'cope'.

I can remember my mother visiting me twice, although later on in life I was told it was more than that. When she came on one of these visits, I distinctly remember her telling me that I will be able to live with her soon. On another, I locked myself in the cloakroom for what seemed like hours, with some of the aunties (which is what we called them) and her, pleading for me to come out, needless to say I didn't. I do not recall seeing her again until very much later in life. I think I decided then to listen to the head of the house, who was to be the nicest, fairest, person I knew. She was a white woman, about 5'5, quite chubby, with long black hair. Age was not relevant, she was an Aunty. When she smiled and was in good humour, all was roses, but when something was wrong, you could feel it in her presence. Her look of being upset, angry, disappointed or concerned, could be felt without a word from her. I started to look upon her as my mother.

School was across the road, set on a common, on the outskirts of a golf course, at the beginning of Epping Forest. Literally a one minute walk: across the road, over a ditch, few yards across the common, over the school fence and I'm there. I liked school sometimes, and sometimes... Well, school was not nice to me. Although at the time, looking back, I think that although they did a good job (of course that's all I new then), they lacked certain things in the curriculum, like in the case of racism, though I don't think I would label it that with school kids. I seriously don't think that the other children's behaviour towards me was out of malice or such; they were rather, just being kids. What, after all, did they care about how I felt? It made them happy. You see, in the home, I was not made to feel different; after all, we were all in the same boat. But in school, every so often I was reminded that I was different. For example (these few I can never forget), it was normal day at school (I was one of the lads). Then, I'm not sure why but I had a fight with a twin, 'T L J'. I won, but the next day I could not remember who I fought, although it did not matter to me. I was given the silent treatment by all the others in the school, my first apparent meeting of racism. I also remember when we had a birthday in the home; we were allowed to invite a few choice friends from school. On one of my birthdays, I remember inviting Mark Buckley, who I considered then, and still have no reason to think different now, my best friend. I used to go to his home and watch the F.A cup final on TV in colour. I also invited the most popular boy in school, Carl, and the most popular girl, and her best friend Amanda, among a few others. After the celebrations we were allowed out to play on the common. One of the games was called 'kiss chase'. I did not get to familiar with the rules but basically, one person was picked and had to run around trying to catch and kiss another, then it would be their turn, to chase and kiss. Even though it was my party, no one even pretended to chase me, but I carried on running, pretending to myself and them I suppose, that they could just not catch me. That did not feel good.

Later at school there was a new kid, she was black, and her name was Jemima Watson, so now there were two of us. Although we weren't bosom buddies, I stuck up for her the best I could, things like 'last one in the class room kisses Jemima Watson'. I walked. I used to go to football training after school that a school mate's dad used to run. They nicknamed me 'jungle bunny'; it felt funny in the beginning, but then it didn't bother me. Not like other names I was called in my early life, like: Nigger, Gollywog, Blacky, Darky, Cat's eyes. Oh yes, my eyes bothered me then, but, they have probably been the biggest physical attraction to the opposite sex for me as a young man. Now, the single most hurtful thing that happened to me in those days, was when it was my turn to go to Desmond Hayne's house for dinner. It was normal then, as it is now I suppose, to ask your parents if you could go to your friends' house for dinner (after being invited). I never did any inviting when we had dinner, guess you can imagine 14 kids under manners might add...well, it just didn't seem like the thing to do. Anyway Desmond was that kid. He was not the most popular boy in school, but he wanted to be, and had to make up for whatever it was he thought he lacked, by bringing in more sweets than anyone else, and handing them out. He also systematically chose someone every so often, to go to his house for dinner, which was never refused. I personally did not think I would ever be asked. Anyway, I could go to Mark's house whenever I wanted to. But one day, to my genuine surprise, Desmond asked me, of course I said yes. What could go wrong? I did not even think about it, because now I was really accepted. I could go to school and tell my stories about, 'what happened at Desmond's house.' So, after asking permission and mentally noting the time of coming back, I set of to my dinner: through the gates of Oakfield, over the road, across the common, passed the school, across a main road, into a block of flats (number nine comes to mind). I knock on the door, a man answers. It's his dad, (I think). 'Who are you?'

"I'm Colin, Desmond's friend"

'What do you want?' Not sure what to say, I ask if Desmond's in, 'He invited me to dinner'. I'm not really sure if he answered, but he said something, and slammed, I mean seriously slammed, the door shut. It closed inches from my face. I just stood there in a daze. For a split second I thought of excuses for him like, 'it was the wind' or whatever, but then I heard words like; Nigger, Wog, Dinner, and, it hit me again. I am not, and never will be, one of the lads. I remember standing on the door step with tears running down my face, no sound, just tears, and thinking, 'what do I tell Aunty Bina?' I cannot tell her what happened, simply because, 'I don't know how to'. I turned, still crying, to face my journey home. When I got half way across the common, I stopped, and sat on one of those logs shaped into seats, and thought 'I have to stay here until enough time has elapsed for it to look like I had had dinner', remembering the stories that had been told to us about the bogie men, and people who take children away and do awful things to them if they strayed alone at night on the common. I am scared. Night is falling, but I'm still not going home, I just sat there in the middle of nowhere, and cried, until I thought it was time to go. I remember pressing the front door bell, which was the first time I ever used it alone. I said, 'hi' and 'dinner was fine' watched some TV and went to bed hungry. Adults can be racist. Kids have to learn.

Dinner time. If fish, I think I will skip it. It's comming up to my phone call, so I will go into the yard and watch the sea, through the fence...Well, that was cool, I got through to Nicky. Wow, another one of those feelings, best described as happiness although different from joy, maybe both. Whatever it is, it feels good. The card only lasted 4 minutes, but it doesn't matter. I spoke to her. Although she was shocked, I'm sure she was also happy. Tomorrow I call J, and Ky. Although brief, today was for Nicky, yesss.

SAT 30TH

Well, as I said before, 'you never know what's going to happen next in here', although, knowing the circumstances happening before the events would give one a better chance of guessing the outcome. A certain man in the cell (Taxi man), who must have been stewing over the fact that I do not talk to him, has been getting more and more paranoid and nervous. I do not know exactly what he was thinking, but whilst I was reading on my bunk, and the others were out and about, he has sent one of his people (that he gives bread to) to clear out his stuff. This 'Taxi' guy, has been complaining about us playing cards too early and draught too late, making too much noise with the dominoes, the light being on late (all cell lights go off at ten) and smoking in the cell. The constant complaining was annoying to the other three of us in the cell. We tried to give him a break, e.g. smoking by the cell door, lights out at about 8.30 which in turn means no draughts, dominoes or cards. I admit we only complied because he only has one month left, but his paranoia got the better of him, so now he has moved into a cell where one of his new cell mates argues for no apparent reason. One is gay (he often said he would never do time with a 'macume') and they all chain smoke. Oh well... No problem. And, they smoke crack. Tomorrow I will start exercising again and hearing from the rest of the block, what he has said we have done. It will be greatly exaggerated, or a pack of lies.

After dinner (it's pork, so I settle for biscuits), I am back on my bunk. Our cell is now the centre of attention, there is a congregational spot, right outside the cell door. 4/5 at a time, they all just stop, to hear what has happened, but very few ask. Most of them just stand there, looking into the cell as if they were waiting for someone to make a speech, but no one in the cell offers anything. All this is happening because 'Taxi' buys the most shopping from the tuc shop and gives most of it to 'the bull' and the other tough boys for protection, which, he really does not need, although he maintains 'it's because they have no source of income'. "Hello!" neither do eighty odd other folks. Anyway, they were disappointed they did not get news worthy of Bordelais, and to my surprise, 'Taxi' was just saying he moved because 'people in the cell' would not talk to him. There is more to say about him, but he, and others like him who have money and power, and pray on other folk, whose morale values, and respect, for other men an women, go way beyond the concept of money and power, do not, in my opinion, deserve even half of the time I have given them already.

A prospective new cell mate came in while I was reading; he looks stressed. 'Can come here?'

"Doesn't bother me". The others are not here, so I assume control (I have turned down three already. One gay (no offence to them on the outside, but here it's different), a nutter, and someone who could do with looking after himself a bit better. I am in all sense, the landlord. My rent is high; common decency. It happens to be the 'Ras.' He is about 5"9, his locks were touching the ground before 'they' cut it at the entrance; it still pisses me off. I have been seeing him around for the past 3/4 weeks. He is about my age, and I have never heard him raise his voice. He fits the bill; he is in, now we can start the 'bonding' thing (no touching). To be honest, I cannot be bothered. I am a bit fed up at being nice to people, even though I have always admired and respected the true Rastafarian. Now, is not the time.

It is Sunday;

I have made it through another month.

I am thinking about the effect that being moved around can have on one, as an adult. Most people try to adjust at a steady certain pace, being polite, understanding, and cooperative, on the hope of being 'accepted' by the new people you are surrounded by. I think it is easier for a child, because... it's easier. You adjust your differences and adapt, or should I say conform. You don't know what, how or why, you are trying to change. You just want to fit in.

At Oakfield, - I have just been interrupted by someone who wants to watch inmates catch a large snake outside my cell window. No danger- _I was the longest serving resident. This is because all the promises my mother made to me never came to pass, good in someway, bad in others. Good in the way, I had a steady place to live. I became closer to the staff and was looked upon as... Well. It gave me a sense of belonging, someone who knew what was going on. The down side was, some of the kids I got on well with, left before I wanted them to, most times back to their mother or family, which put me in a state of depression 'why them not me?' I think at that time in my life I subconsciously believed that people (friends, relationships and families, do not stick around. A small example of change: schools (one primary four secondary schools), leaving old friends, meeting new ones. After learning to accept I was different, as far as colour was concerned, I tried to settle down at my first high school, which had a few more black people in it, and although there was quite a bit of abuse, it never really bothered me because I had others to share and fight the burden with. But I was in for a shock. The old school was across the road from Oakfield, in full view of all but I did not realise how bad that could be, until I had moved school. Only the teachers knew I was from a home, apart from one or two people I got on well with. Until one day, one of the other kids from Oakfield, out of want for sympathy, decides to tell a few of his so called 'new friends' that he and I are from a 'home'. Well, kids will be kids and I wasn't allowed to forget it. As soon as I found out he told them, I got so angry with him that I hit him as hard as an eleven year old could. I don't remember being punished for that._

I do recall being punished for spitting down the stair case, at the school, which I never did. I got taken to the principal's office, a Mr Rouge. He was about 5"7 and had the moustache of a colonel in the 2nd World war. He could put on the old 'Biggles' flying cap and goggles, of the early open cockpit fighter planes era and suit the part. He gave me six of the best lashes across the palm of my hand with a three foot piece of bamboo ('the cane') the diameter of my little finger... perfectly legal at the time. I can remember looking at him and willing myself not to cry, after all, I was right. Afterwards I sat outside the office, apparently to see if I had any short term side effects ("hello, what about long term") and the bursa, nervously over acting a smile, told me: 'That is the hardest I've seen him hit anyone'. I remember getting up and running out of school all the way home and telling myself I was never going back. I can't remember how far away it was from the house to the school, but we took a bus there and back every day, so it must have been some distance. When I got home I tried sneaking in. It was quiet because everyone else was at school, but I got caught by an aunty and was sent to my room for punishment. After a few hours, a heavy set 'Aunty Joy' walked in and asked me what happened. I liked her on a par with Mrs. Bond because I remember having to have my hair combed with an ordinary comb and it used to hurt like hell. Then one day, head lice were going around. We all had to have a special shampoo and comb out. For combing they bought a lice comb, about three inches in length two and a half wide, with small compact teeth made of metal and they wanted to comb my hair with it. This I must say with all due respect to the aunties: they had to literally hold me down and thru my tears eventually succeeded. The next day 'Aunty Joy' (she had just come back from holiday in Ghana) bought me back the best present I had in the home. A soul comb or 'pick' as we called it. At this point I must say I vaguely remember 'Aunty Chris' being there also. She told me, that I should not worry about it and tell them to fuck off. She was white and she was cool. This is important, because it has to be said that most of the staff were compassionate, it's that some just did not understand. She was telling me quite clearly that I should not *let this get me down because I was going to Jamaica in two weeks time, to live with my Grand Mother, Aunty, Bro and Sis (I had heard rumours of this and although I more than half believed, I still had reserved possibilities of being let down again). I don't remember going back to that school. So witnessing as a child and being one who went through the transgression, it's bad but not terrible, sure I had times when I wished I was white. Times when I wanted my Mother so bad I just sat in a corner and sulked for hours; to everyone else I was 'just in one of his moods'. But I also had good times. It's just that at this time of my life, I only seem to recall the sad. So there I was getting used to the fact I am not white and I live in an orphanage. Okay, no problem. Whatever else could possibly not be handled by me? Ah yes, Jamaica.*

Oct 3rd

Started exercising again, and that feels good. Two weeks off and I have not been feeling good overall at all. I'll have to wait for more supplements again, hopefully not too long.

Chi chi has spotted a massive snake from our cell window, just across the yard slithering down the dividing wire fence; it's about as thick as my biceps and about nine foot long. It's about a hundred yards away but it still sends a horrible chill up my spine.

Well, I was right about 'Taxi'. He is telling his new mates, that he "cannot do time in the same cell as hypocrites, people whose breath smells and who influence other people minds" into not talking to him (that one's me). One of the crack heads in his cell has taken it upon himself to mouth off at me in the shower, but it's just talk, so I do not see it as a problem.

I have been asked to help some guy write a poem. Okay, no problem. In he pops to my cell, paper, pen and one line 'me no wan dem fi cum push me ron'. 'What do you think?' "It's okay." 'What do you think I should put next?' Jeez, I swear I look for hidden cameras in this place sometimes. Anyway, he decides to quote the bible, so I write it down for him. I find out he is a good hair dresser (yep, he is also bisexual) so in return he will twist my hair. Hair we go again. I have twice grown my hair to the length of my lower back. It takes about seven years. This is like a physical move, a move that you know what the consequences will be. You have the whole period of your hair growing, to learn to deal with the negative, and live with the positive, or just cut it off. By hair I am talking dreadlocks. Rasta men have sometimes looked at me in a very negative way. Mainly because the hair, I will not insult them by saying I am a true Rastafarian. I have met some (and there are not many) who have been the most positive, intellectually stimulating, full of wisdom, and spiritually conscious, religious group I have met. Maybe some of the other religious sects should take a leaf out of their book i.e. 'Peace', 'love' and 'unity'. Never be mistaken by anyone who has locks, smokes weed and has a big chip on their shoulder, because they are the ones who make up the mythical stereotypical Rasta man. So you won't find many dreadlocked lawyers, doctors, or politicians etc, because it is socially unacceptable. Hell, some schools won't allow it, even in this day and age. But it is common amongst people who express themselves physically, e.g. sport folk, young actors, musicians and the trendy. Although I have nothing but admiration for the true Rastafarian, I personally fall into the latter category. It makes me feel right, and if carried with proper dignity, can open doors. But as I said before about the kind of changes, after looking at the pros and cons, I decided as a man, that a child being moved about and then thrown into the deep end, could have serious effects on his mind when he grows. Remembering, what you throw this young person into is his or her view of what the world out there is like (if you grow up in a war zone for example). A word for parents; if you decide to move your family to a different environment, have some kind of understanding as to what the hell is going on.

I remember being told I was going to Jamaica. I was asked but found out later it had already been arranged by my beautiful Aunt Dell, a Jamaican woman, but to me she had the aura of an African princess. Anyway, they had their best intentions for me. Once I finally understood I was going to live in Jamaica with my Grandmother, Bro, Sis and Aunt I was anxious and excited. I was not only going to live with my real family but I was also going to live with other kids just like me. I am not going to be a social outcast, gone would be all the taunts, my eyes, colour, my home. I was going to fit in.

I can remember getting off the plane in Kingston. I stepped back inside because of the close heat; it was as if I could not breathe. My granny and Aunty were at the airport to meet me and they took me to my new home: '4a Camden Road, Kingston 16.' Situated at the end of a cul de sac, it was a nice house, with four bedrooms, two kitchens, a large dinning/living room, two bathrooms and a wash room area. There was a small flower garden in the front and it had a large back yard, with two massive akee trees and a mango tree that grew out of what looked like nothing that would make anything grow. In the back of the yard was a chicken coup, capable of keeping 400 or so broilers and layers. I instantly took to the job of feeding, watering and picking up the fresh eggs which would be sold locally. I found out later what broilers were, and it was a part of the job to kill, pick and pluck them, also to sell locally and of course, for our consumption. I did not realise that I had to kill them until after I had nursed them from chicks, watering and feeding them, scaring away rats at night with kerosene lamps and nursing them if one got attacked (which often happened). They were, to me, my pets. I could not kill them. This was the cause of the second early discomfort I felt for my Grandma (not taking in seriously that she was single handily looking after her mother, who was bed ridden and dying, and sending to school her daughter, the three of us and a young girl helper, or as it was seen to all of us, someone who Grandma knew could not be looked after by her biological parents. We became friends, more so because I knew what that was like, I wish I knew or understood all of this earlier) and I got my first taste of Jamaican discipline. If I don't kill the chickens, I don't eat the chickens. No problem. I stuck it out for a *few Sundays. Have you ever smelt Jamaican cooking? Especially Grandmas' from down the road and around the corner, after running up and down playing football or something. Well, let's just say chicken is still my favourite until this day. My grandma did everything for us and this chicken episode came and went. But the first discomfort I felt, I still cannot understand how or why, I behaved in this manner. At Oakfield, every one was called 'Aunty' or 'Uncle', so no problem, I grew into that. But Bro and Sis called her 'Mammy'; Aunty Jenny called her 'Mummy' and Dawn the helper called her 'Mrs Ivy'. I really did not know what to call her, so I didn't, which in turn meant I did not speak to her unless I was being spoken to, and this lasted throughout my entire stay in Jamaica. At first no one seemed to realise, but after a while it became obvious and progressively uncomfortable, but as funny as it sounds, I just did not know how to call my Grandma a name. That little misunderstanding had a dramatic effect on my life, especially when she caught on, and decided not to talk to me unless I spoke to her.*

My first introduction to my brother and sister was when they returned home from their Uncle and Grandmother's after the school holidays. I took to my Sister straight away, but the first thing I remember my Brother saying was, "A dat de red kin sitin a mi breada", (is that red skinned something my brother). I don't even know how I felt, but it was an insight to how Jamaican young boys and girls were to be towards me. I was ridiculed from the way I pronounced my name, to the colour of my skin. In England, I went from being; wog, nigger or black, (even though I was and still am brown) to being; reds, yellow man, or English, these being the more respectable names I was called when I was in favour. I never really got over it, I just got used to it. But my school days were fun, especially as I began to grow. English schools, on equal levels, were superior, so from being an average grade student I became instantly above average. This helped in the way of respect but also admiration, I was now for the first time becoming popular, and a lot more self confident. I began to join in more with the others. Girls started to notice me and this was good. At home I still had issues. I decided to solve that by staying out of the house as much as possible, for no other reason than, it was comfortable, Yeah, I enjoyed school. "Roll check!"

Half an hour to dinner, it's chicken. 'Please be fresh'. Sugar, it's library and I have ordered a book that I have already read, oh well; I wonder if I can do what I do with movies that I have seen before, let's see.

I am still trying to get some cigarettes that for no reason were withheld from me at the last embassy visit. The excuse today is, 'it's raining'. I wonder, if they only knew how well trained I am to put up with promises and let downs. *My brother, whom I have started to get along with, now has kind of taken me under his wing. Not that I needed it, though I did feel comfortable being there. We went to movies together, played football and often went to the beach, we even shared the same bed for sometime. He was older and more of a man. I had to look up to him. He was the best of all the guys around me. He was my big brother. But as luck would have it. On the verge of my 'settling in', changes were to come. Just as I was getting to the stage that I could call Mrs. Ivy, 'Mammy,' the past merges with the future (memo to parents: let your kids know the best you can, as early as you can, who they are, and where they come from. That way, they might have a chance of knowing where they are going). The buzz is going around about our father coming to visit us from America. Bro and Sis already knew him, I did not. So them being more excited on the outside and sticking together, with this news, did not bother me. I was just looking forward to meeting him. He is bringing a Ford Mustang with him, so this means he is wealthy, not that I care. He is bringing this and that for Bro and Sis, no problem for me. I am about 13 years old, I have not spoken to him, never met him, so never had the chance to ask for anything. Anyway, I don't want anything except a father, from what I have heard it's pretty cool. So the count down is on and so is the anticipation. At this moment nothing has occurred to me other than, the family is going to be complete, so, he is finally on the island and he is staying in another parish, he will visit sometime in the week. It is about 7 in the evening, and I am doing nothing in particular on the streets when I notice his brother's van pull up, 'Ralph' (good man), parked outside of the house. Bro and Sis were in the house already, but why did no one call me? (At the time only a flashing thought). Anyway, no time to waste; have to rush to meet my father. I ran through the gate, up the tiled path, across the veranda and into the living room. There he is. That moment felt good but I'm cool. He is sitting on one of the living room chairs with one arm around Bro and the other around Sis, no problem, he has only two arms. I can see Ralph leaning casually on a cabinet filled with plates and glasses for special occasions. I can see Jennifer and Mrs. Ivy out of the corner of my eye, their look is saying something but I cannot pick it up. I wonder what I looked like to them. I must have been standing there for longer than I thought because something is changing in me, something is not right. But I had been preparing for this moment for too long for me to see anything wrong. I am just standing there, being ignored by my Bro, Sis and Father. He hands my Bro silver studded watch and my Sister something I could not see, because now the penny begins to drop. He doesn't care, and does not want to know me. I look up to Ralph, who shrugs out of embarrassment and then towards Mrs Ivy and Jenny. No answer there, I turn back towards the family. They have not even seen me. As casual as I can, I retrace my foot steps out of the house and back onto the street. It's dark now but there is a streetlight a few yards away from our gate. I just sat on the side walk with tears running down my face. I cannot remember how long I was there for, but I can remember, after sometime, Sis coming down the road towards me with a big grin on her face. I tried to hide the fact that I was crying, but to no avail. After begging her not to tell them I told her why I was in this state, her answer: "he is not your father, but we are half Brother and Sister". I was not sure what it meant at the time, but it did not cheer me up.*

Oct 8ᵗʰ, at night.

I am lying on my bunk looking up at the pictures of Kayana. I want to write to her but I am not sure what to say. I cannot lie to her but I cannot tell her about the days I spend here, so it's down to basics e.g. 'How are you and mum?' How is school? etc, and hope that these few words will keep me fresh in her memory.

It has been a mixed few days; I finally got my ciggs, needless to say, 'I am popular' again with some, the opposite with others. My phones have also tuned up. I was called into admin to witness them being put on my property. The guard was pissed off with me because I took to the embassy to sort it out and of an act of his superiority, he ordered me to have my hair cut. I was upset at first but I do not think I showed it. Anyway, he got a prisoner who had never used a pair of clippers to do it. He took two big chunks out before another guard told him not to bother. I was also told to write a letter of apology to the admin staff for allegedly accusing them of 'stealing' the phones. I wrote the letter. After all, I did get back my phones.

The Irish lad has finally gone home. Good for him.

I still spend most of my time in my cell and the only thing that bothers me, are the people who interrupt me to beg for cigarettes.

Jackson's (English) phone numbers are not working but I do not think it is on purpose. The little nutter will probably send me a package soon. The Ras is okay and at present it is the best it's been for me with four people in the cell since I have been here. I have finally found some work for one of the lads who insist that I am his boss; he fixed my radio pretty good and told me I did not have to pay him. I gave him two ciggs anyway.

10THOCT;

Silly rumours have been flying around about how 'terrible' we are in our cell; 'Taxi man' is spreading them, so apparently we have enemies. But I am used to them now and to me it seems they are a bunch of pussycats (most).

Someone got hold of a mobile in the cell next to me, but could not keep it a secret. Two days later, prisoners headed by 'the bull', took it upon themselves to search a cell for some jewellery that went missing. A lot of commotion and mix ups left my neighbour in seg for a month because they found him with the phone. Someone grassed. It's quite amazing; I am amongst men who have killed other men. Without guns they are a pitiful bunch, loaded now with only promises of 'what they will do when they get out' and most of the gunmen are small, around 5"7, so if that is not insecure, what is? I wonder sometimes what it would be like to take someone's 'life' and I hope to God never to be put in any kind of situation of such. From what I have heard in here, they have no respect for human life. They used to hang here, and I know there are relevant pros and cons surrounding the argument on capital punishment, but many of the reasons inmates in here give for the taking of a man's life, are as trivial as the punishment they receive. *In Jamaica, while trying (quite successfully I thought at the time) to adapt to the Jamaican culture, around the late seventies, I began to neglect my duties around the house e.g. the chickens, in favour of playing around with other kids my age and finally finding out the pleasures women have to offer.*

My Gran had bought a brand new six wheel ford transit van, for use as a public transport vehicle. She selected a route from Kingston to the country, picking up and dropping off along the way, 'excellent' I thought. Although I was too young and inexperienced of Jamaicans to be a conductor, I would wash the van and prepare it for the next day's journey, my reward being; when they had a special chartered trip around the island, I could go with them, which is how I got to know Jamaica so well. Anyway, she hired a driver, Lee Mackenzie. My brother would conduct and off they would go daily and return in the evening with their stories, always about girls, no matter what they did, girls were involved. By this time Mrs. Ivy had named the van 'King Conscious' , famous among the girls because of Lee and Bro. Famous among the mature people for being reliable and courteous. During this time Lee and I became quite close, although looking back, I became close to him. He gave me my first driving lesson while we were cleaning the inside of the van one day. I was sitting around the driver's seat with the engine on, he was on his hands and knees helping me and all of a sudden he pressed down on the gas pedal and I had to steer our new van out of the way of the large akee tree. He looked up and said "yea man, you will drive." Lee had a new born son, 'Dwight', which is what I think edged him for the job, but he was one of the nicest guys I ever remember meeting. We played kung fu while we cleaned the van together and he would often bring me back something from the country or give me a show fare. If there was an early trip he would stay over and rest in our bed so he would not be late. In these times the political situation was turning sour. We had, as we do now, two major political parties; JLP, and the PNP, (one backed by Russians, the other, Americans). Each would oppress the people and blame the opposition; they also shipped in guns for their followers. It became very, very messy, and I was in the middle of it. I remember playing a game of football on the school grounds and all of a sudden hearing shots being fired. Instinctively, we all went to the ground, looking up to see police chasing a dreadlocked man across the pitch, shooting at him, with all of us belly down, the 'dread' jumped a wall that would have made any Olympic athlete proud and got away. At the beginning of the uprising I was shit scared. I remember distinctively, sitting on the toilet at home one evening and hearing gun shots from every direction and as I sat there with tears in my eyes I prayed and wished I was never there. I cannot say I ever got used to it. I just learned to cope with it even though it just kept on getting worse. The international news had it like a 'war zone' and it was. Even the great Bob Marley got shot. Families *that lived across the road from each other were okay, as long as they did not cross the white line in the middle of it, which was a division of territory. They made raids on police stations to free friends, so the army was bought in and curfews set and broken. The peaceful fun loving island of Jamaica had become a living hell hole. At home the evening conversation became like a stuck record; 'did you hear how many got shot today?' During the day, we all just tried to get on with life. I would still go off to school and off to the more dangerous parts of town to run errands for the family and the van would go off to the country. Meanwhile, Sis is having a relationship with one of the leaders of the local gang, which did not bother me because all I knew was that he was going out with my Sister and our family was protected, or so my little naive self thought. As the violence began to spread to our relatively quiet road, we began to awake to the news of shootings and serious injuries that had occurred on our street the night before and inevitably, it was soon our turn. Two times while my Brother and I were sleeping in the back part of the house, gun men broke in at the front. One of the times, my Gran fought off one of the men who tried to get his hand in the door, screaming and shouting and punching until they fled. I was really surprised that neither my brother nor I heard anything. She really does deserve a lot of respect. Anyway, we now had a routine for the van, which was an obvious target. Even though there would only be a maximum of $40, it was cash that we all survived on, so it must have been quite a lot in those days. Of an evening, as soon as the van came close to the turning that leads to our street, Lee would keep his hand on the horn and we would rush out to greet them (by this time, gone were the days when you could leave your front door open and people who came to visit would literally walk in and shout "anyone home!?" or the nights were so hot you needed a cool breeze). Because of the up serge of violence, the entire house was burglar bared, every window and every door. This may have actually saved my life, because one night while we were watching 'Dallas' (very big at the time) we heard the horn and while every one was glued to the TV, I jumped up and ran to the gates, but I*

86

got slowed down because I had to open the bars. I ran down the garden path to open the double gates, so that Lee could drive the van into the yard and around the side of the house, where it would be parked for the night. As I looked up from the gate, I noticed a dark figure descending from over a zinc fence opposite. He dropped something, which I later found out to be a gun. Not paying much attention, I continued to open the gates (it was normal for young men to jump fences rather than use the gate). As I stepped onto the street, I looked towards the van and heard a loud 'Bang!'. Unmistakably the sound of a gun. The van flew backwards into a wall and my brother came running towards me and the house. I knew what was going on and ran into the house shouting something. A lodger (Mrs Clair) very alert and calm called the police. My Brother came running into the house flapping his ear with his hand just after another shot was fired. When the panic was over and everyone seemingly forgetting about the van for that horrible moment in time, a neighbour came running into the house shouting 'Mrs. Ivy, dem shoot Lee!' I was the first out of the house and when I got onto the street, I saw the van lodged into our neighbour's wall, the same place I sat, under that same light, when I heard about my father. A beam shone through the windscreen of the transit van at such an angle that it highlighted Lee as if he were being spotlighted on a dark stage. I was about half way between our gate and the van (10 yards) standing frozen to the road, just looking at him sitting behind the steering wheel with his head back as though he were resting. They had shot Lee in the face, just on the right side of his nose below his eye and killed him. I have no idea of the time I spent there, but it was a dark night with no moon, just stars. There is a cluster of stars known as 'the seven sisters' but with the naked eye it's difficult to see all, usually you see only six. That night while I stood rooted to the ground I remember looking up and counting seven over and over again. Next thing I remember, I was asking the police if I should show them where his girlfriend and new born lived so they could tell her the news. I was 14 at the time. I had never seen emotion lived out as I did on that night before in my entire short life. And I prayed to God that I _would never have to witness it again. Then I remember all of us huddled together on my Auntie's new hand made bed, just lying there, not saying a word. 'Not a night one forgets.' From what I can recall now, we moved house the next day but we could not have because I can also remember still going to school and dreading coming home, because I had to walk passed some of the suspects houses._ **Until today I still have many of the memories of my youth blocked.** _Anyway, a short period after the incident, one morning Gran just said to us 'we are moving to the country' and we must not tell anyone because the gun men wouldn't want to leave witnesses. So we packed up and moved to Portland._

SAT 11TH

I have been so interested in jotting down my thoughts and reading best selling novels, that when I do go into the rec yard, I hardly recognize anyone. Someone came up to me yesterday and greeted me with "yo English man with no friends". While I was pondering this greeting for a second, another inmate came to me and asked if I had received my bread for that evening (they had run out again and sent for more) "yeah, thanks" I replied and stopped pondering.

Once again, the lack of will power and the want of hearing Kayana, made me phone Emilie. I knew I should not have but there must be no part in this child's life when she can think I did not try to be there, no matter what situation I am in. Emilie got the message from Jackson, good. While I was speaking to her on the phone, I heard a child in the background, I asked to speak to Ky and she said she was not there. Emilie did not want to talk to me so I hung up. Unless things change I don't think I will use the phone to call her again, bar Christmas and birthday. I also spoke to J. And I missed Nicole again. I thought she was staying for weeks or a month or so but it was only a weekend.

It seems, of all the things they can do for inmates here, they have decided to put on a boxing exhibition. Outsiders will be coming in to show their skills in the ring. I personally think that there will be more bouts after they have gone, without a referee.

The gunmen, who committed that appalling crime that took a much loved man away from his journey through life prematurely, were hung. Until this day, I can still honestly say "I would have watched them being hung without any remorse and been completely satisfied with justice". Like I said earlier, there are arguments against capital punishment, but spare a thought for the usually forgotten victims. Not the poor soul who was murdered, for we all have to die, or for the perpetrator, who, I can now say from personal experience, live an above exceptional life here for the crime commited. The two other English prisoners have told me that in here is more like a concentration camp compared to an English prison, but spare a thought for the ones who have had their loved ones taken away and then have to somehow get on with their lives, in their own world of paranoia, fright, nightmares and the constant fear of it happening again. Not for themselves for that would be too easy, no, to another loved one. If you can really prove beyond all reasonable doubt that they cold bloodedly murdered another human being, 'hang em' and if our so called democratic humane society cannot deal with it, for God's sake, don't treat them like the teenagers who have just stolen candy from the corner store.

Mon 15ᵀᴴ

I got up in a good mood. I think it's because I dreamed of Princess Di and I am exercising a little more. I am looking okay even though I think I am now looking my age... They used to say, my son and I look like brother or friends rather than father and son.

All seems well on the Western front; of course it does not mean it is. Here comes another week and I have the library to look forward to (I can understand people belonging to a book club now). I am expecting a package from J soon, and maybe a surprise package from 'English', but the thing I look forward to the most, is pouring my newly acquired tomatoes, pepper chilli, oil sauce (which I obtained for a pack of ciggs) over the bland excuse they have for a meal.

The Ras has just woken up and is looking at me in bemusement, because of the size of my writing; he thinks that I am some kind of genius. Ah well... qui sera.

I have now commissioned a birthday card for Ky, not because I cannot do one but because this guy can do it better. I personally do not like to celebrate my own birthday, because I believe it puts too much stress on one person to please another, especially at a time when they may not be up to it. I do believe however, that children should stay in their fantasy world as long as reasonably possible. I also apply this to Christmas. I buy presents that I see a loved one might like, to brighten up their day or week, on the spur of the moment, because in my eyes, now is the time, not when society, shops and money grabbers say it's time (Oh, there is no reason to believe that Christ was born on the 25th of December, so no problem).

Time for my roll and egg.

The front gates of this block have been opened by 'The men in black', I wonder why? (These are the guys with special combat training).

THURSDAY;

Just finished playing draughts, I won. The guards are downstairs playing dominoes. It's like a sweat box in here. I have called to the guard to turn off the light, which generates even more heat, but they are too busy playing. It's one of those things.

I got in a mood today because one of the inmates asked me for a cigarette "Mr. Collins" he said. I reminded him of the week before (in my own polite way, of course); he apologized and I sent him out. He returned later saying I was his boss, I told him it's time for him to find re-employment.

FRIDAY;

Did not feel like exercising. For the first time we have a fifth inmate in the cell. He seems to be a quiet man, about my age, and he has got the floor. One of the lads in here started to make noise at one of the guards about the overcrowding. I told him to 'chill' because, the way they operate, they will just put a sixth in here to teach him a lesson and then we all suffer: he saw my point. Sometimes I think prisoners in here confront the guards out of stupidity, but now it looks like attention seeking from other prisoners or maybe it's just their routine, which consists of arguing or just shouting all day long, at anything at all that happens: 'lights on!' let's shout, "water on!" let's shout, "they've caught a snake!" let's shout, "Bread's late!" let's shout and this helps them to do their time. Writing and reading helps me to do mine. It's the way to remain sane in here.

The new man has not said a word or been spoken to. I will see how it goes.

SAT 21ST

Up early to exercise. Oh, sugar, I have just realised it's pork today. I do not usually exercise on Saturdays because it makes me hungry. Well, as they say in here, "a jail dat deh".

Boxing today; we get to go out the front, which is still fenced in, but has a larger perimeter than our stretch yard. Maybe we get a glimpse of the women prisoners; I will get to wave at Candy.

I do not think of Emilie as much anymore. I guess it's because I think she is using Kayana to get to me. Not talking to me on the phone, not a line to let me know how she is doing. Okay, in a lot of eyes what I did was wrong and I am here paying the price, more than she will know and if she does not wish to talk to me on a certain level, I understand, but I do not think she should cut Kayana off which seems to be exactly what she is doing. I remember her promising me one day that she would never do this. What is it with women? It's the end of the world if a man tells a lie, because, "we women are not like that" but when they do lie, it's perfectly justifiable and all I can do is sit here in a cell and take it, with no response, because if I do respond, I get to feel I am being cut out even more. So, I sit on my bunk thinking; how a love so good, can turn into something so not good. How do I retaliate? Answer: 'You don't. You chill out, read a book, exercise and don't think of retaliation, even though you have an awful lot of time to. Remember, she is still the mother of your child and in the end, as you and I know only too well, it is the child that truly suffers for the poor and selfish decisions that parents make.'

So we move from the capital 'Kingston' to a parish on the east side of the island. My memory now seems to be disorientated with gaps, as though a dream but not a dream, a thing that happened but did not, although must have, because of the proof of present reality. For example; I am trying to remember if Lee actually had a son before or after he went. Did the mother and son get taken in to live with us when we moved from Kingston or after we settled? I don't remember hearing a child screaming but I do remember a child running up and down when we moved again later. Anyway, the funeral was big. Lee came from the same parish that we moved to and it seemed everybody knew him. Young and old turned out to send him off. It was an open casket and I took my turn to pass and say goodbye. It was the first time I had seen death close up. It's hard for me to describe; He is there, but he is not. For a very long time after the funeral, I always thought he was looking out for me. Somewhere, somehow, something would happen and I would cheat death, I would always think that it was Lee.

So, now another split in the family. My Brother was to be taken away from me again; the people of Portland were very good to us. I got on well with everyone and settled in a new school. In the beginning I excelled in my class, so much so I was the only student to take final exams in a different school because the exams they were giving in my school were considered below my par. I played a lot of football for the school and became popular with the girls. I think a lot of this had to do with my English accent and the fact that we were popular because of the van, which still did the same trip, only in reverse, and also because Mrs. Ivy happened to rent the biggest house in town. So I guess one could say I had things going for me (I am 15+). It was a two storey, four bed room house that stood just off the main road, lots of space at the front and sides and a hill at the back, leading miles into the back bone of Jamaica. Ideal for my seclusion zone. The town is called 'Boston Bay' famous for starting the 'Jerk seasoning'.

On our side of the parish, there were roughly 12 small towns that the van passed through every day, bar Sunday, on route to Kingston. The van left at seven in the morning and returned at about three/ five in the afternoon. I can remember if I was not on the van returning from school, I would be up on the balcony with everyone else, waiting for 'King Conscious' to return. This was done religiously, somehow we were all together, no matter what we were doing, we would hear the van's horn from about a mile up the road and shout "Conscious is coming!" This was mainly to do with the fact that Kingston was getting worse and we all knew the possibilities. Despite this, my grandma used to drive the van and she became a regular heroine throughout that part of Jamaica.

My brother (17 at the time) was the envy of most his age and older because he had unlimited access to girls (mainly school girls but the best of) and because I was next in line as 'most eligible' bachelor... At this time in life I am making the most of good things, making good friends and having a good time. Once again I found my calling towards the streets; peoples' houses were always open to me. During the day, if not at school I could be found playing football or cricket on a pitch that we cleaned out from some neighbour's piece of bush land, we dug it up then levelled it and played the sport according to the season. We would go fishing down by the rocks across the road from us about half a mile through bush land and we would run up and down catching (or trying to catch) wild goats and every so often, we would have a cook out and just chill, giving each other jokes . On hot days we would go to the beach (literally 5 mins walk from the house) and swim, surf and play. Thursday nights we would go to the local cinema (which was our open air dance hall ,transformed, by putting a big white sheet across the back wall and re- arranging benches. It was always packed with the same people but we enjoyed it. The movie was always Karate or a western and afterwards we would fight each other with our newly acquired skills all the way home, very often hurting each other and not really caring, we just had to practice more. If the show was not on, it was guaranteed there would be music playing, just to hang out or dance to, or both. Failing this (a power cut) we would 'hang out' at our meeting place, in front of our neighbour's ('fatty') house and just be teenagers .

Not all houses in our town had running water or electricity but there were stand pipes at regular intervals along the road and just off the road side in some front yards, this is where the young ones (my age) would sometimes have their evening washes. It was around this time I became more interested in the female structure. Although the pipes were just off the road it would be normal for the girls to just strip off and bathe and we would play our little games, getting closer to our goals each night. From this episode came my first ongoing relationship with a woman.

22ND SUNDAY MORNING;

I have just scrubbed my cell walls and metal bunk, had my morning shower and decided to sit on a small railing, near the outside washing. The sky is scattered with clouds but it is a warm sunny Caribbean day. Inside, the usual banging of dominoes is taking place. The phone is relatively quiet since I Cry took over as time keeper, some of the others are playing draughts or chess, while outside I sit and observe the sea across the hills of green landscape; looks calm, no whales today. There is white smoke drifting across the flat at the bottom of a hill where a tractor has made a clearing for a future road through the hills. Hanging on the mesh fence, the top of which is strewn with razor sharp bits of metal, is some inmates' laundry; towels, sheets, pillow cases, the odd pair of socks and a few bandanas. My washer man Blaze (a big East Indian type fella with constantly blood shot eyes) passes me by with a smile and a nod, while he hangs out my washing, as if to say 'I am worth the pack of cigarettes, in' it?' I nod and return an appreciating smile "yeah man, das good" is unspoken but heard. Within the perimeter of the fence, other inmates sit in small groups of twos and threes, backs up against the fence appreciating the cool breeze and little shade, offered by the shimmering laundry, made so by the wind sweeping in from the Atlantic. On the concrete ground of the rec yard lie trainers and bits of towels that have been washed. Dotted around them like an exhibition of modern art are sponges 6 by 3 (the size of the average door at home) they are the mattresses which have been put out to sun to be relieved of the sweat inevitably accumulated over the past few days (or weeks depending on the owner). As I glance up from my thoughts I notice a Rasta man; half bald with one short matted lock at the back of his head and a moustache that almost covered his mouth. He was walking towards me, almost in slow motion, steering through the sponges as if not seeing them but not touching them either. He glanced at me as I was checking his six pack out. He is older than me, my guess 6, 7 years but he outdoes everyone with pull ups and sit ups, although you would be lucky to actually catch him doing them. I wonder, as I look for a second, when will my physical look stop responding to my early ongoing morning sessions of routine exercise? Well, at least six or seven years, I think to myself. Then I kind of gazed up, still deep in thought and at that moment, our eyes made four and before I could think of anything to say he smiled at me as if he knew exactly what I was thinking. I smiled back and once again, within the space of a few minutes, on this Sunday morning in the 'Bordelais correctional facility' on the island of St. Lucia, so much was heard between three human beings, without a word being spoken. Time to eat, it's lamb today...

Dinner went well. I called Sis, apparently she got wet waiting for a date, nothing unusual there. I think she took her part of what life threw at her, in a similar way to me.

WED 23RD

I am really fed up at the moment, why? I am not sure, but it's nagging me, maybe because I would like to be alone in my mood but as I lay on this bed of metal trying to stabilise my thoughts, inmates just have to wonder in, to say or talk about the same boring things that they have been talking about since they started to talk to me; There is an inmate, very muscular; he is always on the phone and for the last three days has turned up at my cell to talk to me about the said phone and how he has enemies because of it. Sometimes I can put up with it but I have nothing much to say to him, even though we all need a shoulder to cry on. So when he stops talking it is quiet for a few (to me) uncomfortable moments, so I pick up my book and start reading. He gets up with a half smile and says "I know what you're going to do right now". "Good" I say, "so leave". After he leaves, someone hovers over me with a request form for me to fill in for him; he seems to think that this task is more important for me, than what I am doing for myself. I decided to fill it in because he was just standing over me, watching what I was doing. I figure if I say something about it now, it will come out all wrong and some part of me is saying "he does not deserve it".

THURS 27TH MORNING.

W.I. play India in cricket and it's relatively quiet. I am still a bit moody but not as much as yesterday. *At Oakfield,* _when I was in one of these moods, I would just find a corner in the big house and sulk for hours. In Kingston, I don't remember having times for moods and in Portland, it was great. Across the road from us were sparingly separated houses, some concrete, some wood, some mixed, all homes in their own right. All were doted about, just off the main road, so you would see, more often than not, a packed stone wall, with a gate or log across an opening. The space or 'yard' in front of a house was always well kept, no matter who lived there. Some had nicely mowed lawns, big enough for us to play 5 or 6 aside football and some, just dirt yards with various fruit trees scattered around. Beyond the back of the houses was the best part for me, because gradually as you walked down towards the sharp honeycombed rocks, which end with a sheer drop down to the sea, the trees would slowly become more dense and the undergrowth much thicker (what we call bush). This is where we spent most of our time (if away from the playing fields and beaches). Down in the bush were countless coconut trees, mango trees, etc and when I got moody I would climb to the top of a special coconut tree, with a knife, and sit in those long, slender, elegant branches and sway in the wind while drinking the fresh water from the young coconuts. I was often so relaxed I would sometimes fall asleep._ **Excellent therapy for bad moods.** _I don't believe I have mentioned that to anyone before now. Where the bush got the thickest, people would tie their cows and goats out to graze and when we had time (which was often enough) we would help to water them. This was hard work, but not for sixteen year olds who have a lot of energy to use up. We would carry wash basins and bath pans full of water from the house, through the bush, to the cows (cows drink a lot of water, so it was often two or three trips), but it was all fun for us and we would always make some kind of game of it, in the bush, with the girls (if they were there) and I was 100% a part of this. In fact, this time around, I was the main catch. But we all had fun._

Some nights we would go crab catching. After a heavy rainfall, with our kerosene lit lamps and large sticks, off we would go, into the moonless night "stopping" crabs as they scurried across *the road, trying to find safety amongst the rocks on the other side (funny enough, they remind me now of a younger Kayana chasing pigeons in the park). We would end up walking at least 8 miles in one direction before we turned back, stopping and playing on the way home, where the next fresh meal was of course... 'Fresh crab.' Most of my little gang had a time limit on them, or they imposed it upon themselves. I still had problems with calling Grandma a name, so if the doors were locked I would simply sleep outside. I figured it was a good deal; after all it was never cold. So once in a while we would go night fishing, from the rocks beyond the bush, we would pick bread fruit on the way there and make a ridiculously large fire to roast them on , then set about trying to catch fish, 70 or so yards from off the rocks to the sea, with our fishing lines that where wrapped around a stick , stones for a sinker, and hooks bought from the local hardware store. We would sit for hours on these sharp honeycomb rocks, not catching anything and blaming it on each other for either making too much noise or moving too much. Then close to sun up, when the breadfruit was ready to eat, we would eat until our stomachs were full and wash it down with home made lemonade and off we would march, home to tell our other friends about the ones that got away. Of course these adventures took place all year round but during the holiday season it was more so. Take the beach; just because we had one of the most beautifully untouched beaches in Jamaica, on our doorstep, it would surprise some people to see it empty most of the year round but when we did go, it would be for the day; snorkelling, surfing, and diving for treasures, left behind by careless tourists. It was a cove and we could swim to the mouth of it, climb up the rocks, dive back off and race to the shore. We would play football and when the evening came the beach became more secluded. Well, you can imagine: a coved beach, the cool turquoise Caribbean Sea swishing up to and unfolding on the golden grains of sand. Hills of green in the background looking out to see the sun setting, and the silhouette of a young beautiful Jamaican girl innocently smiling and playing bare breasted in the rippling water. There is no need for words, there is no need for courting, we are friends and this is a way of life.*

We were very promiscuous and it was never really frowned upon, as long as it was done with a certain amount of respect (you don't go of bragging about sleeping with someone if they are supposed to be taken. Although if you found out, it should not come from the horses mouth, unless of course, she/he was new in the area, and that would lead to a fight, instigated by the rest of the gang, after which the outsider was generally accepted). These were not so much happy times in my life as they were tranquil. It took my mind off a lot of other issues, which were really getting a hold of me. At home, Bro and Sis did their thing. Brother, the grown up, would often be out on the van or with his age group. We had time for each other but not much, I think at this time we were both just 'trying to get on with it.' I think I really stopped taking things in around the family. I was not angry with anyone and I don't think anyone was angry with me, I just preferred being outside. So looking back now, although these next few incidents happened, it's hard to put them into comparative time zones to other incidents, in other words, right now, it all just... seemed to have happened. My Great Grandma died. As I said, she was bed ridden ever since I went to Jamaica. I can remember her telling me stories of Queen Victoria. I spent time looking after her as did we all. I don't remember Bro having anything to do with her, though. When she died I watched Gran cry over her as we stood and watched the last breath leave her body. Her tears though, I thought were more of thankfulness for the ending of the suffering. I went to the morgue (I don't know why) and watched them dress and make her up for the funeral, which was somewhat different to the other one. It was held in her home parish, there were drums beating (kumina) sacrifices of chickens and lots of rum and People were performing rituals that had been passed down from generations.

Through the cell window I can see them rigging something in the rec yard. The boxing was suspended last week so I guess it's for that.

This weekend; the non speaking man from my cell is outside working already. Apparently there is an abundance of work (like searching for and killing snakes close to the perimeter) for those willing; it's just the majority refuse to work for fifty cents a day.

SAT 29TH

The boxing exhibition was okay. The highlight being when the woman officer (who had the misunderstanding with my phones), wearing a tight pair of pants and a loose at the sleeves but figure hugging top, passed by the inmates to an onslaught of whistles, clapping and shouting, all in good taste. She is about 48 but she does have a good figure, shame about her temperament. The lads came back to the cell sparring along the way as I did when I was in the island. A few fights were on the verge but nothing unfolded.

Mrs Ivy's husband had come back from the States when we were in Kingston (he was not my grandfather, thank God) and with all the trouble going on he added to it. He would come and go when he felt like it and was always drunk. He was not there at the time of the shooting but turned up one day when we had moved to the country.

Gran had a few acres of land in the country, about 17 miles from the house and he used to farm it: bananas, yam, coca ect, -in the earlier days we used to collect the dry coconuts and sell them by weight which was used for copra to make oil-. When he took over, he behaved himself at first, then more often than not he would come home really drunk and start arguing with anyone for nothing. Then he would start on grandma, who I believe was 54 at the time (for some reason she was always that age whenever someone asked me). The arguments got worse and even the police were called in. The police throughout the Caribbean are known for their tactics, it's accepted as a way of life, not surprising being how small the country is. Everyone knows everyone and who does not, knows someone who does. The police took, not what was seen as bribes but as money to help them with bills to get by, because, of course, the salary was never enough. We had a love hate, no, an all right hate relationship. They did not really protect us but our van was popular. By law licensed to carry 12 passengers at any one time and bearing in mind that we had to 'pick up' and 'drop off', it would be impossible to run a bus like this and survive, so as all buses in those days did, we stopped for all the passengers and if there was space, we asked if they did not mind the discomfort for a while. Very few said no, we were known for racking, stacking, and packing passengers, in fact, when I took over from my Bro I was known for driving outside the door with my foot on the sliding step, one arm over the open door and the other braced against the inside to stop me from falling, just so we could fit more passengers in, and this was the norm at 70, 80 miles an hour . The police knew this and would set up road blocks. But we usually got warned by oncoming traffic, a flash of lights or a quick hand signal. When it was time for them to have money they would stop us for anything, then they would explain in front of the passengers, why they stopped us and what law we were breaking and the passengers were made to believe that the van would be seized and their journey ended. Then an officer would call the driver around to the back of the van and remind him that it was Christmas or such and after a quick exchange, all was well. There was a time when I was on the van and an officer caught me outside. He counted 48 passengers, turned to me and said he could "not be bothered to count anymore."We went to court that day and were charged $30, and resumed work. Sometimes we would be on the way home, with a van full of passengers, and certain police would be drinking in a bar. They would stop us, all smiles, and ask or tell in their polite way to 'have a drink' with them, we did. If we did not, they would be waiting for us the next morning. This was all done with an understanding, it was through this; we got to know the police quite well. Sometimes a sergeant might say he is 'coming to dinner on Sunday' which I thought was pushing it, so I was quite surprised when they were called to the house for the husband's behaviour; they told Mrs. Ivy that they could do nothing, unless *someone ended up in hospital or, if she was raped. 'It's a matter of domestic violence that should be sorted out at home'. So when the fights started, and they did, even though the whole town knew. It was a household thing. It would always start behind the closed doors of the bedroom; voices got louder, words got stronger and then the scuffles. Jenny (Aunt Jenny, his daughter) would always try to stick up for her Mum and Sis once hit him with a large rock that was used as a door stop, but with blood oozing from his head, he carried on as if nothing happened. I was not always there when the fighting was going on and did not really partake in it. I did not have whatever it takes to fight anyone at that time in my life. My brother, on the other hand, did. I remember coming home to hear him screaming, "Mammy! Mammy!" I ran up the stairs and into the house to see the two of them seriously fighting. The husband had a machete in one hand, which Bro had a hold of and the two just wrestled, with the machete flying every where while we watched on. It was the first and last of the machete in a situation like that but there were more scuffles in the near future which Bro always came out on top. The husband was not tall but at 5"8 he was very compact and strong and I think the reason Bro always got the better of him, was because he was always drunk and I guess after the shooting incident, my Bro probably thought he should have been dead already, nothing to lose. This made me proud to have a big brother like him although I think he saw me as 'just a waste of space,' unless that behaviour is typical of the big brother little brother syndrome. In any case he would not have anyone mess with me, so a joke at my expense, I could live with that. While all this was going on Bro would be taking special trips to Kingston. As an eye witness of the murder, he was picked up, dropped off and taken care of by the island's police. He would tell me stories of his weekends under police protection; riding around in the back of a Toyota crown and watching the bad boys being interrogated, J. A style. He glamorised it I'm sure, but at that age, which teenage hyper man would not? The case was tried (I was not there, I had nothing to do with the case whatsoever, I was not even asked if I saw the incident or if I was, I do not remember), the murderer was hung and in exchange for his testimony, he asked to go to the States to 'cool out' on some kind of witness protection scheme (I must add, he would have testified anyway). After the case was over, I don't remember him going. I just know he did (I am 15/16).*

Sis had other issues. She was beautiful and she knew it. She had won prizes in the schools she went to for being the neatest student. I don't think she set out for any prizes, they were just a result of the way she naturally acted. When we attended the same school together, which was about 28 miles away, we had to catch a 5.30am bus to get to school for 7. I used to be out of bed at 5 and do not remember ever missing the bus (all buses on our route knew us and would give us a friendly blast on their air horn when passing. So our bus would be bellowing its horn at least a quarter of a mile away to give us final prep time). Sis would be up at three in the morning, and very rarely caught the bus. She would usually get a ride from a neighbour who if I missed... ,no, if the bus never turned up, would tell me he was full and that he had to pick up other people along the way (to me he was just a dirty old man and worse, good friends with the husband). When on some mystical day she did catch the bus, it was an amazing act of self indulgence that really had to be witnessed; in the house, the three of us shared the downstairs. Sis had a room next door to ours with a toilet and bathroom, (we had a massive room with a toilet and shower) so she would wake me up with her antics (ever since the shooting I have been a very light sleeper. My brother could sleep at the base of an erupting volcano undisturbed). She would spend her time in the shower, which, as far as I know, only gay men and other women really know what goes on in that room of theirs. Then she would reach for her uniform, which was always ironed the night before at around 11.30, and go over it again, if in her eyes it was necessary. A Persil white blouse and a maroon skirt with a top like an over all, (a square front patch with two length of strip material that crossed over each other at the back and was buttoned to the patch at the front of the skirt). A nice uniform and Sis would have made the designer proud. She wore a high afro, we're talking seventies, Jackson 5 stuff that took forever to comb, well not actually to comb but to get every hair in place and stay there. With a flick of the pick (or soul comb) and a patting down with the hand here and there, her hair was always combed. But it had to be neat on leaving the house and all this was done seemingly without forethought or effort (and no, not all women are like this. We are talking extreme). What I used to like observing the most with amusement, was the effort she used to keep her socks in place. White socks, which unfolded as she put them on and came up to just below the knees, were with great precision and care, neatly turned back down. Each one twice, with about a two inch fold, each fold, being smoothed to her leg. On the bus, if she sat (not for lack of seats but not to crease the uniform) there would not be a crease in sight. Of course she would always see one and harrumph! to herself while I looked on unnoticed with a smile on my face. After the bus journey, we faced a half to three quarter mile walk, on a road through a sugar cane field, to where our school was situated. I never liked to be late because I liked school back then, but I also always liked to walk with Sis, which really was annoying, because even when the bus was on time she would be late. She would first get off the bus, straighten out her uniform and fix her hair, even her folder got due care and attention. When she was satisfied, off she would strut like a teen catwalk model in slow motion. But that's not what made her late; after every so many steps, she would stop, give me the folder (if I was close , the embankment if not)and roll each sock back up to just below her knee and do the same unfolding process, 'because' she protested, they were riding too far down her legs (you had to be there).

Thurs 3ʳᵈ

Another eve falls;

I am a quarter the way through another book 'Over Load'. I have not long finished a romantic novel 'Outlaws bride' by Joan Johnson; it's the first romantic novel I have read and was surprised at how much I enjoyed it. Her address was in the back of the book, so I wrote her a quick note stating just that. I hope she replies, it would be nice to get a letter from someone who is not going to piss me off.

The last few days have become to me, what's known as 'the norm'. A big fight broke out downstairs, apparently one of my 'employees' did not like the way his cell mate was misusing the disinfectant we get issued, steal or buy (ciggs), so he thumped him. A few more joined in but no blood flowed.

Apparently an inmate was taken to hospital and diagnosed with T.B. His other four cell mates went in for tests but it's being kept quiet. I wonder what would happen if an epidemic broke out in here. Wow! That would be a sad end for someone who decided to turn his life around.

We are in the cell. The cricket crazy Ras wakes up 5 o' clock in the morning to listen to the ICC competition and he does not mind making as much noise as possible, to let everyone know he is enjoying it. The others, I think pretended to be asleep through it, except Chi chi, who sleeps through anything this place has to offer. Myself, I just get up half an hour earlier and exercise. The Ras is funny, I like him. Just now as I write, someone has blown their nose really loud and Ras is saying something, I'm not sure what, but it included "is everyone here in the cell garcons!" The way he said it just sounded very funny. We are all getting on very well in the cell and today the new lad said two sentences; one, in reply to me telling him he could "use my bucket to bathe in the cell after work" if he liked. I asked as politely and un-embarrassingly as I could, even though the body odour of a working man in a cell with 5 inmates such as this is awful. The next day he came from work late and just as they were about to call 'Roll check!' he said to me in half English and half whatever, that he could not bathe yet, but would use the bucket when the cell reopens. For some reason I felt guilty, but it passed. The other thing he said to me was while I was reading in the afternoon, "excuse I want to shit please".Oh well, I guess his tactical politeness and mine tend to differ some what. No problem.

The boss man was in a good mood this morning. He stopped me on my way upstairs to enquire about the health of my family, "fine" I said and thanked him for asking. Then I got back to my cell and although J has got his problems, Nicole won't return my letter, Emilie won't write and tell me how Kayana is doing and, I have not heard a word of support from any other member of my so called family. "Yeah," I guess I just have to keep telling myself they're all 'fine' as well.

I was wondering what some of the guards think of me, especially 'Boss man'. I tried to look at my self from their point of view. The outside looking in. All they know of me is that I am a drug trafficker from London with possible connections in Jamaica and the USA. I am quiet, I don't respond to provocation and in their sight I don't break any of their rules. I always say good morn or afternoon and thank them for their time, if I know I am going to address a guard I don a shirt and comb my hair, and I only speak to them when spoken to. I sometimes show humour but do not joke with them and if a guard does decide to converse with me, we chat for a while and I usually end up finding out more about them, that they would sometimes like to reveal. I know the Boss would like to converse with me, but I will not approach him and I would not allow him to approach me. The other day he asked me when I was leaving, I answered and he paused as if he wanted me to add more, I held the pause as if to say "Anything else?" He smiled shaking his head and off he went. I wonder if he knew I was messing with him, simply because; I know that the inmate's departure dates are on the office wall in front of his desk chair. "I like this", it gives me an aura of mystique to him. I often catch him looking at me from his office window when I am whale watching.

This evening I strolled across the rec yard to my whale watching spot, did not see any, but I am also on the look out for a small marsupial type animal, which apparently frequencies the outskirts of the perimeter. It was described to me by I Cry as having two long hind legs and two short front legs, which made it fast up hill and slow down. I haven't seen one yet though.

24TH.

It's time to leave my friendly bunk and go forth on my routine quest for my friendly whale. I don my worn out but friendly flip-flops, take a quick glance in the warped 6 by 6 piece of glass on the wall above our tiny sink, turn right, out of my cell towards the four showers, which I avoid by turning left and descend the 13 steps to the ground level, noticing, but avoiding, the loitering inmates, all dressed in blue shorts and tops. Some have pretty hair styles, many having tattoos, some with serious looks of intent and some obviously thinking of the time already spent. I pass the domino players and men on the phone talking to friends and family, wishing they were home, through the two large gates that open onto the yard and across from which nature is, but we are barred. Once again I look out beyond fence, across the hills of green bushes and trees, out, scanning the Atlantic sea, caught up in the confused feeling of freedom, bought upon me by the cool Atlantic breeze. I did not see my whale; instead I saw two birds courting, with a matching rhythm and coordination that would make Torvil and Dean in their prime, envious. One propped upon the top of the razor wire, head aloft bobbing rhythmically back and forward, mouth agape meeting and accepting the beak of its partner, which is flertisly hovering just out of reach. But every, what seems like few seconds, but looks like split seconds, the other descends obligingly, teasing its partner with a game of 'it is, no it is not'. The bird on the fence takes flight and amazingly enough the mate is not following, but is flying by her side, darting from side to side up and down. Not maybe more than 6 inches apart, almost matching speed of body and equalling each other's wing beat, mirroring their flight path in a magnificent Ariel display of fondness for each other, so perfectly. I could not only see them I could actually feel them.

There they are, two birds above, playing out the game of love, being oblivious of their surroundings, ignorant of me. Just two birds in love, happy and free.

TUE 7ᵀᴴ

I have seen the little fellow known by the name of 'Agouti', an inmate threw bread over the fence for it at midday during Rec time. He appeared at tea time to retrieve it, with a crowd of spectators looking on in awe. They seemed to be as fascinated as I was to see the little creature, yet I was told they were as common as chickens on the island. Intriguing. I think they were bemused to see the Agouti because most of the inmates have not seen one in a long time. They are becoming a rarity, no doubt due to the islands rapidly growing development and the ever increasing tourist industry. One time in the past, inmates may have seen the occasional 'Agouti' pop up in their back yard for a bite to eat, just as a neighbouring fowl might do today. They are now only (it seems) seen deeper in the bush, since the prison is surrounded by bush and the only humans around are safely behind fences, these inquisitive vegetarians can sneak a bite and at the same time sneak a peak at this hostile environment's co inhabitants. Oh yes! I must not forget. They are edible.

I have just come back from the yard, handed in a book, now I am on the bunk waiting for returns. Time for thought; while I was in the 'Rec yard' a tennis ball bounces towards me, from the other lads in Bravo -who are separated from us by one of the fences- an inmate beckons me to throw it back, a distance of about 60 yards. So, I am picking up the ball, thinking if I should throw it back over the fence, or, give it to someone nearby so they can return it. If I gave it to someone else, how would the inmates see it, simply, 'I cannot throw a ball over a fence' or would some remember I told them I had problems with my arms (I know most, if not all, the yard was watching because it was a tennis ball. Main use, trafficking) or some would be drawing other conclusions. These thoughts are happening as I am catching the ball and throwing it back. What did not occur to me at the time was that I didn't know I was thinking (or calculating), for the throw to be precise. I had to think and calculate the distance of the balls flight, the velocity at which I am going to hurl it through the air (1, to not fall short, 2, to not overthrow), the path of flight (not too far left or too far right) and the resistance and opposite of, to make sure it stays on course (the wind flow). I had a direct hit, the receiver only had to move his arms and hands a fraction to catch the ball. And while accepting an unseen nod of approval I was also thinking of the pain in my arm while calculating. With all this going on in split second timing, it is actually possible for me to get the ball to the intended target. Hell, I know we cannot all knock the coconut of the pole at the funfair, but if you can think about it, isn't it amazing what we think about, when we are not thinking about anything? I saw a mind game on 'Friends' once, involving Joey of course, the same, I think, psychiatrists use for their patients, though they also use flash cards. The idea I got from 'Friends' is that if you answer a series of quick fire questions without consciously thinking about the answer, it would be true and should reveal a lot about your state of mind. What are the questions really revealing though? I did a quick test on myself (I thought about doing the test and completed it before I could consciously think about the questions or answers). One of the questions I asked was, "What's my favourite fruit? Banana," was the answer. I stopped the test realising it was not the right answer; I prefer mangoes, pineapples and grapes. The reason I think that the answer was wrong became clear; Since I have been here, I have only seen Melons and Bananas, Bananas twice, which were over ripe and smelt as though they were fermenting. Hence, subconsciously, fruit, Banana. This leads me to the question. How would a person benefit from a question unless he/ she knew the social life you had been in prior to the question, to ascertain weather or not you were subconsciously telling the truth? In prison or not, what would be the point of the question in the beginning, if he already knew your state of mind? Just a thought for today. So, now I am thinking.

Library is here, time to read 'Alistair MacLean' and 'Lesli Egan'. The first I have heard of, the second I don't think so, or... do I? I could never tell what my grandma was thinking, she would just do things or things would just happen. *Before we left Kingston she told my sister that she was pregnant , this I could not understand because although I used to carry messages back and forth between Sis and the boyfriend I could not see how she could find the time or the place. Later in life I was to find how deceptive young girls can be when it comes to boys. Sis refuted the accusation and nothing more seemed to have been said (at least that I knew of) so she went to school normally (for her) until it started showing. It was around that time in life I saw changes in her. She took the looking after herself and extended it to the house and would clean, clean and clean on her hands and knees, and we had no carpet (Caribbean style). We had square marble like tiles, no hoover. Instead, we /they used the husk of a coconut with polish and she would shine those tiles until you could see your face in them. With this she grew a temper and an attitude with us. No one bar grandma could go near the veranda when it was clean, which seemed to be all the time, if we did, me and Bro especially would get a mouthful that could be heard a good quarter of a mile away. Her favourite, "oonu cum ofa di veranda!" Later, my mates would be laughing with me saying "Kay catch you again". I think I got the odd slap but it did not bother me. My sister cleaned like that up until the time she had the baby.*

It was about 2/3 in the morning. She was calling through the door that separated us and Bro told me to go and tell Grandma. Although apprehensive for a split second (still not being the first to talk) I went and called her. It was one of the few times I did break the silence between Gran and I, but for some reason still unknown to me, I would revert and very frustrated the block would be there again. (I still cannot figure that one out). This night there was an electricity blackout (the norm for J.A at the time). I was told to go and call 'Fatty' our neighbour and helper from across the street (I still have time for her and her family when I visit Jamaica). By the time it took me to go upstairs, call Mrs Ivy, and go across the street to get fatty, the baby was crying. Sis had the baby in the toilet room, her excuse for that was; she did not want to get the "sheets dirty". Fatty took care of things and Bro and I chatted away for the rest of the night. Although this was Grandma's first Great Grand child, she could not have the son of the man whose gang she thought (with good reason) killed Lee, in the same house with her. My recollection was she and the child had to go, "where?" anywhere. Within the next few months, my sister, fifteen, and her newborn son, were gone. She did not know then and still doesn't know now that I cried for her that day, because I knew what it was like to have your family not want you. I did not see or hear from her again until 16 years later.

Not long after the court case was over, my Brother was flown to America to stay with his Dad. He kept in contact with a few letters here and there and he sent me the odd U.S dollars also. He had flung himself into business and although he never finished school, he was later to become very successful. In the months during and after the pregnancy, while Bro still worked on the van, there was a period of searching for drivers so Mrs. Ivy could take it easy. There were a few applicants, one of who was called 'Reds'. A hard worker and a good mechanic, he always seemed to find some reason to pull the van's engine to bits and then some how manage to put it back together. He and Bro got on well together, I think, because the two had a similar appetite for girls. The only problem it seemed was that every time the van went out while he was driving it, it would crash. I think Mrs Ivy kept him on because he was a very hardworking man, however, due to Jamaican superstition and belief, the word was out that 'Lee' was the cause of the accidents from beyond the grave and did not want 'Reds' to drive the van. And so Mrs Ivy regretfully let him go. Before or after he drove I can only remember one accident with the van, thankfully in any of the circumstances no one was hurt. So now we needed a new driver.

Bro goes off to America and I became the conductor, excellent (or so I thought). I get the chance to emulate in my brother's foot steps. My first driver, outside the family was Lee's brother Mr Panton; A nice guy, with a dry sense of humour and very professional. Even in just driving the van, he did not, but struck me as the kind of person that if asked would gladly wear a tie to work. He was nice but I always thought that I would have enjoyed more and ironically felt safer if Lee was driving. There was one problem and that concerned the safety of the van and passengers. It was the fact that he was an active PNP member. We rode our luck standing on the fence (we were a JLP family) and went into town every day as usual, hearing about and witnessing all sorts of violent acts. There were constant army road blocks and check points where they would pull us over and search the passengers one by one and the van for weapons. We never once had a problem with this; our main problem was where we parked the van at the end of the line. The bus terminal on West Street, down town Kingston, a large cafe type building with seats for quite a few people but very rarely used. Most would buy a quick lunch and sit on their bus and eat because it was safer. There was a big yard for the bigger buses and the mini buses and taxis would park on the side walk or the street outside. There was a street market going back the way we came and on the other side of the terminal the infamous Trench town, Rema and Jungle (which was and up to date still is, by far, the most violent place in Jamaica) split into territory by roads. PNP and JLP vying to win the election by shooting and killing each other.

Friday;

It's another hot day in St Lucia. I have taken some of the morning sun in an attempt to tan slowly over the next half year, for the journey back to England. The usual hurling of soaps in plastic bags with their other contents swish back and forth overhead. I find it strange, it seems today more than any other the inmates are missing their catches and falling short of their targets.

It was tuc shop yesterday, the normal people ask me for cigarettes in return for favours i.e. someone lent me a radio, someone else is fixing the old one , my antenna wire which leads up to the roof has snapped, so someone is looking out for one for me. I Cry has borrowed my last phone card (he has a $50 card but does not trust the guy with it) so I will smoke tonight, I look forward to it. Of the two books I borrowed from the library I did not take to any of them, so I'm thinking, a boring 5 days ahead. But strangely enough a lad downstairs had the same problem and showed me his books. Susan Tamaros's 'follow your heart'. After reading the wording at the back of the book, I thought, I have to read this. What caught my mind was, "while reliving everything that happened to her, she seeks to remind her Granddaughter that the one worthwhile journey in life is to the centre of one's self. Reflecting on feelings and passion and how failure to communicate leads to futility, misunderstanding even tragedy". This is one of those times when a percentage of me believe in destiny and that something, a force of some sort, is ever present. Looking over us and playing what my simple human brain conceives as a game. I shall read the book.

I have reached page two in the book and the lad who lent it to me has just entered the cell and asks for a pack of biscuits, I gave it to him; he has already earned it.

Sat; Day of the pig.

Last night we played dominoes, it's the Ras's last night. I have been observing his actions and I caught him off guard twice doing a little jig, it was fun to see. I tried to help him out in the domino game but really he should stick to draught. 'I cry' sent over a little weed, but the Ras does not smoke with ciggs and neither does Kenny, Chi chi said it was too small and so I had it all for myself. During the game, downstairs in cell

7, my once friend André was banging the metal stool in his cell. It was ignored at first but as we all begun to find out that someone needed medical attention, we all joined in with one hell of a racket. The guards who were off (probably playing monopoly) came after a long while and he was taken to the hospital in an ambulance. My evening was spent in solitude after the smoke; I started to listen to the radio and reading the book which has been written similar to this. The main character is at a stage in her life were she finds it necessary to write a letter, in the form of a diary, of her past and present, to explain to someone she loves (grand daughter) what was thrown at her and what paths she had chosen. Well, she is a writer and I am just me, so where she may describe and put pen to paper more eloquently than me, what I am writing is an honest account of what happened in the journey of my life. I am half way through the book and it appears to me, that I have been through a hell of a lot more at my half way stage, but I understand, sometimes one thing can lead to an accumulation of things and an accumulation of things can lead to a single outcome and the pain or happiness can be equal of either cause. But trying to read the book while high was pretty much impossible, as every time I tried to read a sentence my thoughts strayed. So, whatever the outcome of this book of life will be, the questions asked are "what ifs?" Suppose they take this from me at the gate when I leave... This would be a disaster, because this cannot be done again, by me, or anyone else. The time for this, would have passed forever. Oh, I could explain vocally to my kids and loved ones, but it would not show the same picture. How would my kids receive the book? And three (it appears I am stoned now), suppose life is a play, a joke on me and none of this is happening? Suppose I wake up and everyone I have known before I came here, said I never left? Of course this would be a conspiracy to drive me crazy, but suppose it was so. Then my thoughts went to counteract the plot with proof, and I did, but that will remain my secret, just in case. Four, what if I did publish this and it became a best seller? How could I judge loved ones and family on their behaviour to me? If I had not told some people that I needed help, they already knew it. Some played on it and took what they could, others left me to my own devices. The bottom line is; I asked for help, for help and understanding and only one person came through for me up until this date.

As much as I love Emilie. I don't know how I would treat her if things got good and she wanted me back. I, knowing Emilie like I did, it would not be for the success of what proceeds may come, and I would like to think that if the family and close friends spoke ill of me (forget what joy I bought into their respective lives before my time here), that she is woman enough to remember when we were in love and that I told her I was going to get better at any cost for the sake of my kids and myself. Then I thought that the Emilie I knew, would not have (as it appears at present) stopped communicating with me and leaving me out of touch with Kayana. So how could I then know, why she came back? (Assuming of course that she would), I thought to conquer this puzzle and I think have found a solution. See, life is a funny thing and one thing I have learnt, is that anything in life is possible. So bearing this in mind, this is my wish: "Be I live or be I die, I would like all proceeds, to go to my son Junior, who shall, with the integrity that I know he has, share it between his Sisters and Brothers. With a percentage put aside somehow to go towards benefiting children and adults who have gone or are going through similar things that caused or led me to my present place in life. That if all goes well, I will personally set up, my reward being that through my worst time, I pray that I leave here alive, if not... This that I have written should reach my son." I thought about this entry last night, but being 'high' I declined, it was a wise thought.

I woke this morning to see Ras, cleaning his trainers. I was so happy for him. Kenny however did not seem to share it, I didn't linger on it, I suppose everyone has their own way of saying things even if they don't speak. But I like the Ras.

He told me he plants weed in the hills and sells it for a living, he detests violence, and he has nine children with the same woman and has lived in the same house in the hills with her for 39 years. Now that, in my mind deserves credit. When he was gone, an inmate (who I cannot stand the sound of his voice and happens to be gay) came to the cell demanding the bucket the Ras had left behind. The Ras had left specific instructions not to give it to him, simply because, when they shared a cell together the guy would continuously steal his belongings and sell them for ciggs. The inmate decided to make it a problem, telling Kenny, my cell mate, to "tool up" because he was going to, and when he comes back, he was going to take the bucket. After quickly thinking of what our cell would become if he or any one thought they could just walk in and take anything, I voiced my opinion. Knowing he was wrong and anyone who backed him would be wrong. I had a quick look around to see who else was close enough to take sides, calculate the odds and positions, and told him in Jamaican patois loud enough for all to hear, that he should "no bada cum back" and that this was the only warning he was going to get. He told me what he was going to do with me; I told him I was ready. I went to my cell he went to his, returning instantly. And now, what I have tried with all my knowledge to avoid was going to happen. Time to get physical. Outside of the cell was getting crowded, people in here love to watch a fight and this morning they would get to see mild mannered English in one, or so they thought. I could feel the adrenalin in me and when I saw Kenny looking towards him (the wall blocking my view) and telling him not to enter, I timed him blindly and on reaching the cell door threw enough weight on him (similar to an American football barge) that it took him back a few good paces and off of his feet. I think he was shocked by my strength and also by the fact that no one intervened. Now it was his time to weigh up the odds. Me and him one on one, he declined. With the assurance it was over, I went into the yard to smoke. On the way I was being told that I should have beaten him up properly; my reply was "I don't fight unless I have to."

The outcome of the confrontation left me feeling quite good. Not because I came out on top, but because I realised if I was right, it would always be a fair fight and no side would be taken. As one lad said to me while he was in the shower just afterwards "yo English you have a problem?" "No problem" was my reply, but in here, you still have to be on your p's and q's. Because as with the tossing of a coin, it may fall on heads 99 times out of a 100, the last toss is still 50, 50.

Sun 11th

Had bread and cheese. Spent the rest of the day reading and writing, to me, an important letter to Emilie. The thought of me still not trying with Kayana is overpowering me not to contact Emilie. It's funny how what's important to one, is of no concern to others. I don't believe this trait follows me, although I am sure many would bid to differ; I was speaking aloud, asking myself if I had written in this book today. Chi chi, staring out of the gap turns and tries to convince me I have. Now even though time here is repetitive, I thought to myself, "No, I haven't" simply because there was nothing to write, instead I had to read the book and write the letter. I turned to tell Chi chi he was wrong, and, happy with what I wrote, was showing him the pages (not the letter), just to show him what I had done today. He showed no interest, just kept on gazing out of the slit in the wall to what he has been looking at for the past two years. He was obviously deep in thought (I think a waste if he was not) but in those few secs, it would have been nice for him to acknowledge what I had done. In here you need that. Sometimes it helps: if I am writing and he enters, having just spoken to his family, I will stop, not because I want to, but because in here for what ever reason, it's something you want to share. I think this of the outside world too. Many people think too much of their need and forget about the needs of others.

MON,

I woke up to exercise, ended up doing thirty push ups and did not have the feeling to carry on. I think because of the letter I wrote to Emilie, it was something to do with cause and effect. It bothers me how she will take it.

While I was sitting on my bunk brooding, I remembered something I read in the Bible a few nights ago. A major politician, while giving a speech at a university, was quoted as saying to students "if you do not study hard you could end up in Iraq" of course there was uproar. The president said he should apologise and the soldiers were offended. The guy tried to tell the people, he was not talking about being a soldier in Iraq, he was not referring to that, his colleague went as far as to say "In his defence, he did not mention the word soldier!" Now come on, who is he trying to fool? If he made a mistake with a speech in the heat of the moment, that I can understand, but to turn around and defend it like that, after having time enough to prepare a response is ludicrous, unless he had ulterior motives. What does he think of the ordinary people and voter's mentality? As a BBC spokesman correctly put it "I don't think the students had plans to go there on their vacation". Personally, I think, he thinks like most of us: The War is no good and the troops should not be there. He wanted to voice his opinion but was not brave enough to stand by it. But if he is as smart a politician as a politician should be in his position, he should know that he has already planted the seed. He is just leaving it for nature to grow. But why not just tell the people what he meant and leave it at that, surely if anyone of us has a chance to put some substantial input into the stopping of friction it should be done proudly. Colin Powell got into trouble at the end of part one of the war by stating publicly (in my opinion rightly so) "We should have not pulled out then but finished the job" thus giving Saddam no time to reorganise. He was made to apologise, but why? If the president of the USA is wrong ,then he, the most powerful man in the world, should he not be man enough to admit it and then go on to rethink strategies instead of the me, me, me? I think the president of the good old USA cannot be seen to be wrong. Hello Mr President, how is your first visit to planet earth? Cause and effect; Saddam once warned the president "it will be the mother of all wars", you know I believed him at the time he said it. They have been fighting since Biblical days. How many people involved, speak or understand their language and culture or their country as they do? Did they, the Americans, not learn from Vietnam? Did you know? The Vietnamese did not have a single war plane to fight the marines, come on guys you should have done your homework because look where *you* ended up.

During my time on the van I was once again surrounded by the horrors of violence and what it brings; Kingston had been put on the map, not by Bob Marley, but by the sheer uncaring attitude people had for life. It's a fact that doctors used to go to the hospital, armed, in case the gun men did not finish the job they started on the street, or, for the fear of his own life, if the doc did his job too well. I would not be exaggerating if I said "for a good period of time I saw guns or heard them being fired every day". Going into town never really bothered me, I was careful and always alert but in the back of my mind I always thought I had a guardian angel. This may sound strange, but like everything that I have written, it's true. It happened one evening while I was in the house in the country sitting on the sofa facing the door leading to the outside. I was upstairs so all I was really looking at was space. Then just to the right of me I see this figure that appeared, like a woman kneeling down in front of me, with her hands clasped as if praying. She was dressed in the kind of gown and head gear that Mother Teresa wore. I slowly turned my head towards her and she kind of floated up, not like a balloon but as though levitating and she moved towards the door on my right. Not losing my line of thought

I got up and followed her, but on reaching door and looking in the direction she went, she had vanished. I said nothing and have told only people who I did not fear would ridicule me, for years after that I had this ultra strong feeling that I could not die. Weather it was healthy or not I don't know but I had it, so going to Kingston was okay. When we used to park the van and wait for passengers for the return journey, I would often take a stroll to the market to buy things for people who were either afraid to go themselves or just because of convenience. A new me developed then, simply a caution to ensure survival. I started growing my hair (not locks, Gran did not approve), walk with an attitude. I would not react if I suddenly heard my name called (you never know, mistaken identity) and other small things. To blend in for the van I used to wear a green shirt, the colours of JLP and underneath a black and red vest, red being the colour of PNP (you could be shot wearing the wrong colours in the wrong zone so I wore both). If someone hailed you and your natural reflex is to put up your arm with your fist clenched, that also could find you in a coffin. I also made it my job to educate the country folk who came into town unavoidably; things like: don't wear jewellery, stay on the main road and try to stick with the crowd. I remember telling two such young men, similar things. One hot day we were parked, waiting as usual, the two back doors of the van were open for breeze. I always had an eye on it but many times a passenger would put a suit case or a bag there without my knowledge and at the end of the journey find it missing. Now, these two young folk were well known in our town and they came to Kingston on business. They sat at the back of the van across the aisle from each other, counting money. I was honestly taken back by the ignorance and sheer stupidity of the scene. I actually marvelled at the sight that was taking place. Not only were they putting themselves in danger, but there were also us and other passengers. Looking around quickly for what I now had instincts for, I told the lads to put the money away until the van was on the road. You know, one of the lads said to me (in patois) "what's up conductor are you afraid?" I think at that time I subconsciously hoped someone would rob them. Anyway, they paid me no heed, so I let them think I was ignoring them while still keeping an eye on the back of the bus. A few seconds later a boy of about 12 appeared as if out of thin air, his eyes only on the money about two feet away and his arm poised to grab. I should have let him take it but based on my reaction I quickly shouted in respectful patois (yes respectful) for him to leave. The two men looked up startled and the boy came towards me hurling abuse "jus wait, I soon come, I gonna shot you for taking my dinner away!" and off he went towards Tivoli. Not taking his threats lightly I told the driver what had occurred and I was told immediately to lock up. We left half empty. The following day while going for lunch in the terminal the assistant told me the guys (gun men) came just after we left and 'were shooting up the place'. He even showed me the bullet holes adjacent to were we park the van. Funny enough, one of the lads came to town a few weeks later and asked me to show him where the chicken hatchery was, and guess what? He had on a tight T shirt (which I never wore because any one could see you were unarmed) with a small left hand top breast pocket with a roll of money turned sideways making the material bulge out on both sides. I did not say anything to him on purpose, time for him to learn a lesson. I walked him through a slightly less violent part of town, nevertheless, still quite bad. I felt okay because it happened to be not far from the school I attended while living there. I took him down a side street and sure enough, two lads came out of a derelict building and told him to "cum ya". First, I asked if they were talking to me. "No, him" said the guy and actually walked over to him, grabbed his pocket and took the money. He wanted to go after them into the derelict building, I advised against it, this time he took my advice. When hit suddenly by actions unfamiliar to oneself, people do and say the strangest things: Another day in Kingston (Trevor was driving now) we had just passed the market place, heading home with a full load when straight out of the street where they took that man's money, a man came flying across the road, gun in hand, glancing back shooting at another man chasing him. He had to put his arm on the van to avoid being knocked over. The other man was closing in on him, shooting in the direction of the van. Trevor stopped the van and waited, as if he was waiting for a traffic light to change to green (I always admired him for his coolness in any given situation). In the van, most, if not all, were experiencing this kind of action for the first time. They all ducked and I heard one passenger shout "they're shooting!" And another answer "and they're real bullets!" This was said out of fright and not to mock the first statement. I thought the whole scene was quite surreal.

Trevor had started driving the van after another day of surrealism. On the way home one day, after passing the outskirts of Kingston (where people live mainly off the road, in houses in the bush), are opportunist bad boys. They don't really ever leave their surroundings and rob; they wait until their quarry comes to them and being there is only one road from Kingston to Portland (on this side of the island), a relatively small winding road with thick bush on either side, we never pick up or drop off here for obvious reasons. On this day, as we came around a deep bend, we saw a massive tree log and rocks blocking the road, men with machetes and riffles but what I remember most clearly was a small boy of about 5 or 6 maybe 7, trying to approach us, while we came to a screeching halt, with a bolder that he could hardly lift which looked twice his size. Once again, I wasn't particularly frightened. While the passengers were screaming I quickly took my green shirt off, pulled off my vest, threw it under my seat and put the green shirt back on. It was a JLP road block. This would mean, if we stopped they would approach the van and take out known PNP supporters and beat them probably to death, but Mr Panton had different thoughts (remembering he is PNP), he slammed the van into reverse and drove about a quarter mile back down the road and we reversed into a police station. Times were so mad in those days the boys would even attack the police station, with the excuse that they needed more guns. So it was no surprise to see the army there. The soldiers acted really quick, got all the passengers out and before you knew it, the driver, I, and a van full of soldiers were heading back towards the road block and all I could hear at the time was the constant clicking of SLR machine guns being

*set to fire. When we got back to the scene even the road block
was gone, the soldiers jumped from van and ran towards the
bushes. We picked up the passengers and continued the journey
home leaving the sounds of gun shots in the back ground. Mr
Panton would understandably not wish to drive the van again.
I remember getting home, jumping out of the van and making
such a big deal out of the incident, not even remembering I had
been through worse. To be honest, I think I was just looking for
attention. Anyway, Trevor said casually, "I'll drive." That was the
interview. He got the job.*

*Because of all the excitement I had made earlier, including
saying that I would not go back to town , "it's Russian roulette
out there" I felt pretty cowardly when Trevor said he would drive,
so I got up extra early and shinned the van mirror like and sat
waiting for him. Trevor was all right, he was humorous but not
playful, and it appeared nothing fazed him. He always seemed to
be one step ahead of everything. Until this day, I do not recall him
raising his voice; to know him was almost impossible. He gave me
the feeling that there was something about his past, not hidden,
but not spoken. Apart from the prior incident, at this moment,
I do not recall seeing violence on the van again, but Trevor's
actions were intriguing. One day we picked up a passenger who,
on reaching the end of the line, refused to pay (this did happen
but not as often as it might have). I would usually disgrace them
in front of other passengers or take something until I was paid.
Sometimes I was approached first and I would take into account
the amount of passengers on the van; if I said ok and the van got
full, said passenger would have to stand, but this passenger acted
like he had paid already. I told Trevor and without emotion or
looking, he said "don't let him out." We drove this guy all over
Kingston while he was begging to get let out. I followed Trevor's
lead and said nothing. It takes a lot to frighten a real Jamaican,
and this guy was scared, remember, he has no idea what part of
town we may end up in and people like him have enemies all over.
Finally Trevor stopped the van, turned to the guy and said "gimmy
your shirt". He took of his shirt, gave it to me, stepped out of the*

van and we drove off as if the whole incident did not take place. I thought, 'I like this guy'. I had passed through Trench Town and so, before it got violent; but it was a no go area now, you just did not go there. However, during our break we rarely stayed at the terminal. We drove uptown for Chinese food and then often to the telephone company where he would spend hours (he used to work there). Every so often he would drive straight to 'Rema' in the heart of bad land, park up, and say to me "soon come" (to give an idea of his 'soon come' I once heard him tell a friend, who was expecting something from him that day, "soon come". I smiled; I knew he was going to Miami that afternoon). So I would sit in the van watching the guys go about their normal everyday life , I can see now a dreadlocked man, shirt open hand in hand with, I expect his daughter taking her to school. When the breeze blows his shirt open, I see a gun propped out of his waist ready for a quick draw should the occasion arise. One day while I was sitting in the van, I heard gun shots, as if it were Bon Fire night, coming from the adjacent street. The police and army had surrounded a house where Claudi Massop Jamaica's 'Most Wanted' was sleeping. They did not take him alive. You know what I found strange? There was this clean, almost new van in the heart of a serious ghetto with gun men strolling about and me sitting inside and no one ever bothered me. It was as if I was never there, I knew I could not die but I did not know I could become invisible also. It never bothered me and I never once questioned him or spoke about it. I suppose it never bothered him when I went to watch the matinee during the break and would miss the van back home. I can just imagine him not giving me five mins. Whenever he was ready, he would go and would never say anything when I turned up on a late bus. I never complained. That I can live with.

MON, EVE.

In the cell Chi chi is learning English Bible studies. Monero quiet as usual, sits on a bucket by the gate.

Yesterday I asked 'Octave' (head guard) if I could get a blank piece of paper to design a birthday card for my daughter (I ordered one from the tuc shop but it did not turn up). I told him it was "important to me", he told me he would "take care of it". I did not think much of it; I would get paper from somewhere. In the evening he came to my cell (sat eve) and told me he would 'sort it out on Monday'. Intrigued, I thanked him. Lunch time today, another guard came to my cell "Collins what's the occasion for the card?" "Birthday" I said "she is four" then went to lay down. About an hour later Kenny tells me that Octave wants to see me. Donning a shirt, I run downstairs not knowing what to expect and he hands me this pretty birthday card with a designed envelope ("Thanks Mr Octave, I really did appreciate it").

I had many indifferent times with the van, some, upon reflection I may break out with a little smile, others upon reminiscing a few tears come to my eyes. All in all it was another building block to what I was to become. I stopped working on the van and for the love of God I cannot remember why. It still went out but I was never on it, I think it was once again to do with me not opening dialogue with Mrs Ivy or maybe (I think I am closer now) because I caught a dangerous virus called 'Dengue Fever' and literally could not get out of bed. At first sight you could not tell what was wrong with me. Trevor and Mrs Ivy thought I was acting up a bit, it happens that I was not, a few people had died because of the fever as it spread through Jamaica. Bought on by mosquitoes the fever was a class 'A' epidemic. Finally to get rid of it, the government supplied trucks, with what seemed to me like tar, and pretty much smoked out the whole of Jamaica. They said if you caught it twice it was fatal. I recovered after a few days and just did not go back on the van. Once again, nothing was said so nothing happened. Well, that's not entirely true; I felt that I was getting further and further away from her and although I truly wanted to, I could not bring myself to call her a name that I would feel comfortable with and so I spent more time on the street during the day and my time at dances during the night.

Being locked out of the house had now become the norm. These times were unhappy times for me although I am not sure I showed it. Sometimes I missed dinner, it was always there for me but I would have to pass Mrs. Ivy to get to it and I could not, so I did not (anyone reading this might think; I know why you could not. Well, so do I, but it's much deeper than that, my question is: "How comes, 'I', could not?"). So, Trevor moved in with us after marrying Jenny who gave birth to their lovely little baby (Tanya) that I was quite fond of. Blossom and her daughter Val was to come and live with us (daughter and grand daughter). Bro and Sis had gone and for some reason, due to a spiteful landlady, we moved home again, about two and a half miles down the road. A nice spacious house; I had my own room, although there was a bathroom shower toilet on suite and also had a door leading to the outside, it was never private. Anyway, I was hardly there so it did not matter. The beach was a bit further away but just around the corner was the famous 'Blue Lagoon' so we would swim there. There was a hotel with a private beach even closer, 'Dragons Bay' (where 'Cocktails', with Tom Cruise was shot). If you have seen the movie you know how beautiful it is. I would spend many nights on that beach alone on one of the sun chairs looking up at the blanket of stars asking questions we all ask ourselves sooner or later. "Why am I here? What is the purpose for being?" Later on in life I would lay under the stars, which looked like a black blanket with silver glitter and think some more, only this time it would be of a woman left behind in the whirl wind of this life of mine, never forgotten, just filled away. I wonder what, if any impact I had on their lives, I wonder: Do they sometimes lie under the stars reminiscing with the occasional thought of me? Do they sometimes hear a record and get transported back through time to when I was very much apart of their life? Does a smile appear or does anger grow? Do they even think of me at all? Have I subconsciously or consciously been blocked from their minds? I realize now, that maybe I have caused pain to people (girls) along the way, but it was done unknowingly without malice. One thing I think all would agree; if any woman shared a part of my life, they could not say it was boring. As I think up until today the causes of people and the effect of my outcome, was not done with contempt for me, but merely out of conditions they had to deal with also. After all, I am not their life, I only passed through it . *Two major things happened to me at this period in life: one, that everyone could see and the other one I cannot explain, and no one would know. They happen pretty much at the same time.*

WED 12TH

"Stop the press!" I must digress. While exercising this morning and casually thinking about my life I have just realized two important issues which have just crept up on me. The first is; I happen to get a flow of incidents in my mind with my mother in them. *I was in Wales on an army barracks with her and Frank (her husband and father of Donnia); I fractured my arm there crossing the road by myself. I had gone to the shop to get some sweets and ended up buying a magazine with the Jackson five in it; I was so in to the Jacksons for obvious reasons I just did not pay attention to the road... Next thing I know, two elderly people are asking me if I would like biscuits and tea, all was well. Another time I was on an army barracks in Germany. Frank showed me the inside of a tank. Once again on the street alone, probably looking for more sweets, I was chased by a bunch of white kids a little older than me. I did not leave the house again. I am beginning to get quite angry with myself now because I know it was Oakfield time, and Wales and Germany are two different countries, but I cannot remember right now seeing my mother there, or doing anything with her. I do not think Frank would have been allowed to take me there by himself (I have just paused not realising it, playing back time looking searching for my mother but she is not there). I also remember getting a Timex watch from her for Christmas, but I don't remember her giving it to me. It would be unfair not to jot this down, as I intend to send a copy to quite a few people and although this is what happened*

to me, through my eyes, I feel it would be being bias or unfair to my mother if I did not tell the full story as and when I remember it. I guess she must have tried; she just did not get through. Any suggestions Freudians!? The other thing which is strange in another way, I remember Dell taking me to Jamaica and actually taking me to her Brother's office to introduce me to my father. He was sitting behind his desk in white, with steths around his neck. He gave me $5, quite a lot then, but I really did not need money. He told Dell he was busy. Later, when I actually moved to Kingston (this would have been after the event of my Bro and Sis's Father), I tried to contact him. I found his number in the yellow pages and phoned his surgery. Of all the things, I told him I had a cold; to this day I still feel stupid. Anyway, somehow I got invited to his house in the then posh Beverly hills; over looking the National stadium and famous for the crown house over looking the town (later to be squatted in by gun men) for a week end (now I remember, I was so happy because I understood who my real father was, now all I had to do was meet him properly). I went by myself (I am maybe 13) but Kingston was nice then. I am now at the door of a quite ordinary house and a beautiful young woman answers the door in what I would assume is his shirt. I know she has a nice face but I really cannot see it, although her legs, I recall, were long, shapely and smooth. I don't remember there being any furniture in the house but there is a mattress on the floor and a TV. I am not sure if she was embarrassed by the situation but she handled it well and I was happy she was there. You know, my father never showed up for that whole weekend. I went back home without seeing him, I guess that was when he left my memory; or maybe not. Years later at the house in Portland as I have said there was an election coming. There was a new party forming and the members were looking for supporters. The house we lived in, I guess made us approachable and Jenny was now a teacher. One night, as the norm, I was enjoying myself at a local dance about a mile down the road, when one of the gang (Jason) came storming through the crowd calling "Colin! Colin! Mrs Jenny wants to see you, it's important!" This, you must understand, is unheard of in Jamaica;

everything can wait, you could get called for dinner but it can wait. No, a dance was something not to be interrupted, so you can imagine. I ran out of the dance and sprinted the full mile to the house and up the stairs, passing three gentlemen sitting on the veranda, I politely said "good night" and proceeded through to the living room where Jenny was talking to another man "Hi what's wrong? Good evening sir" I said, still out of breath. "I would like to introduce you to your father." Those were Jenny's exact words. What happened a few seconds after has not come back to me yet. I don't remember a dialogue; I think I said "pleased to meet you" and then I went back to the dance as though it never did happen. Looking back, I think it was then (how do I explain), full up sounds about right. I think once again not consciously, I just had had enough. I was next to see him twenty five years later (after careful deliberation, yes, twenty five years). Maybe a start to my organisation would be to open a web site for people who have had similar situations: talking to someone does help but you have to have the right listener, in my case, me. Maybe it would help if people spoke to others, like themselves and me on a site; I bet there are people in all walks of life that just need to empty their glass. Remember, I only ended up in prison, think of the other means of escape that may have been used by similar circumstances. The world is upside down, I do not have to name any of them, be brave you people out there, say 'Mummy' or 'Grandma,' it could make all the difference.

First incident, Lavern was pregnant; yep, I was going to be a father. Fern and I had, I guess, a normal relationship. She is one year older than me. We used to play around on the beach and down in the bushes, she would be my date at the dances and we would argue about nothing constantly. She was pretty and had a great body; no one was to know she gave me my first French kiss. It was good, even though up until today I am very selective about whom I kiss. I was one of the last in our community to find out she was pregnant. When I did, it was one of the girls across the road who told me, laughingly of course. Fern and I were not talking at the time, so there was no need to tell me something like that, but that was Fern and this was me. I can remember when I used to sneak into her parents' house at night, when they had gone to bingo or out for a drink, I would hear a motor bike coming down the dark path towards the house and quickly pick up my clothes and fly out the back door through the bushes and around the long way home. The first time I pulled that stunt I had forgotten that the house was built on pillars about 3 feet of the ground. I must have looked like a cartoon, shirt in one hand pants in the other, flying out of the back door which had no steps and running in thin air, before my brain would tell me there was no ground beneath my feet. Needless to say, we, through our limited selves, had a good time together. We complemented each other. In fact, she now has another family. I took a trip with Jana and my son to the island and for the first night we stayed at her place with her man and their children and we had the master bedroom. We were treated as guests of the family, genuinely warm. I wonder how many of you could say that about a previous 'Baby mother'. Well, through out the pregnancy I did not mention it to Mrs Ivy. Once again, not because I did not want to, but because I did not know how to start. I knew she knew and she knew I knew she knew but in Grandma's ways she kept silent. The second incident was happening parallel; I can remember this because... well, let me explain; when we left the first rented house, Mrs Ivy decided to build her own house, bigger and better than all of the houses in the area. In fact, where she proposed to build it the locals said it was impossible. Up a steep hill at the base of the foot of the mountains over looking everything and out to sea. The first stage of the house, big rocks and boulders were needed to be moved manually from over the hill to where the house was being built, (for a boundary wall) so Grandma proposed I should get some friends and take care of it. It was one of the most enjoyable jobs I have ever had, up at the crack of dawn with a bucket of water and bottles of lemonade we would trudge up the hill and start displacing boulders, of course in our own style, because through watching the movies once a week we became karate experts over night, jumping from rock to rock performing katas, which would invariably end up with us hitting the bolder as if it would fly off the hill and land in its place, just like in the movies. Well, they did not, but we kept it up until there were no rocks left and only stopped for lunch which was chicken back (donated by my favourite aunty of the time; she used to sell it from the back of the veranda) and dumplings, all cooked in the bucket, washed down with the sugar and water, served on large leaves with sticks for knives and forks; all this done in the green hills of Jamaica in 75 degree temp overlooking the Caribbean sea. Now, that job was fun. I did not ask for money, not this time because of name, that was going to be inevitable in time, but because Mrs Ivy and I knew that this was my only source of income, and through my whole stay in Jamaica, I never really needed money. Everything material and food was provided for, but we both knew at the time of the birth I would need to do some shopping, so all was good with me.

On the 6, 6, 1980 my son was born in Port Antonio hospital and his mother called him Damien. Now, that I could not have, two sixes and Damien was not on, so I immediately went down to the registrar office and changed it to Junior. Fern would often bring him to the house, Oh yes! The day I got the news I went straight to Mrs Ivy and said with abated breath "Mrs Ivy, Fern is in hospital, can I have some money to buy things?" She got up went to her closet and took some money that looked like it was waiting there for me. After thanking her, off I went to the hospital flowers and all. Fern used to bring him to the house and I would often come home from work to find the two of them laying on my bed, it felt good but I was truly lost inside, I could not see a future for us, to be honest for me (for me to be able to help them in Jamaica). Yes, the house was coming, where if I stayed, I would be guaranteed my place in it until I could build my own house and yes, the van was still on the road, but I was 21 now and England was calling. I was to find out later that Mrs Ivy had a plan with Trevor, that I could have easily fitted into, but we hardly ever spoke, so how was I to know... I worked on the house and told Mrs Ivy my plan. I could tell she did not agree but she did not say anything, so I continued to work and save money. I *remember being very impatient, bugging her when I could to get me the ticket, and finally, it came. I don't know if I was happy, sad or excited with the thought of leaving but I was going anyway, and, do you know something? Of all the things Mrs Ivy did say to me, six words have rung in my ear ever since she spoke them: she handed me the ticket when I was ready to leave, and said to me out of ear shot of anyone "I don't think you should leave." I do not remember the journey to the airport but I do remember Trevor's parting words "when you go behind those screens you won't see me again". "Yea I know", I said absent minded and I still do not remember going through customs getting on the plane, being on the plane, or getting off. All I can remember are those six words "I don't think you should leave". The next thing I can remember was looking out of a window and seeing a clear blue sky from Mrs Bonds private live in accommodation of a new children's home. I was back in England.*

THURS, 13TH(ISH)

For the first time I exercised with Chi chi, it was all right but not much was done (by him). I was interrupted by the memory of a lucid dream; being in a shopping centre for clothes which turned into a fruit and veg market alternately. I heard the howl of market traders trying to gain the attention of a beautiful eastern European woman. I thought 'no chance' but there were three equally less beautiful women behind the one, and looking at me, signalled to the other, that the men were calling to her. She smiled knowingly and went on. Just that they got a smile startled me, a girl like that acknowledging wolf whistles and shouts, only really done to show off in front of their friends. I understand some women might feel flattered and (in England anyway) rejected if it did not come their way but she was of a different class, why? I had to see the faces of the men, so I went to where they were sitting and standing. They looked Greek /Spanish dark and hairy, moustache, short sleeve shirts, and ordinary bodies. I was still puzzled "you have to know how", one said, and I woke up. What I thought about; in all my dreams someone has at least a small resemblance to a single person I have met or seen but these guys did not. They looked Spanish/ Greek and they looked and 'felt' perfectly normal, but no clue of anyone I knew, to have taken that role in my dream. I was about to relate the computer to the brain. Most people know you can't get out of a computer what you do not put in, so I put it to myself that I must have seen this face before, for the mere fact that he played a prominent part in my dream, but I have seen millions if not more faces in my life. Forget Waterloo, London, and Blackfriars bridges during rush hour, forget the Notting Hill carnivals, and forget the different countries I have been to. What about the movies, news reels, TV, documentaries that my brain must have registered. I thought maybe the brain, knowing the physical make up of the human body could just put one together, but no, there must be a reason. The brain is too complex to just throw something like that together without reason. And besides, something would not be quite right, something would... seem wrong. Then it hit me. In 1987 while at college (hotel & catering), we were preparing, cow's liver, when another student came to me and said "I drink blood". His face was pale and he had a moustache, tiny blue veins lined the skin on his face and his eyes were blood shot. I believed what he said but not to that extent, so I got a plastic cup, burst a hole in the liver bag, filled the cup and offered it to him and he drank it. For those people who do not drink blood like that, you can imagine how I felt, but what I'm getting at, is that 1) I was right; The person in my dream was the spitting image of Kevin the vampire only now healthy looking and able to attract the most beautiful women, and 2) the computer (brain) did not just make something up, it was already there, I just had to press the correct retrieve button untwined in a complex code that would reveal the correct answer without going through the same disgusting feeling I had all those years ago. Looking at this dream; I may have discovered a path on another clue to the direction I must take to unlock this deeper more complex code I have stored in my brain.

SAT 18ᵀᴴ

I have woken up feeling quite good; it's raining heavily and the bread and tea are late, no problem. Over the past week I have been thoughtful of Junior's situation but my hands are tied. I have not phoned for fear of the worst but this morning I will make an effort to try. I have just looked out of the cell towards the phone downstairs but the only people I can see to put my name down cannot write. Usually if our cell is near last to open the list will be full, maybe I can get a squeeze from someone.

Well, two hours later, my slot has passed (earlier I Cry had seen my plight and had put my name down for 10.30) the guard had told me it was 9.20, and after reading for about 40 mins and checking the time from a different guards watch, it's twenty past eleven. So the only time one needs the time in this place, you cannot even get that.

The other day, on the same day, 4 different inmates came to me to tell me their heartache stories. I listened to them for different reasons. One, from 'I cry' (because he is the only person I trust in here). His was about his mate whom he has been feeding since he has been here, up until he received his own money. Now he has, he cannot see fit to give 'Cry' any ciggs and then he called him 'Red Eye' which is like adding salt to the wound, so 'Cry' has sworn their friendship is over. I am sure, although he is sincere now, come tuc shop, all will be forgotten. The second is 'Blaze' now, he is the one who sees fit at whatever time necessary, 5 in the morning or 12 midnight to shout a sermon to the whole block about whatever is on his mind, so for some reason he has come into my cell to tell me plans of a robbery for the hotel being built across the way from the prison and that he would take a gun and shoot the people he was robbing. I tried to reason with him, stating that, if he planned it properly he would have no need to shoot anyone. Later, after explaining to me that it was because no witnesses could "finger" him, he went on to tell me of a robbery that he went on (very descriptively) from start to finish; How much money he got away with, his escape route and how someone got shot. He was telling it as how a man might tell his spouse about a typical day in the office. Anyway, I had hoped he would see reason but the blood shot eyes tell me; even if it's not the hotel, it will be somewhere else. Visibly shaking my head I thought, 'here stands a murdering gun man who does a very good job washing for me three or so times a week for one packet of ciggs a fortnight...

So now I am once again living with Mrs Bond & her family. Her son, who I was trusted with to take to school once in a while, has grown into a young man, and her husband, John, still a devout family man and 9 to 5er.

My first thought of England now was the cold fresh air. Even though the sun was shinning and the sky was blue it was bitterly cold. I spent most of my time sussing England out, trying to get a job and being as helpful as I could around the house. I also found out that London had hit the 3 million unemployment mark, so getting a job was near impossible for me. I tried the Army (for discipline more than anything else, I figured I could do with it), but to no avail. Anyway, the Falklands war broke out a few months later so I was quite relieved. I would fight for England or Jamaica but only if it was imminent that they were going to be invaded. I also, after flicking through the adds for countless days , found one for a poultry cleaner, great, not the most ideal job in the world but I could do it, after all, I had experience. I went for a trial, picking and plucking chickens and although I did a pretty good job I did not get it. Disheartened only until the next day (oh, I had my thoughts as to why I did not get the job but I did not air them) I got up and racked the paper again. In the mean time, I discovered that if you are not working in England, they gave you money. Bad idea I think, but great, I'll take it. So there's me with money for myself (I would give Mrs Bond half) and London there waiting. One day I got lucky, an add in the paper for waiters and bus boys, chefs and bar men at a unique pizza restaurant called 'Pappagalis' so I donned my best clothes (Jamaican style which was England ten years back) and set off for my interview (I had a brief stint at a hotel in Jamaica and acquired silver service skills). At the interview I was bubbly and very, very energetic. I knew I had the job, so much so that when the interview was finished I could not stop talking to the interviewer about how good I would be for the restaurant and that they would not regret it. It was true, I became like a son to the couple who owned it. I could do no wrong in their eyes and vice versa, so much so if there was a drunken disturbance in the direction of either of the two (not that they may have needed it), I would step in with my 6.4 slim but muscular frame coupled with a Jamaica attitude and defused the situation before it got out of hand. The restaurant was designed for couples and small families in mind but we had all sorts of customers, who were, for the most, well behaved, good mannered, and welcome: suits ,ties, or jeans and T shirts all were welcome. I got the job as a 'Bus Boy' and basically filled coffee cups, cleared tables and before the place opened for business, cleaned the toilets and the floor. It was a new restaurant and I had the pleasure of helping to add the finishing touches. My first job in London. I was as proud and as exited as anyone .The first day at work, the rest of the staff, all young and new like me, were also filled with the same energy and we really were like one big happy family. There were budding models, painters, actors and me, all of what it takes to have a good time, and I did. I was never late (which would surprise anyone who knows me now) and when ever there was a spare shift or someone was off sick, I would be the first to fill in. I would strut around that restaurant as a Bus Boy as though 'I am the proud owner of this fine establishment,' as my boss would put it. It was at this time that the clubbing started in my life. Wednesdays, Fridays and Saturdays, clubs with the crew and private parties in between. From a little village in Jamaica, I had reached the bubbling town of London with the grand neon's of Piccadilly Circus and the bright lights of the West End. I was where I belonged, at least at that time of my journey I was. Women I really did not court, they literally came at me, beautiful young and ready for fun. My relations were fun but never lasted which was good for me and the women involved at the time. Everything really was perfect in my life then, or so it seemed. I often thought of Jamaica and my son and wrote a few times, nowhere near enough and excuses are shamefully not there. Not that I didn't love my boy. I really had wanted to forget about Jamaica in a way, and have any joy that was happening. I had promised when the time was right my boy would come to England , but apart from the fact I could not possibly look after him then and he had a good mother and large family, I wanted him to grow up a Jamaican man not an English man, and so I enjoyed myself.

There was good old Sonja (whose dad apparently wrote the tune for the Magic round about). She was a young man's dream, a German (which I had always had misconceptions with since my only visit there) who hated the German accent and who always tried to emphasize what cockney words she could, her favourite being, war-a (water). She was pretty witty and fun to be with, very sexy, 7 years my elder and married to a gay man with a son. She often told me that the marriage was not proper and I should not worry about it, so I didn't, although one night after work, she invited me home, saying that her husband had gone to France for the weekend on business. After a really good night, at about 7.30 in the morning, I hear the front door opening "God it's my husband!" How cliché that sounds now. Anyway, looking quickly around for my pants and a weapon, I calmly told her that she should go to him and tell him, that it was me and that he could come in and hit me if he wanted to and I would not strike back but if he used a weapon I would retaliate (and I meant both). For what I always had in mind of gay people was that they were, well, gay, just feminine males; how could he possibly hurt me? In fact, I actually felt sorry for him. Anyway she told him and he just said I should be out of the house by the time he made a cup of tea. If this had been Jamaica the situation would have been bloody, however two reasonably intelligent young men caught in a situation, did not resort to violence. I got dressed said goodbye to Sonja knowing she would be okay and jogged all the way to the train station giggling to myself along the way thinking, this life is fun (although I must admit I drew the line at married women after that). Me and Sonja remained good friends for a long time after that. As always, like so many of the good folk I had met in those early days, she just drifted away. (I won't excite you with details of all of my great on and off relationships for each one is a book by themselves and I just want you to have an idea of what was happening to me at this time of my journey). By now Mrs Bond had gotten a job elsewhere. I had the opportunity to go with her but I declined thankfully. It's time for me to be alone; although for a young coloured man in those days getting a single room, even though I had a job, was somewhat rather difficult. So I had found 'Ossie' who was the husband of Blossom and father of my two great (as in wounderful) cousins Valerie (who was still in Jamaica at the time) and Angela, a somewhat troubled but genuinely nice girl. I told him my plight and he let me crash on his couch in the front room of his small flat.

'Ossie' was old school, a young good looking black man who refused to lose his Jamaican accent over the years. He would sometimes beat Angela when she knew she deserved it. He wore a suit and hat every where, like the 50s Chicago gangster, he was never involved directly in anything criminal but because of his life style, knew everyone that was, ergo he would know about everything going on in the black side of London's underworld. His stories always intrigued me because he had this uncanny way of telling these sordid stories in such a funny way that he could share the stage with Richard Prior, again, I could write a book about him also, but I find the need to just briefly explain, although I blame nothing but causes for my outcome, this man had an impact on my journey. He slept through most of the day and during the nights I believe he was second to the owner of a very trendy black night club which is where he got all the info from (does Casa Blanca come to mind?)And whenever I was there, I dressed from head to foot just like him, different colour material but same style,

I got treated properly. They would have champagne on the fridge for me and my guests and always had a table reserved. It felt good, if anyone famous came to the club I would be introduced to them matter of factually though it might have been. Although I could not take the restaurant crew with me for reasons that were understood, Sonja was always treated like one of the family there. Of a night time Ossie's associates would come to the house for a game of poker and drink brandy and lemonade. So, here am I dressed like a gangster only drinking champagne or brandy& lemonade, sovereigns on my fingers and a Gerry curl look (I had never felt so uncomfortable in my life but that was the image of the day and I played the part, literally played the part great). After a year or so Ossie got me my first room from a friend of his and the novelty of the clothes wore off, sadly though the booze did not. Ossie was and is a good man at heart; it's just that he lives his life the only way he knows how, just like me...

Well, its Sat eve now. No dinner today (pork), so I wrote all afternoon.

I just finally got through to my son; he gave me some not bad news.

I have had a conscious relapse of writing recently because all I could think of was the end result of my time, the years before coming here, they were not all depressive; Suppressive yes, but depressive no. *Ossie's daughter Angela was my first girl who was a friend; we spent a lot of time together in clubs, parties and so on. She was not working at the time so I used to enjoy taking her out and made it a special date to see Eddie Murphy in his new movies in the West End whenever they were released. After parties, we would sit up in her bedroom and chat for hours until she made us a wicked fry up. She had problems with her dad which I understood and tried to help her through those times. Although cousins, we are still very close and she is the only one who* really tells me off when I am stupid or wrong (usually both) and then forgets about it.

I had a few girlfriends in my time but not many that I did not end up in bed with, Karen for instance, beautiful, lovely and intelligent. We even slept in the same bed together but contrary to believe we never, 'slept' together, she was just fun to be with. But more over I guess I was a play boy.

I had gotten promotion in the restaurant within the space of two years and really had my heart set on head chef but the owner had different plans. Richard hired an Italian, who I got on well with, for the job. But I was disappointed, and when his wife 'Barbra' decided to cut their long hours, they hired a young manager and although he was alright, I felt let down, especially because he had his name on the licence over the front door. I thought it should have been my name, and because of this I became more challenging to the owner. I was still very good at my job but my heart was no longer there. I had a verbal dispute one day (I was wrong) and the only way he could save face was to sack me (the row took place in front of the staff). He actually told me he was sorry in private and that I should leave and return some time down the line. I was heart broken but it did not last long. I came to like the idea of cooking and went straight to college. College seemed to follow the same path as work I took it seriously and partied more so. It was during this time I had moved from my room in Shepherd's bush to a brand new council flat in Kennington 2.4.84, which I got through a girl I charmed in a the housing office in less than three weeks. I had planned to take her out for dinner, but as was becoming my trade mark, never got around to it. After college I got a job at the Piccadilly hotel. I was first commi and got promoted quite quickly to chef de parti of the exclusive brassiere restaurant and health spa. I also did work cleaning the saunas and around the swimming pool, which meant that I could chit chat with the likes of Bonnie Tyler and George Michel. Being a chef in a hotel has its perks; the odd chicken salad in pita bread slipped to the house keepers outside lunch hour would guaranteed me a very nice room for the night, with a guest *of course, room service, and the mini bar. Well, 'everybody gots to eat'. Clubbing also became a bit more exclusive, because we were a club, so other club managers would come to our place, eventually there were no queues for a certain number of us who came from the Piccadilly, which was especially fun on New Years Eve, when the 'West End' is choca block. The hours were long but the job was not difficult and I was learning all the time so I still have no idea why I walked into the chef's office one morning and gave him two weeks notice. I had enough money to play with, so I did. There was a guy who was having a hard time finding a place to stay so I put him up for a while. As far as parties and women go he and I had the same appetite, but that was all we had in common. This is around the time I met a cute fiery Barbadian, she looked about 18 and that is what she impressed upon me. I was later to learn that she had lied to me because she wanted to lose her virginity before she was 16; she did, with hours to spare. I did not find it funny and really laid into her (not physically), then she decides to tell me that she lives in a children's home. After the shock and memories had passed, I quite level headedly started to visit her at the home and with the consent of the people in charge, I would take her out and have her back by a specified time. At 16 she was no longer responsible for care so I had a meeting and officially became her guardian, whether it was right or wrong I don't really know. What I do know is that I saw in her, what I had in me, a lack of family love. So, she moved in with me until she was to get her flat. She would enjoy cooking and cleaning for me and we had a loving relationship. When she got her flat I began to let her go, as was the plan, but she said she had fallen in love with me. Now I was back at 'Papa's' and wished to resume the life styli I had put off to take care of her. Of course I had no experience of this. My heart was there and I did what I thought was right and good for her, I did not gamble on the love or hurt part involved and only realized it when I met Alison.*

Thurs 23rdish

Tuc shop day again, usual nonsense; there has been trouble brewing on different parts of the block. Recently three inmates even tried to come into the cell and get Chi Chi involved, he had the sense to tell them it was none of his business. 'I cry' was involved again; he carries his pre-fight boxer's look around more often now. I have seen it before in other fighters, if the time comes I am ready, willing and able to help but it seems he is taking on friends that he knew from the outside. Shame, I thought he could hold it down a bit more.

Three in the cell now and I have a cold, which is irritating more than anything else, the coughing and throat clearing during the night etc, but here is one for the books; I was reading through my monthy edition of 'Reader's Digest' (for probably the third or fourth time). As much as I try to focus my thoughts away from the young ones, destiny rears its indiscriminate head; of all the magazines I could possibly get sent from P.A, this month's edition just happens to have a picture of Emile in it. I don't know how I missed it the first few times. She is looking good (of course). Memories flow, I hardly slept last night, I want to phone and tell her she is looking good, but if I get the reception I have been getting, I feel I will go into a state of depression for a while and I really have no need for that. I bet she had no idea I would see her picture in a cell half way around the world. I'll probably send a complimentary note in Ky's Christmas card or tell Junior to pass a message on. Oh! Here is a good example. Here is one of those 'roller coaster' feelings I wrote about; one minute I'm at the center of a hot dispute, concerning cigarettes, the next I'm staring at the love of my life, upside down in full yoga gear in a magazine. I am a bit ashamed of myself actually, I acted uncalculated, I showed her off to two cell mates, but I just had to tell someone. The thing is I just don't know what to do with it now. I was considering putting it up beside Kayana, but that would not make sense, then I thought about sending it to her... nah. Finally I just popped it back into the envelope it came in and tucked it away with my other stuff.

FRI.24ᵀ

Well, nothing worked and I am in the middle of *the* great depression. I have gone into sulking mode for the first time in years. I suppose drinking stopped that, which could mean one step forward and two steps backward. I feel drained of everything. I am not hungry and the food is crap so that don't matter, there is little much to do, so I can't do anything, so that don't matter, and now I hate myself for letting a stupid picture of a girl make me feel this way. This, I fear, has the recipe for disaster; if I don't somehow change the pattern a bit though, I will be like this for sometime, but that would take distraction and I think the kind of distraction offered here, well... Maybe a letter from Nicole, maybe I just carry on writing. Oh! I can't do that, I've 14 lines of paper left, my pens are finished and my pencil is as short as my big toe. I think I will lie here with a face as long as long as an elephant's trunk and sulk until the weather changes. Don't worry, it will, I have to get to the end of my story don't I?

SAT. 25ᵀᴴ

I am just getting over the cold, had a little help from my washer. He came into the cell, and after telling him I was not well, he went and returned with a bottle of rum, vinegar, oils and lotion, and gave me a serious upper body and head massage. It still boggles the mind, how he, without being asked, sincerely (I believe) cared about my health. But without thinking how precious life is, would shoot someone in cold blood.

Alison: beautiful, temperamental, intelligent, a smile that could stop a raging bull at 50 paces. Alison. We met in the restaurant. I remember the day she came at the interview; the boss uncharacteristically interviewed her on the restaurant floor, rather than in the office (personally, I don't think he wanted to be caught alone in his office, by his wife, with her, however innocent he was). The kitchen came to a stand still, and the crew were peering through the serving hatch, and passing comments to me. I took one look at her and decided, yeah. But this girl, you could see, had an aura about her, so I ignored her. It worked but I was still trying to be nice and gentle with Amanda, and contrary to popular belief (and of the girls who had lived with me), even if I went abroad, I was never unfaithful, but we would spend a lot of time together. When Amanda finally got her flat, it was time for me to move on. But she had other ideas, which left us in a situation. On one hand, I knew I wasn't ready for a life time commitment. On the other hand, I did not want to add to previous pain. I did explain this to her, but to no avail. I did not sleep with Alison, until one day, Amanda came to my flat, and found us (I think drinking coffee). That's when I first saw a woman show that kind of passion and jealousy for a man. To say she lost it would be an understatement. She headed straight for the kitchen.

Sun, 2ND

I still have no pen or enough paper, but I woke up feeling good for some reason. I remember why I was down, but that at this moment does not seem to matter. I have been wondering this roll check, what are actual feelings. What really makes them work? Emotions? Sure. But what's behind that? To know we love, hate, envy, and are jealous of people and their things, you can categorise them, but there are others that can just come upon you, and if you stop to consider them when it happens, it can throw you (well, it does me anyway): feelings tend to follow a process. You love someone; he/she is seen with someone else, you are jealous. Ok, no problem. But here I am totally down the last few days, and I wake up feeling, I don't know: good? Happy? No. Quite content. I am in prison; my two daughters are out of touch. Well, you have read my life so far and there is more, but I am sitting here in my cell, quite content. Why? Surely the feeling should be opposite. At least until a visit or phone call.

WED 6ᵀᴴ DEC.

Well, I have received my embassy visit, got my ciggs, earphones and most important, writing paper and pens. I have felt truly despaired without them. For you who are reading this, it was probably only a few seconds ago but check the days, maybe only two or three for you, now maybe try to stay in your house and do nothing for those days. You can go to the garden for a few hours a day but no gardening, fixing the bicycle or car and no, no phone calls, you get the drift. Ok.

Well, the unit's been quiet (not literally). There has been another English man on the block for two days now; I did not see him on purpose. I figured, let him cope by himself for a while see how things are. I saw him today however at admin, gave him a pack of ciggs and a quick run down. I missed Candy (pity) but she left a note with English asking if I got the earphones and pens along with a message, a few words of encouragement. I don't think I need it but the thought was very much appreciated. Meanwhile, now, where was I? Ah, yes.

Amanda; after seeing Alison perched on the end of the bed (fully clothed), off she goes straight into the kitchen (remember now I am a chef by profession)and picks out my largest chopping knife, holding it with intent and coming towards me, to get to her, with a serious look in her eyes. Until today, I am still certain that if she had got passed me, Alison would have been in serious trouble, although I think from my point of view, she handled it as I would have wanted her to, she did not get hysterical or perceivably frightened, she remained nonchalantly calm which may have pissed of Amanda, had she seen her, but of course she did not pass me, I held her with both arms, ushered her into the bathroom and finally put her in the bath still screaming about what Alison had ruined. For the first and only time in my life I hit a woman but it was rational and although I regret it, it really was necessary (at least it was from my limited knowledge on the subject). After she had calmed down she wanted to talk to Alison. With her being calm and without a knife I decided, with Alison's agreement, it was okay. For about five minutes all was good then Amanda just went for her. I happened to get between them and part them and just for the show of strength, to get absolute attention I struck the mirror on my dressing table and it shattered. Yep, I had their attention but there was blood pouring from my hand, which looking at now, I can still see the scars. What I found interesting, was that one of them called the ambulance and the next thing I remember I was in the back watching two beautiful girls pampering me and chatting to each other like the best of friends, I have to admit, it did feel good. After that scenario, Amanda invited me over to meet her family, Mother, Sis, Bro ect. I was advised against it, but as I told Amanda, "they know what I was doing for you when they could not" and although the break up was hard, it was never meant for a life time in that way. If they understood that, then I had nothing to worry about. I believe Amanda had a son some years later and moved to Barbados happily. I and her mother still bump into each other and all is good.

Alison and I became more involved; she lived with her mum but spent most of the time with me. We quit 'Pappas' for a new expanding chain of pasta restaurants and because the head waitress of 'Pappas' 'stole' us. I was made head chef of the Kings Road branch. Alison was a waitress and every thing was grand, or was it? Once again I have to smile at these next few years of my journey, it seemed I could do no wrong, I was head chef of a restaurant (albeit pasta) I had my own flat (albeit council) and I had a girl friend who seriously looked and smiled like Julia Roberts, need I say more, yes I need . Well, I had my beloved triumph 2,500 TC, good to be in. So, restaurant, house, car, girl, is this not what you want at 24? I don't know. Even though all was going well, there was still something missing, a certain, je ne sais quoi, but I was still suppressing it. I had parties regularly, which Alison enjoyed, being the social type she was. I was promoted to, I don't even know the title, but I no longer stayed at Kings Road. I was now in charge for recruiting staff for existing and opening restaurants and designing the floor space, making it most accommodating for the chefs, and now we had a central kitchen to make the food for all the restaurants thus making them uniform, generally keeping the standards, I had set for all. Quite easy and enjoyable, I had an open cheque book for supplies and equipment (which I never once abused) and although my hours were long, they were my chosen hours. During all this time I was still in contact with Mrs Bond and would often spend weekends with them, doing the gardening or odd jobs, it made me happy, I always felt I owed her although I am sure she did not see it that way. Her husband, I think, suffered a stroke at this time. I readily volunteered to take him to and from work, until he was a bit better, and I did. I got up extra early in the morning and commuted to Kingston (Surrey), took him to work (just until he had the confidence to travel alone) and stopped work to pick him up from the office and assist him home. The only thing that worried me about that was Alison had convinced me to grow locks. She said it would suit me, so I did. Mr Bond worked for a prestigious insurance firm (for over 20 years) in the city of London. All I knew about that lot was that they had loads of money and went on the rampage in their suits and ties in the West End on Friday nights, and they were snobs, so I felt embarrassed for John, having me a young black dreadlock walking into the building with him, but after an introduction, all was well. I was in touch with Jamaica but not as often as I should have been by any means, but as poor as a reason or excuse might sound to some, it was not on purpose or with fore thought, the time just seemed, to go by. Alison and I were enjoying life and that's all that seemed to happen. Meanwhile in the restaurant a trainee manager had to get kitchen training (as they all did) via my supervision. They spent time on the pots, pans, dishes, cooking and cleaning etc. I remember just coming back from John's office because I had to meet him again. But there was also an Earl's

Court branch opening up, so I was pushed for time. I got to the kitchen and saw this spiky haired, big nosed, short white guy with a solemn look on his face. I introduced myself and apologised for being late and told him to start on the pots. You know? I completely forgot he was there until a week or so later when I passed through on a routine check and saw him elbow deep in suds scrubbing a pile of pots. I just burst out laughing, I am happy to say he saw the funny side of it. Anyway, after a quick word with the chef, to see how he was getting on, I decided not to let him go through the rest of the course. I spoke to my boss and she agreed to make him assistant manager of our busiest restaurant (Irving St, West End, Leicester square). Customers literally queued down the road to get in. Of course, it took the most money, but for a place like that, to work in, you have to have a team of staff like the old restaurant, hard working, good at their job, patience, a good sense of humour and above all, comradeship. I employed foreigners, young (as I was) Italians, French/ Algerians. They came from places where their wage was not enough and the English equivalent was ample for their needs, basically paying the rent and having a good time. I found myself spending more time in that restaurant than any other of the five. One morning (I think a Sunday) I was just strolling the West End and happen to pass the restaurant and to my surprise, I found Andy in there, it was too early on a Sunday for it to be opening, so I asked what was going on. "To be totally honest" he replied with an embarrassed, shaky smile, "I have been sleeping on the floor since I've been here and I crash with a friend from time to time". Without thinking, I told him to pick up his stuff and he could stay in my front room until he found a place to stay. He was there for almost a year. He got promoted to manager and we basically claimed the restaurant. I even started to cook from time to time just to show the lads I had not lost it. Although I recruited them, I could do what I expected them to do, it worked, and we had a great bunch of lads. There were nights when we never closed (to the public yes but not for us) we would grab fish and chips from the best in the square, wine from our cellar and party all night and in the wee hours of a morning we would stagger home; through Trafalgar square, down White Hall, past the houses of parliament, over the river, to my place, where we would finish off, chill out and freshen up then head back to work without missing the proverbial beat. So now I have a good friend to add to my tally. But things were still below the surface and I am now beginning to drink more than I should, not enough to interfere with my job, but enough for me to realize that I should slow down. But I did not, the life I was living required drinking, yeah right. Marijuana was also socially acceptable so there was always weed around. In fact, it was known by people who I recruited, if you could do your job to the equivalent or better than sober, then I would turn a blind eye to smoke or drink but if one offence was committed under alcohol or weed it was instant dismissal. I never had to fire anyone in the 3 years I worked there. I think good examples of, 1, commitment and 2, comradeship are; one morning after a heavy night on the town, Andy and I were in the restaurant when the porter turned up for work, "you're early" said Andy "I know" says Lielo in his Italian accent "I sleep, I don't wake up, so, I come to work." So me and Andy start to laugh with each other.

"why everybody this morning they laugh at me?"

"Where are your trousers Lielo?" Lielo looks down "Santa Maria! I forget." So, Lielo came on a bus and tube from home to West End in a shirt and long johns. After telling himself off, he turns to Andy and says "I still work, no?" We also had people who forgot what shift they were on and turned up for work (remember no mobiles then, if the phone was busy that was it), saying that they would rather turn up and not work than their only excuse being that they did not know . The second being when Andy was fired, no one could believe it (some big shot took over management and wanted to make changes by throwing money away). That day, the restaurant closed and the staff smashed every plate, cup, saucer, and microwave. Anything that could break was broken. Irvine St. was making the highest gross profit but it had to pay for the other restaurants that were not up to scratch. The staff, with no union decided that they would work for no other management. And so

it was, we had a good party that night. Nowadays I think there is too much distance between management and the rest, but in restaurants for sure. I think they call it professionalism, but if you make yourself a dictator, it does affect the staff, which inevitably affects the service, which affects the customer, which affects the takings, which in effect should cause the owner to change the management. You cannot dictate to staff how to create a good atmosphere. If you employ the correct staff for the idea of your establishment, then the staff will create the atmosphere themselves and, believe it or not, save the management a hell of a lot of time, trouble and work.

In the latter times of my journey with the restaurants and the Alison thing was beginning to decline, but not beyond repair yet. Alison and I had fun together and I think even she would admit, sex was not making love, sex was just fun, a hell of a lot of fun, but never the less, fun. We both liked to be with each other, when I was working late and came home, more times than none she would be doing something artistic with the flat. One night I had returned from work and she decided we must design the garden so it could accommodate plants and the Alsatian puppy I bought her for her birthday. That was funny; she came home from work one evening to find this puppy sitting in the hallway with a big pink ribbon and a card around its neck saying, Happy Birthday. She was livid, "How could you do this!? We do not have the time or the space! Or" blah, blah, blah. Then she took time out to meet the puppy and that was it, but I digress. She put it to me that we should acquire some pavement slabs from up the road where the council was repaving, so we both, under cover of darkness, 'acquired' the slabs and she designed the back garden, which is still as it is now. Other days when I forgot my key (which I still do) she would come to open the door in a bathrobe that I 'acquired' from the Piccadilly (if you look for the same scene in pretty woman with Julia Roberts and Gere, you will know exactly what I am talking about) although the robe was two sizes too big, it had the look on her that most men would want to see when coming home of an evening. But all good things come to an end and we started arguing over, nothing really, it was just that she was as stubborn as I was and in a relationship, that just does not work. Someone sometimes should concede, or at least agree to disagree. We never really loved each other; I think we were just each others playmates. She kept telling me she was leaving and she did, but she kept coming back, which really did not bother me. Then, one day she left and I had no contact with her for months, until one sunny afternoon, while I was sitting out the front of the flat, she turned up in her car, dressed like one of the girls from the Dukes of Hazard (for those who don't know, blue short shorts and a shirt, tied up under her breasts, it's sexy) and after a brief hello to a friend I was with, she strolled off into the house, inspecting as she looked around. Something about a record I had that when she heard it, it reminded her of me, then I built a spliff. We smoked, and she leans out of the bedroom window, which is waist high, observing her garden. Leaving me on the bed observing her, then she just came over, lay on the bed and after talking for a while we just fell asleep. I never saw her again after that, though she told me she was going to study to be a children's nurse. Sometime later I went to St. Thomas's Hospital to remove my wisdom teeth, I went to the nurses live in accommodation and there was her name on one of the buzzers. I was happy for her and left it at that. Lucky children, lucky doctors. Somewhere in between I had learned of the changes that were to be made (not about Andy) and I did not see myself as a part of the new system, different bosses trying to prove themselves without meeting the staff who made it possible for them to be there, so I resigned. So now I have no job and no Alison. No problem, sign on for a while and party. I remember one time in particular, one late evening, two girls came to the flat with a bottle of J.D and said they were told there was a party tonight (they were from one of the restaurants). There was no party, but they were invited in anyway. One was Chinese, the other English, I will leave the middle to your imagination, but the next morning as we walked towards the River Thames, Andy says "fuck I'm hungry, man, I could do with a Chinese". Without dropping the flow "don't be greedy you've have just had one" says the girl he was with. We had fun, after some nights of smoking, drinking and driving to Gatwick at 2, 3 in the morning with 'Brothers in arms' by Dire Straits blasting from the tape deck, just to watch planes take off and land. We decided to work on a cruise ship together, it sounded fun and there was nothing wrong with our credentials, it was just that Andy had eczema on his hand and failed the medical. I passed and made the decision to go, regretting very much leaving Andy behind.

THURS 7ᵀᴴ

Tuc shop; I spoke to English again, gave him a little advice from my experience. And now I have the perfect example of a phrase Grandma used to use, "who can't hear, must feel." I was sitting on my little perch, watching the football, and he comes and sits beside me, putting me between him and the game. So, he is yapping away about something or another (I am sure he was just happy to talk to an English man) but I am watching the ball and it appears that he has the same habit as another inmate had, which is touching me every time I am not looking at him. I explain to him to stop it because, firstly, I hate it and secondly "if you don't keep your eye on the ball you could get seriously injured". He, is telling me, who has been here for ten months, that he, will warn me when the ball is coming. I told him he will not have the time to warn me, "All you will do is feel the ball in your face and hear; Salope!" (Fucker)You know the man did not believe me. Two minutes later, from the corner of my eye, something. I had enough time for instinctive reaction, I did not even look towards the path of flight, I just leaned back a few inches and wham, smack in the face, left side, "Salope!" "I told you," I also told him he could not react; it's one of those things.

My status has gone up again. One of my so called employees has taken it upon himself to rid anyone of the inmates who continuously get on my nerves for cigarettes from my cell. It costs me less now that he does something. Maybe he is paying me back for when he did nothing and I gave him ciggs.

Fri. 8ᵀᴴ

Woke up this morning, same ole routine, different thoughts. Thought for the day; do you really think you know your friends or your family? (I would leave yourself out of this one) even if you are given a brief history of a said person, do you really think you know what's going on inside? I think I have just tried to find out about someone, by trying to place myself in that person's surroundings of that time. Kind of astral projection combined with meditation and a link that I must have. I will explain more later. For now; I have been in my block, a select few (myself including) received cigarettes from the shop, you may think lucky me, but if you recall the hassle I get when most of the others get them, well, you can imagine the traffic in the cell now. But not to worry, the boys are in town. We will see what, if anything happens when they start to get edgy, but for now, roll check and I have time, without interruption, to tell you more of my journey. I hope you understand. So far my time back in England would seem to others to be, good, to say the least, but as I said earlier do you think or care to know what's going on inside, then again why should you care, it's more than likely you have your own issues anyway. Maybe if I popped into your life for a brief period, the part of me you met may have been better for you than the part of me you never saw. Please do not misunderstand me here, I mean I was having a good time but what I did not realise is that I was not thinking about life properly. *I should have been paying more attention to Junior(even though I knew all along that when he became older I would see that he came to England, of course no one else knew, but I did and that was good enough for me, whether I was right or wrong). Anyway I was thinking along the lines of having a house rather than a flat and all that goes with it. Well, to be honest, I was never going to be a nine to fiver with a mortgage, I could not stay still long enough. I would be self employed or have a job with hours that suit me, not the boss. After all; I want to work to live, not live to work. And so I got myself together for the trip to Miami. We partied for two weeks as a fair well bash and off I went to America. Via New York to drop in on friends and see the sights, Check out Brooklyn and see if it was as bad as they say it was (to me it had nothing on Kingston). Then I stopped in Philadelphia for more friends from the hotel and I did the 'Rocky' thing over the benches and up the steps of the museum, jumping up and down like I was on top of the world. It was a good feeling. I felt as I thought Stallone wanted to portray this feeling. Then, off to Miami.*

Carnival Cruise Lines, excellent. I had no doubt about my capability of the job in hand, Trainee Assistant Food Manager, but there was something I had not banked on and that was my incessant need to keep my mind off something. I did not know what then but I have an idea now, and if you have been following you should have an idea also. Anyway, I have been booked into the Ramada hotel, lovely thing, and of course I knew about hotels and restaurants, so it did not take me long to settle there. I was supposed to be on board in three days time but I still had some energy to dispatch, and this particular hotel was a stop over for air hostesses and ship crew, so I fitted right in. Now the cruise ships probably have, on a whole, the cleanest service area, food prep and storage in the world, for a public. An example; every Thursday the passengers were allowed to tour the kitchen (there was always work going on but it would be minimum). An ice carver with a chain saw would demonstrate his skill ect, but what was quite impressive to me, was that given the size of the galley and the amount of equipment (space easily more than half the size of a football pitch) and the sheer turn over of food, was that passengers were given a prize (not sure what) if any or all could slide a finger anywhere in the galley (kitchen) and find a film of dust or grime. I challenge all who wish to take me on, to check your kitchen, home or work and I am sure it would not take long. A few places you might check; behind the fridge there is a motor or grill thing, there will be dust on the ceiling above the cooker, for sure, you might not see it but its there, and try the top of a lamp or bulb, anyway, the galley was clean. So it follows that they have their own private medical centre where every working person is checked before being allowed to board. No problem for me there. I had my check in London, just routine I thought. So, here I am in medical; this obese, ill mannered, uncaring, (you can make up the rest yourself) woman takes and tests my blood, comes back to me and says "you can't board the ship this week, you may have AIDS" well, I do know that I was instructed to go back to the hotel and wait for a week for the final results. But I do not know if I said anything to the nurse or not. Please bear in mind the year is 1987, AIDS is seriously getting its due promotion around the world. It's not like now, when every so often someone famous may have caught it, or it's 'AIDS Awareness Day' or some kind of promotion, No! What happens, how it happens, what it does to you, or how to prevent it. 'NO CURE' was in your face everyday. Anyway, shell shocked would be the word (yes, I would have deserved it if it did happen but read on) to describe it. When I found myself again I was in my hotel room with a litre bottle of brandy, quiet sober, but still not quite there. Then I started to think, if the test is positive, do I call all the women I have been with and tell them? Of course I will, then try to track down their numbers, and then how will they react. Allison was first to come to mind and I really felt sad about it, funny enough though, I did not feel too bad about myself, I reckoned I could face death with as much dignity as death would allow. I thought about who would miss me, who would have felt genuine sadness, or happiness, or maybe even a certain amount of relief. I thought of how my parents would think, and how they would think of how they both left their son to the government to bring up, and he ended up dying of AIDS. How would they feel about not getting to know their son, not playing any part in my life? Then for the rest of the week I was between the bar, the swimming pool and my room, with the brandy, waiting for the phone call. On the Friday I received the call and an assistant said to me "you do not have AIDS and you can leave on Sunday." I was too relieved to hear the good news to be upset about the nonchalant way she delivered it. I asked her what the problem was and she asked if I had recently been 'partying'. Of course I had! Two weeks for a fair well party. She told me; "When the body has exerted itself in this way, the white blood cell count, lessons, which is the same signs as the early stages of contracting the virus". Well, looking back, it's almost anticlimactic, the time I had on the ship. We went around some of the Caribbean islands, including ST. Lucia. We worked 18 hours a day and our day off, was as long as the ship stayed docked on an island. In shifts, one island of choice per week, sometimes 9 hours sometimes five and then back to work. We also had to write reports of what we thought of the job and suggestions, if we had any. I remember my first day off; I must have finished work at about 2 am and the ship docked at 5.30. So I sleep and get up at what I thought was 5.00am and while walking through the corridors in my shorts, with towel in hand, looking for a way out, which is not easy considering the size of the ship and the fact that I had only used the 'in' to get on . I noticed by looking through the port hole that it was all sea. I thought I was just on the wrong side of the ship. Then one of my colleges was passing by and asked me what I was doing. I told him it was my day off; he said "no it was yesterday." I had slept through the early morning and the following day and "the staff captain wants to see you". Well, that was the first time I was spoken to by the captain. Another time, I arranged a staff party for the department (no, not all). The entertainment, the chefs and us, (there were six, I think, of us. We did not really get to meet anyone else because our 18 hours were spent mainly in the kitchen (99%). They did have a small staff bar, where I met a few people, and there were the people that you met while eating lunch but that was it really. So, the party on the beach went down okay and we were to have a few more, but when I got back to the ship, I could not find the staff elevator. So I used the passenger one, of course against regulations, but the ship was in dock so most of the passengers would be on the island. So I get in the lift, wearing a pair of shorts, bare chested, with a yellow towel wrapped around my head, balancing two large plastic containers on top of it and on the very next floor the staff captain walks in with two aged passengers and a look of dissatisfaction. I promptly got off on the next floor and after dropping of the equipment and a quick change to uniform (white jacket, trousers and black tie) went to the kitchen to find my boss waiting. He had a soft spot for me and he told me the staff captain said he should have a word with me about a certain situation. "Okay" he said "I've had the word, don't let it happen again, especially without permission". Another time someone suggested I should go to a certain beach on the island of ST. Thomas, called, 'Morgan's Bay'. He said it was ranked, by some reputable magazine, of being one of the top ten beaches in the world. I believe 'Round tree' did some of the adverts for Bounty Bar there, and if you have seen the bounty adds, need I say more; When I turned off the road and passed through a coconut grove, in my hired jeep, I stepped out to have a look around and I'm not sure I if I saw the water or the sand first. I just remember falling to my knees in awe. I mean, I had been to many beaches in Jamaica. Boston and Nigril in their own respected times were two of the better beaches in Jamaica. Dragon's bay, French man's cove, to name a few others, but this beach is the kind of beach you could only imagine being a best, only to find out when you get there, it surpasses your expectations. The tiny white grains of sand seemed to find and take over the natural dips, curves and crevices of your feet almost like a liquid would. The two sides of the cove are covered with thick deep greenery, stretching backwards into the not so close, mountain range. Beyond the water, barely trickling up to the sand in almost silence, stretching out in different shades of green and blue but so clear. You can walk out, 20 or so yards before the water reaches your knees. One day I saw a yacht anchored in the middle of were the imaginary line might form, at the end of one point of the cove to the other. It looked like a yacht from the rich and famous and I could hear music, so I thought, 'why not?' and started to swim for it. I got to about 50, 70, 80, yards from it, then I saw a sign in the water. "Do Not Swim Beyond This Point". I never did go back to that beach, but I would still say, if touring that part of the world check it out. Hopefully they have not slapped a big hotel on the grove and over crowded the beach with too many little touristy things. Oh and I think that developers should not be allowed to take over what remaining beauty some of the islands still have left. After all, the cruise ship passengers are on a package thing, they are pointed in a certain direction and they go. As do all the exclusive lot, they do not really care if the beach their hotel is on or the beach the tour guide suggested is a natural beauty or not. What they care about is that they went to a wonderful 'looking' beach, weather it is natural or not is irrelevant, what is relevant to them is that they can send pictures, or have them for their family photo album to say,' I was in this island on this day on this beach' you guys can develop beaches for that. There are so many locations around the islands that can be transformed into fabulous beaches exclusively for those who don't care about nature, yeah you guessed it. I don't care for the people who come to me, knowing that I have spent time in Jamaica. "Oh, I have been to Jamaica, I had a wounderful time."

"Where did you go? What did you see? How was it?"

"Oh, I took my family to Sandals, it was wounderful, and they loved it. It was all inclusive; we did not have to leave the hotel. (To the kids, tell them you want to go to a place to see the place and meet some people. It's not that difficult, just tell them to be adventurous. And to developers; please don't give these people any more of our few lasting beautiful natural beaches it's really not fair). Anyway that's how I spent most of my time on the ship in-between night clubs in Puerto Rico, San Juan to the beaches of the Virgin Islands and St Thomas and apart from the tail end of a hurricane we passed through, it was quite an uneventful part of my journey through life. It finally broke the donkeys back when my cabin mate (sea term) told my boss I had been smoking weed in the cabin, which is a widely done thing; you just were not to be caught, although they had sections. Example, all the cooks and most waiters come from the islands, entertainment and management from Europe, the captain invariably being from Italy. So I was issued a cabin with the Europeans. I used to pop *down to the Jamaicans because some of them were from a nearby town to where I used to live. You would find them literally by following the sound of the music and the smell of marijuana, but they were never bothered. I on the other hand was expected to behave like, well, different. I did not blast my music but I did like to light a joint and smoke it up on deck at about 1,2am, lie down on my back and look at the black blanket with the silver glitter sparkling over head, with so many shooting stars you could forget how many you saw, even if you were counting them, because at that time in life, if you are anywhere that drops the kind of feeling I had with the stars and listening to the bow of the ship cut through the waters of the Caribbean with almost no existent sound of the engines, alone , then somewhere in between the counting of the stars, your thoughts tend to drift on others you would like to share the moment with. And while currently drifting in a world of tranquillity, whooshhh, another star goes by. Some nights had passed of the same routine, until I was grassed on for the weed, and back on the next flight home, which really did not bother me. I would never do it again, but I am really glad I did it. To me, there was no real purpose being on the ship, yes I had a job, but that was it. I could not help believing that there was something missing from my life. Every time I achieved, or was on the way to achieving a certain amount of what society says is success, I either stopped the process or semi consciously found a way of being stopped. So I went back to London to figure out what is halting my journey, what force unknown to me is blocking my effort to continue on a straight path through life, I mean, I had the youth and vigour, any get up and go all sussed out and knew where I had to go and who I wanted to be and that did make me strong in some way and weak in others example, I was proud of myself for just getting to where I was without Motherly or Fatherly advice, or pointers along the way. Fair dues, I was thrown into most situations, but I survived and my consistent question has always been, why? I also thought of my upside to a bad situation, example; I would never feel what it's like to lose a loving Mother or Father and in a very sad way, that's actually comfortable. I know now that I would like my children to be sad for a while, rather than the initial feeling of 'comfortable', so I do understand what's wrong, but I don't know why I can't fix it. A little later in my journey I realised I had to go deeper, do some research. I had to find out where my Mom lived, but first; I had to see Andy and family, get an income, live in a squat and meet a future wife.*

SUN 10TH

Little Ky's birthday; I phoned J the other day to ask him to leave the answer machine on so I could leave a message for her because I really do not want to go through anything that will mar the happy thoughts of Ky's birthday, like Emilie telling me she is not there, or refusing to talk to me. Meanwhile, J has told me he has won his previous fights and maybe a challenger for the British title one day. Well, I am glad that he realises at this early stage in his life that anything is possible, you just have to want it bad enough. Anyway even if he does not reach the top he will be able to look back on his life and say: "I gave it one hell of a shot though" and giving it a shot is all you can ask of anyone. Funny thing just crossed my mind, what happens to those who try and do not succeed? Those who ask for help, only to find there is none there, or not available, or who need support to cross the river only to find the bridges that were there have been washed away or broken through too much use. It's rhetorical now, but it was not then.

I find using the phone now a bit less demanding. I find this is because the amount of inmates that have left, compared to those coming in, is leaving more people who demand use of the phone, and they are the majority that I have of course known, so I am in their category. No one who came in after me (or after my settling in period) can be allowed to jump me in the queue, and the few that can, have manners not to now, so that's not bad. I also realise it's not because of a problem erupting by the phone why the lifers do not have to queue, it's because they have been here the longest. What a reward for the loss of freedom, huh.

Mon 11th

I had a smoke yesterday and sorted English out; I have been showing him the ropes. He is having a problem with lack of ciggs and wants my advice on who to ask. I told him; "you do not have to do without; you just have to program yourself". Now, I fear he is the type of guy who chain smokes. I do not think he and I will be seen together much, simply because when the time comes (and it will) when you have no ciggs, you tend to behave in a manner unbecoming of a British subject and at this present time in my journey for many different reasons that have become apparent, and because of the circumstances and surroundings, I can say, "I am satisfied being British. I will serve this sentence with the resolve and dignity that should be expected of any British prisoner abroad to the best of which my ability and circumstance allow."

Tue 12

Its library day and I have decided to stop with the thrillers. They are good, but I have gotten used to the pattern, in their place I have picked up the Bible, which I read a lot of during my acquaintance with Rastafarianism. Now I have the time to maybe understand what it's really about (although I doubt it very much.)

Yesterday the cigarette tension began to over flow, with arguments and fights breaking out. But the general election seem to have bought all together, I would not call it harmony, but together none the less. Bets were going on through the evening and we had an armed team of specials' parading the floor for a while, I think just making their presence felt. The party in power Ken Anthony (whom I was told by a guard this morning, actually served time in here some years aback)against a former prime minister of 30 years prior and is now 82, Fredricks , he won 11seats to 6. While I was in the cell listening to it on the radio, we heard the unofficial results and the prison was quiet. We were listening to the opposition being congratulated and being interviewed and it was still quiet for about an hour, even Chi chi said to me he does not understand "why no noise." My answer, "I still can't figure out St. Lucians."Then I heard Icry from across the way shouting "11 to 6! 11 to 6!", and then the noise; Juice boxes bursting, banging on the metal stools as drums, the kegs also drums, cups running across the iron bars of the cell gates, shouting and screaming. Anything that could make noise did. They actually outdid the cricket matches and the world cup. I had my earphones on and I could not hear the station, so I gave up and after a brief look around the block. I lay down just to listen. Have you ever heard so much noise, that it becomes almost melodic and some what soothing? No matter how incoherent, a football stadium crowd comes to mind, sometimes you have to consciously listen to make sure they are still being noisy, it kind of blends in with other forces that are around and becomes rather tranquil. Well this was the case, and it went on for hours. I ended up falling asleep to the sound of music. This morning however, back to norm; the loud talking and slamming of dominoes with the added attraction of prisoners impossibly trying to debate the election. I think I will remain in my cell today, for I have learnt from the past that it is almost impossible to debate politics and religion with people of political or religious persuasion, you either agree or you don't.

So after I land back in England, I head off to my flat to see how things are there (I had left my flat with Andy's brother Mike and his girl friend Karen). They had made it quite comfortable and being as I was not due back for some time, I told them I would stay by my Uncle Ossie and Angela. Actually I had no intention of doing that, but they were nice people and I did not want to make their life uncomfortable. So I stay with Os, for a few days and I get a job as the Head Chef of a cosy restaurant, in front of Charing Cross hospital, not far from Ossie's. Now, that was a strange restaurant. On my trial shift, the chef, who was supposed to be there for a week to show me "the ropes", walked out on the first night, just as it was about to get busy. At this time I had only been shown a menu, no recipes, and no method. I did not know what 'mise en place' was in which fridge. I did not even know where some of the fridges were. But as any chef can tell you, this can be the norm in some restaurants, actually at some time or another most. But no problem, because when you are good at a job, these are the times you grow admiration from your fellow workers, if they cooperate. It just so happens that my salad chef, unknown to me, was a needle junkie and although I had the support of a dishwasher, he was no chef. So I would call things out like, lettuce, meat, pots and pans, etc, he would bring them and I would do my best. At first, the salad chef was helping and we were coping, then it started to get busy (as we were just around the corner from the Hammersmith Odeon) and Jessie started to panic. I had no idea what was going on, I just tried to focus on the incoming orders, then all of a sudden, Jess picks up the small radio that was playing and hurls it towards me, missing me by inches and before I could retaliate he was sat down in the corner of the kitchen on a milk crate, shaking and trembling like a leaf. I knew about powder coke and had a line or two prior to the ship (do not condemn me for this, you may be surprised how many people had a line or two of coke in those days, it was not like the epidemic of crack today) but this, no. I honestly thought he was dying and it seemed everyone was too busy to explain to me what was happening, or to pay Jessie any attention. So in a lull in the orders, I literally picked up Jessie in my arms and took him across the road, via the back door, to the hospital, where I went straight to A&E (still in uniform) with this guy barely conscious in my arms and literally ran into a doctor. Without questioning me, he looked at Jessie and said "you've done it again, huh." Then he turns to me and tells me he had a 'bad hit', which means he liquidised the powder for the syringe and air or something got into it, so I left him there and went back to work. When I got back to the restaurant, it was half full and getting busier, so I told the manager to close the doors for a while and explain the delay, in what ever form he wishes. If you are a good manager the problem we had is a challenge but by no means impossible, if you can relate to your customers " certain difficulties", they, unless they have a deadline, would like nothing more than to sit with a date or company, drinking complimentary wine until the situation gets under control, but this manager could not, instead, he kept coming to the hatch where I served the food and stood there demanding certain tables, leaving customers querying about their food, thus making the amount of food to be served at one time, impossible. So I told him to leave and talk to the customers and he leaned through the hatch and said "you call yourself a fucking chef." The adrenaline hit me one time, I had a large bubbling pot of bolognaise on the fire simmering and in one movement, picked it up and hurled it towards him, he ducked and the pot hit the wall behind him, splattering everything in its vicinity. Then I just took off my uniform and headed for the door. As destiny would have it, as I was reaching the door, Cousin Angela turns up with her boyfriend for dinner as a surprise. I spoke with her for a little and told the manager I would finish the shift and be off. That's when I really noticed the head waitress, slim, elegant and seemingly the only one with her head screwed on. It did not seem to be the place for he, I thought a maître de, at some swish place where you book even when you don't have to would suit her more. Anyway we got talking and I quite liked her. The next day I told Ossie what happened, and to my surprise he put his hat on and took me to the restaurant. I don't really know what he said, but the scene was like a mafia boss reprimanding a lesser about him disrespecting the family. Personally, I thought it was quite funny, but the manager was really shaken. He asked me to come back with a rise I accepted and stayed for a year or so, within which time I made friends with the salad chef, and porter and we all ended up squatting in a house just around the corner from the restaurant. The squat was just squat living: police came, *chucked us out; we would get back in and so on (I could go on about stories in the squat but they really are not that relevant, for this part of my journey). Deidre and I became close and although I was not seeing anyone at the time just as I am now (well you know what I mean) I could not stay indoors or in one place for long, so we would see each other, whenever. But in these times I still had it in mind to track down my mother so I really was not taking any one serious then. And although she was and still is I believe a good woman, she knew this. So it was a bit of a surprise to find out from her that she was pregnant. Now I am getting confused again and really did not know what to do. Her parents being catholic, I decided to do what I thought was the right thing to do at the time and asked her to marry me. It was not a disaster but I was seriously no one to be married to then, I am sure Deirdre took it like me; let's see what happens. So we had a small wedding and I asked her to move in with me. By this time Karen and Mike had moved out of the flat, Andy had married a beautiful Spanish girl and moved to Spain, I was the best man, and I remember throwing a brick through my work place window and pretending to cut my hand just not to miss the wedding. But I still had issues in America which I had explained to Deidre and had her support in going. I was not sure what was going to happen, I just had this feeling of needing to see my mother. So off I went, I do not remember the first meeting but funny enough I can remember as I write that I had seen her on more accounts than I gave credit for. Once when she worked in a cinema (when I was at Oakfield and must have stayed for a weekend with her) and at a time in Kingston; I remember her making me breakfast, sausages and eggs, my brother was pissed off because she was paying more attention to me, so I asked for an extra sausage (sorry Bro) and I remember my little sister Donnia in a pram, maybe more will come before I finish. I remember bits and pieces of seeing her in my stay in America. This is due mainly because when I got to the states, I found out that my bigger Sister was living close by and quite well off (money wise.)A nice house with a swimming pool and a basement decked with two bedrooms, a music room and hair* dressing space, which is what she did best, so I moved in with her, or let's say I stayed with her most of the time. I don't think Mum really appreciated this but I did feel more comfortable with Sis and to top it all, on the first day I saw her, I hear a deep voice from the front room. I said "Corries' voice cannot be that deep already" and to my total surprise, it was my Brother. I was so happy to be there with them again and for that reason, my mother took second place, which was not intentional, but I really wanted to be with them and they did not mind my company. This is not to say we did not hang out with Mum. There was a party and I was an honoured guest, we went shopping and my Sis, being her, and, in America, never cooked, we always ate out. I was there for my birthday and they booked a really nice restaurant, where the chefs cooked and served on the tables. So, this is the first time we were together and I was okay, until I had to bring up the reason why I came. Maybe I should have left it; after all it all seemed so good at the time. But I think I realised I needed questions answered and my mother, I thought, had the answers.

So, on the ship was the first time I used a drink for comfort, and Sis liked to drink , now this is not to say I did not drink a lot, it's just that it caused no outside problems , and so me and Sis were at it everyday, but really just enjoying each other's company . My brother was too busy with other things to be caught up with our care free lifestyle and so one evening I decided to stay with Mum, after she made it clear that she felt away with me sleeping all the time at Sis's house. So after a couple of bottles of probably rum or brandy, knowing me now, probably both, I asked "Who is my real father", because up until now no one had claimed me, (strange sentence that one, "no one had claimed me") none of the two are dead, both apparently living okay, one getting up to more mischief than the other. Personally, I have an inside feeling that it's him, just because of the way he acted, he can't stay still either. Anyway I don't know and that's exactly what my mum told me "I don't know" (memo to kids of mine, as terrible as you may think I am, you know I am your father and I have never done or acted in any way to make you think different) and she told me the *story of being a young girl with a fine husband and kind Father of their two children, but he worked too much or all the time (or however you, women, put it when you find that rare breed of man that works as a devoted family man and it still is not enough),so she found , or visa versa, a young good looking charismatic young man and had an affair. Things could have been resolved there and then, but cause and effect of one's, certain journey, start right here: My mum falls pregnant and I am on the way. The husband has suspicions and wants me aborted, Mum can't do it (a good decision on your behalf mum, memo to husband; it's a good thing my brother is not writing this, he is not so forgiving). Mum is now having a nervous break down, good, in the way that it means she cared. I end up in a home, if I did not go to a home, husband divorces Mum, all the kids end up in a home. 'The sacrifice of the few for the need of the many' (Spock from star trek). I cannot write about how I felt because I do not remember, oh yes I do, I punched a hole in her wall but that was more or less it. The three of us niggled her a bit and I started to feel sorry for her. After all, I am beginning to see that she did care and that was a lot, but she does have a way of putting her foot in it; prior to this she told me, that I came to the states to "get her back" and I could not convince her otherwise. If she had known me at all, she would have known that I am not capable of hurting on purpose, or maliciously, without someone, purposely, or maliciously doing something to me. The fact that she could not understand that hurt me more than the news of the two men. However, this was enough for now; I had some answers, but not what I needed. I needed more info. That cup that had overflowed could now take some more, but not yet, and were could I get a refill? Oakfield maybe? For the mean time, I enjoy the rest of the vacation with Sis, Bro and Mum, and I did, until I had to cut short the time and return to England. I do have to say though while I was in America, Sis decked me out in new clothes U.S style, Jewellery, subtle but expensive, I drove the new ford Taurus and sometimes the prize winning Camara, which was first of it's type off the production line. We went to the best clubs but I have to say, money has never been seen as a value in life to me (That does not sound right. I'll come to back to that one, let's say for now, that I have never owned a credit card, which a lot of people find amazing. I do not.*

WED I 3TH

Ciggs or lack of them is causing tension to run high, as predicted. There was a good fight on the floor space this morning between the guy I gave my shoes to (he did not sell them) and another inmate who has been here as long as I. It was good in the way that they were boxing, no weapons no kicking or biting, they had a good crowd and a guard came by to silently oversee (good move). It went on for a while, good punches were thrown but they were getting tired, then the one who had the upper hand put up both hands in a sign of 'enough' and the other agreed, to my surprise, the clapping of hands, hugs and smiles bought on a round of applause from the other inmates. I spent the rest of the morning having my hair done by the man who always wants me to write his letters. It's been twisted for dread locks. Throughout my journey I have been most comfortable with my locks, my plan is to grow them again, but in here, if I have to go to admin for a package my son has sent, over six months ago, and I meet the wrong guard, he will surly have it cut.

The other night I had a smoke and a question came to mind (and for those who have smoked weed you know you can really break down a question, pros, cons and all the rest). I'll give you a summary; should I make this book public, how would the people involved feel and react to it? Would it have an effect on their life? What effect would it have? Then I look at me, what about me? First I am doing it for myself, a self therapy course I could call it, so what I have written is what I have experienced, then,, it's for my children to decide (whom I will ask how they would feel if I did publish it), for it is for them I need to know how important family values are. And even if I was not there every step of the way, they must try to understand the reason, not excuses. For there are only reasons and there are no excuses. Thirdly, the book is not meant to condemn my parents. How they acted was not my fault, even though of course, it was because of me. I know some people tried and put themselves out for me. For them, I have nothing but admiration, even if it may not have sounded that way back then. It would appear to me that the only people that had the ammunition for my fight were my parents and they have not used it properly, probably because they did not know they had it. Money and material things are truly not every thing in life and anybody who knows me, will know that I really don't care about either of them for myself (that's what I was trying to explain earlier). So how will people think about my parents? How will my parents think about how other people think about them? Well, to be honest, it should not bother them. Now, its how I feel about them and how they truly feel about me. To get somewhere on a given journey you have to know where you are coming from, or how can you know what direction to take to get there? By going through my life, things are emerging, certain thoughts are receding. I truly am, feeling better within. It's been a hard slug, but what's happened has happened. Now if nature is good to me, I have the other half of this journey to fulfil and for this part, I can change direction. For I am beginning to feel for myself deep inside, and for this reason if only, my parents should be happy for me. It has just occurred to me, that comfortable feeling I spoke of a couple of days ago, has something to do with this. So you see, I am not bull shitting, something really is changing for the better. My hope is now; that Emilie will understand, even if she has found someone else. I have to play the part of the Father, in her life. So I weight up the odds and for said reasons, about people thinking I did not try hard enough or I did not care about anyone or thing, or even if they think I am just looking for an excuse for my incarceration, even if no one buys it. For the sake of my family and others, this book has to be published... I just had an interruption from the Ras (my former teacher);

he came in to ask something, but got side tracked into a nice reasoning about life and people. Well, we have similar views so I won't go into it, but he did say he is a close friend to a guard who he likes to reason with and I came up in the subject. Her evaluation of me: I am intelligent and have a good spirit. I don't cause problems and it looks like I can take care of myself, also I've a good up bringing. Well, 4 out of 5 ain't bad, but enough of this, let's see what happen next.

So, I am back in England and am seemingly full of vigour. I am keeping in contact with both sisters. Donnia, who I have always loved but spent so many years apart, although I did spend a few days with her and her husband (interesting that three out of four got married and neither of the others knew or got invited to the wedding). Kay, who I can remember cleaning more obsessively, is spending money getting drunk with me. I remember one day literal falling down the stairs in her house, spraining my knee and going to bed laughing myself to sleep because I was so happy and broody Bro, who always had something else on his mind and never quite showing how much he cares or hurts. I remember telling him I was gay, just for a laugh, and I put on a really convincing show, the disappointment was easy to see, but he said "your my brother and I still love you" but when I told him I was not gay I was only kidding, after an embarrassing smile he went back to normal. I also phoned Mum a few times and she, I. So I thought I was feeling okay. During this time Deidre had gone to Ireland to have Nicole which I thought was a good idea. When she called me I think I was two days late to get to Dublin but I got there and we stayed in a little hotel in Dublin for a night. I met her parents and family who were okay. I could see her mother tried her best to make me feel at home, although I got the distinct feeling that her father would have preferred if I had not met his daughter. For example, he took us for a drink at his local (the only) pub (or place to go to for miles)and there were two sides, one empty the other one bubbling , and I do like to meet ordinary folk from different countries, if only just to see how they get on. The Father told me it would be better if we did not go to the other side because, well I don't recall how he put it, but it was something to do with my colour and/ or hair, but he put the blame on his fellow Irish men, when just a few nights earlier I could not buy a drink with my own money at a pub in Dublin, crowded with only Irish folk all being very nice to me. A few days later I won first prize in a karaoke competition in a large club kind of thing amongst only Irish, so I was welcomed by all the other Irish folk I met, genuinely and warmly. And he met me at a time when I was okay. Although I guess you can't help what you feel, I don't blame him for behaving that way. But I am willing to bet that now, he would be telling his daughter how right he was and how he knew I would end up something like this. I just hope he does not go lecturing his Granddaughter on those thoughts. Let her grow and discover the beauty of individuals not the ugliness of a group of stereotypical people, because as you see me as being bad because of colour or creed, I in turn could see you as being bad because you are Irish, and we both know neither is correct. So, we go back to London and I am going to attempt a family life. We both worked at one time or another, and I had my share of dirty nappies and although I did not drink continuously then I had my fair share of hang over's (memo to new fathers do not get a hang over the morning you have to look after your baby). It's very difficult to try and hold your breath, to try not to look in the nappy while making an effort for the contents not to leave the nappy, and trying not to throw up, while changing the nappy. But it was done and we were a family, for a while. I remember her first tooth, and her first step was at, 10.10pm, 17th Feb in the kitchen. Deidre was in the front room, with her cousin. It was quite funny, I was priming her for ages because I wanted her to walk before she was one year old, she would be a fast learner, and when she took the first step, I shouted out of excitement and she just dropped, plop, on her bottom and started to cry. I picked her up and went to show mum but she did not walk again that evening. She was a beautiful baby and I sent a picture of her to Jamaica and Aunt Jenny's comments were "she looks like a TV baby." I took them to Spain to see Andy and Chica and we had a good time. To be honest I cannot remember having an argument with Deidre. She did not do anything wrong. She and cousin Ange became good friends and later on had more contact with them than I did. I watched and helped her learn to speak English (although Sesame Street was excellent) and we, Nicole and I were good. I loved her then as I do now, as the love should be from father to daughter. Now this is where things start to go a bit weird. I was neglecting Deidre, not because she had done anything wrong; I just started staying out late drinking and smoking I was never with another woman although I don't think, looking back that she will believe me even now. I did flirt a lot but I was always like that. I just was not treating her as she deserved, though I have to say in defence of myself I did not treat her bad just not as good as a husband should treat his wife. Inevitably she left me, but stayed in London and we saw each other often. I would sometimes drive Nicky to school or travel by train to pick her up from school when Deidre could not (she lived about five miles from me and few hundred yards from the school but sometimes work would get in the way) I remember one day Nicky came home from school quite sad and after asking what was wrong, she told me that a boy in her class or another, was bothering her. Now, I could be quite intimidating to adults then, 6"4 I worked out, and my hair was flowing, so I asked her if she would like me to stand by the fence at lunch time and she would point to me saying "that's my dad", but she said that it was all right "I have a friend in the next form and he won't let anything happen to me" (she was about 6 at the time). I was quite proud of her, she was learning how to take care of a situation, before having to run to Mummy or Daddy, which reminds me of a time when Deidre and I were in a MacDonald's in the west end; while we were queuing there were two or three big African men in front of us, in a very joyous mood, not drunk, just exited. We got kind of talking and as you may know, many cultures express themselves with a lot of figurative hand movement and although I am sure it was not malicious, he emphasised a statement by slapping her above her chest with the back off his hand, I immediately pushed him away and told him that it was my wife he just put his hands on, he *apologised and I accepted, because I believed him, he even wanted to pay for the burgers (I did not accept but not begrudgingly). I am not looking for praise for this kind of action, nor should one receive them for protecting your wife and offspring. Knowing this however did not stop what ever it was inside of me driving Deidre away. I had to go back to America but I don't even know why, I was drinking more now but not enough for people on the outside to think much of it. The big difference with this trip was that I knew I was drinking too much and I thought I could stop if I was with my Mother. I did talk to her but nothing really hit home. I stopped drinking for six weeks before going home. When I got there, Deidre and Nicole had gone back to Ireland to live (she did tell me she was going and I thought it would be better there than London for Nicky). It's almost as if I had the freedom to drink myself silly and it would not matter to anyone. So I did just that, only this time I started to drink from the off licence. It would start with a can, every so often. Then one particular summer I became a part of the people, who would stop by after work, and chill out on weekends, I would spend afternoons there and when I lost a job, days. Around these times I found out that Cousin Val and Ange had stopped inviting me to their birthday bashes because of my worsening and bad reputation at particular social get togethers. Now, bearing in mind when I appeared to be okay, I hosted their 18th & 21st birthdays at my place (great party).*

These bad reps came (from my point of view) from Ossie's mum's funeral: All his family are there and I am somehow stupidly thinking, that apart from his immediate family I was the closest one to him. Okay, so I've had a good few drinks but not enough to not know what I was doing. When I heard Ossie and a guy my age arguing (at least I thought they were arguing, Jamaicans have this way of being like that) and he said something that even in jest, he should not say to Ossie. Now, being his age group I took over the case and really had a go at him, I even offered him outside to 'settle it', I don't think he did not come because he was scared, I think he did not come because I was drunk and misunderstood the context. After I had calmed down I asked Ossie why he did not speak up for me, and he said to me, that that man was the same to him as I was and he could do or say anything because of the way I acted. Although he understood why I was doing it, it was not necessary. That man would no more be rude to him than I would. So I went home and drank some more. There were other times but you get the drift. I was still close to Ange and Val but I never asked them about parties again, when I heard they were having one I would just not go. So now I am following a pattern of drink but still very capable, although something is still driving me to the edge. But before I get there, I have a few more cards to play. I had taken acting lessons while I was with Deidre but did not really do anything with the skills. So I decided to take another classes in a college close by. My tutor was a certain Craig Snelling, wonderful man born to teach that subject, such passion and energy, and he was gay, a good combination if handled correctly, which he did. Not to take anything away from my previous teachers, but Craig taught me something deeper about acting, something he thought I could do really well and it gave me not only confidence to go on stage, which is different from confidence in life, but it also gave me the chance to leave myself alone, and become somebody else, I enjoyed it so much, I joined a small drama group that put on little plays in fringe theatres, which was really fun, and I think I found what I needed in life. I got a full time job in an exclusive restaurant in Sloane Ave. somewhere along the line it's where I met a lovely girl called Christian. Stop press! Indeed, time out to explain something very important that no doubt contributed to my journey to the present. From the time after the incident with Ossie until I went to my second drama class few incidents took place. My problem is I cannot pinpoint the sequence of events so it may appear that the next few paragraphs are mixed up or do not seem to follow, e.g. mood pattern behaviour ect, I have tried to focus on the main points and work around it but, although I know it happened, I cannot place a time within a two years bracket (approximately) in my mind. At present I am quite confused about what led to what, so I will attempt to break it down and when I catch up with the flow of time I will give you a holla.

I remember specifically being invited to Mrs Bond's house for dinner, which was the norm, there were gaps, but not long enough for me to be a stranger. I went with a new girl friend and as usual I tried not to be late. If it was a mere visit it would be in the afternoon or morning sometime, but dinner I know, (unlike me) is a family occasion. So, one is not late for dinner. For years now(in my own environment) I had not eaten pork, but whenever I came to her house I would eat it without saying a word simply because, hell, I don't know, not wanting to upset or disappoint her, doesn't make any sense now, but it's like that anyway. I was late and it was pork. I remember telling the girl I was with, that I was going to get a telling off but not to pay too much attention, she means well. We got in to the house and she unleashed the wrath that I very rarely saw at Oakfield, along the lines of; "How could you be so late!? Do you not think about others!? You should get it together," and, blah, blah, blah. Well I was in my early thirties, and I stood rooted to the ground. I have no real recollection during that incident concerning the girl. It was as if she was not there, I just stood there, all 6"4 of me, a grown man with two children, and just burst into tears. I have no idea were they came from, I do not recall crying like that since the other dinner incident (stop press, now that is interesting). Anyway, it really was uncontrollable, I was a mess. I don't think anyone expected that least of all me, but I understood why it was happening. You see, Mrs Bond had stuck by me through everything and I tried through all the ups and downs in my life not to disappoint her. She never once saw me drunk, although it was sometimes difficult, after the wine at dinner, I would sneak out for a quick beer to top up my poison. I was always being very, very controlled. How trivial it would have been for me, if it was any one else on the planet (and I am in the text of a simple dinner)apart from her, it hit me like a sledge hammer, she led me upstairs, into her room out of embarrassing eyeshot and soothed (I think is the word)me. We spoke for sometime but all I can recall her saying was that "It gets worse as you get older" (if she only knew) from that day things did not really matter to me which ever girl it was I was with I stayed with her for some time. I don't remember which girl, so I don't recall how long, but I tried consciously to make the relationship normal. But it was with the added help of my poison, and that, although I could find no other alternative, was not right. Once again in this mixed up period, I tried to overcome what ever it was. I had a good relationship with Christian but lost my job at the restaurant , however that did not bother me, I only really needed money to drink and put in the car to socialise and drink, yes I drank and drove a lot but understand this, and it's no excuse what so ever, one should not drink and drive. But if you are an alcoholic you are not constantly drunk, because the drink in your system becomes normality. You just need to top it up sometimes, if you do get withdrawal symptoms you start to shake and your mind wonders, usually to where the next drink is coming from. So having a drink calms you for the time it takes to take care of your task (imagine this the English man just came into the cell, to talk, just to pass the time, I half listen to him for a while and then I had to excuse him, anyway I shall not digress) *literally it is better and safer to have a drink than not to (however do not try this on a long journey, the possibilities on making it before the craving begins again are slim). Chris was a very busy girl, always doing something or meeting someone, most of her friends or people that she met, seemed to be well off as far as money goes. There was an occasion we drove to Guilford to some relative of hers. The man seemed to be okay, he had a farm with stables, a swimming pool, tennis courts and what have you. I remember him casually shooting a rabbit from the upstairs window with a double barrel and using mixamytosis as an excuse, but what changed my favour from him, was that he had a brand new Austin martin. The car was something to appreciate, I don't recall the model but somewhere in my head I recall hearing that only ten had been built, Rod Stewart had one and the Sultan of Brunei another, the others I'm not sure. Anyway, Chris and I took pictures of it and then another guy came to join the BBQ. Another guest just like me, a friend of the family and he invited him out for a drive in it. I must admit I would have loved to go for a drive also, after all, it was the car of James*

Bond, but the guy was white and I was not, now please understand this, I don't think that the man was racist, he was very hospitable when I was in his home, what I think his issues were, is 'what would other people say' and I don't think he could allow himself, a person of his stature, to allow local neighbours to have anything controversial to say about him (memo to that man, it's okay we don't eat people any more.) Anyway, most of her rich folk were okay but I tended to only see them once. They do live in a different world and I really do not care to share it with them. Now Chris is not only in the story for mixing with rich folk, she also had a passion for art. She painted, had exhibitions and also loved photography. She would love taking pictures of me, literally hundreds, which I built a port folio from. Because now I had calmed down again for a while, one of my cards to draw on was acting. I really believed I could be as big as they got. It would take work, money, and time but I had what it took to make it big time. Somewhere along the way, for what reason I know not, if I did know the reason, I could categorise the time but somehow the knowledge came to me through my questioning: that I could find out what happened to me from the day I was born until the day I left Oakfield. Thought and feelings do not come to mind at the moment, just a chain of events. I went to an official place in Hackney and found almost weekly or monthly reports, hand written photocopies of what happen to me and what behaviour patterns followed, very interesting reading. Oakfield for example; I was not as nice as I thought I had been. There was quite a bit I did not remember, e.g. visits from Mum, spending a weekend with an aunty going to see my grandma (Mum of Mr. charismatic) etc... Of course all this was enlightening, but let me fill you in (stop press déjà vu. I have done this already and written what I am going to write) on the office I was in while receiving the records. It was white, with large filling cabinets a large table with chairs and coffee and biscuits were served. The staffs I do recall were introduced to me by profession, a long the lines of; the person in charge of the files, security, counsellors and someone with something to do with the law (a witness). A rule of me obtaining the records was simple; it had to be read in front of these people so that they could determine weather or not I was stable enough to leave there without being a danger to myself or others. I don't remember if it was me reading or someone else but it was read, not word for word (I could, because I still have the records at home, but that would be cheating. I am trying to show what happened in my life as I recall it) but among other things, here is what stuck out the most; the part that said 'Colin was brought to Hackney police station,' so much months old such and such a time on such and such a day by a certain gentleman. He was wrapped up warm and had a toy and a bottle. Now as I write, I recall getting the rest of the story from my mother, so it appears that I spoke to her a lot more when I visited her, what I recall her saying at the time that she got pregnant, was that she had a nervous breakdown and when I was born, because of the threat to the rest of the family the only thing she could think of doing was to dress me warm and make me comfortable (thanks, and I'm not being sarcastic) and take me to this other man. It just so happened that he was not in, so she left me there apparently knowing he would come back. I cannot voice what I think, should or should not have been done, this is just what happened, I am now 30 something (stop press! Question, don't you think this would have some kind of effect on you?) Anyway, after the reading, questions and advice, a woman who was present, told me she was amazed by how I turned out; "many other people would have been in prison by now or become, difficult (huh , if she only new). It was recommended that I see a counsellor- something along the lines of me becoming a human time bomb- which I did. Weeks later I was in another white room with bars , but I was relaxed, I had heard counselling was good and although I knew now everything, it was still advisable. When I got into the room, she introduced herself and visa versa . The woman asked me what the problem was, so I told her. Then she tells me how long the course would take and what she could do. I think I misunderstood this. Because, after the intro there was a long uncomfortable (for me) silence, then I blurted out my life story in that first session and that's when she tells me how long the

_course will take. I figured I had nothing else to say so I left feeling
let down and I never returned. I thought that now I know what I
know, I can forget about it and live properly. It just happens that
I was still in contact with my African princess Aunty, and she was
in touch with her Brother. Every so often she would get a letter
mentioning me (memo to father: why did you not just write me?).
One particular letter stated plans he had for me and that he was
a successful professional, quite wealthy and I was somehow to
benefit. But the only thing I had to do now was to change my
name to his, okay you might think, but I was having none of it. I
was going to be a successful actor and my kids were going to be
proud of me, but Aunty, as persistent as ever, convinced me
otherwise bringing the kids into it saying, "if not for me, for
them." I conceded after sometime but with a promise to myself; If
I was to receive anything from him via a will I would pass it on
directly to my children in an appropriate way, so under the cover
of me changing my name to his I used the excuse of acting purposes,
and I chose his mum's last name and put it first because I remember
her being kind to me, she also told me a bit more of her past,
which included a Scottish head of a plantation very wealthy or
whatever , he took her grand mother and got her pregnant. They
where allowed certain privileges, with the understanding that the
Scottish side of the family must be forgotten. I think they were
from Edinburgh. My Gran died and I promised I would pursue it
no further. However, she said that I had six fingers just like some
prominent figure in British/Scottish history. Hence the colour of
my eyes, but I'll leave that there._

_I then took acting quite seriously, going to all the auditions,
keeping up the portfolio, I even gave up a steady job because of
the way auditions were spaced. I could not keep taking time off
so I joined an agency for chefs, this way I could work whenever
and without hindrance. It would be an understatement to say I
worked in hundreds of establishments and although the auditions
were not as regular as I would have liked, I had mediocre success in
music videos ,English soaps as a 'glorified extra' and commercials,
the best being Reggae Hits Volume One, by Island Records. With_

Bruno and his mate in charge, there were posters around London and it was on TV. I was on the cover of the CD and tape, so I knew I could do it, I just had to keep at it. I did a memorable 20 min play with an actress friend Enid, called "your obituary is a dance". We had the audience in all sorts of an emotional tangle, silence, laughter to tears that, for many reasons was of my best performances as far as I am concerned, but more was to come. Stop press! I am now back to being unconfused, events continue as follows; *it's time for Christian to go back to Australia and we part as best of friends. I continue my search for glory and in keeping in contact (which is not normal for me). Chris phones and asks if I would like to visit her down under.*

SUN, 17TH

10 month here. It's not all that bad. I have become used to my surroundings and the faces keep changing, of course I would not like to stay here too long, but being here has done me more good than bad. I cannot sum it up now because it's only half way, but so far, over all, I'm okay.

Yesterday I made the mistake of asking a question about the Bible. When I questioned the answer, the inmate I asked acted totally out of character; shouting at me and calling me a disbeliever, it didn't frighten me, I'm beyond that now, because I have studied them. The people who I could be frightened of have no reason to behave in a bad manner towards me and the people who try to frighten me have not got what it takes, so no problem. What I did feel though was disappointment, although I would guess that this man (my knowledge is more wide spread) and a few more are the only people I can approach for an opinion of a subject outside of guns & violence in here; the thing about it is, I did not know he was on crack, before he admitted it to me. In here is the best place to clean up, but only if you can rid yourself of all the demons. You can get anything in here and he got his poison. I have watched people make my poison. I have smelt it, I have watched people get drunk and apart from the first week I came here (so Jackson tells me) I have not wanted to even touch it. It's been hard, not the temptation of drink, but the closing in of another reality. Look at it this way; I lost something I had found but could not find what I had lost. And that is a lot harder to balance than it might be to decipher. Anyway, normal tensions are still high in here, two guys fighting over peas but it's fundamentally about cigarettes. With 5 days to go who knows, as much as I have learnt to predict certain actions in here it is still an unpredictable environment.

TUE. 18ᵀᴴ

We received our Christmas treat yesterday, a small bottle of fizz, an apple, a slice of cake, two sweeties, a small pack of peanuts and a wafer biscuit. What can I say? It's the thought that counts. I was expecting a card from Kayana but, c'est la vie, I don't really expect from the other two, they know Christmas is not really my thing and I don't really mind. Kayana though, I thought her mum might have said something like "Come on let's send Dad a card for Christmas", it seems at the moment I am being banished from her life, I really don't think she or I deserve that.

TUE 19ᵀᴴ

I am feeling very agitated, things are bothering me more than the norm (of recent) I am trying to read a book (The massiac legacy by bright &co)that I find very interesting it has 490 pages and I have 4 days to read it (it does not come from the library), "Easy" some might say, I have all the time at present, but I don't, remember I have to make time during a day to queue for bread and dinner. Twice, I shower, fill buckets and bottles, I get interrupted to write request forms for prisoners, people constantly interrupt me to ask for cigarettes, even though I have told them previously that I have none, a friend may need a shoulder, I get interrupted to use my so called wisdom to sought out arguments, for example; my washer came in yesterday for me to teach him how to read Psalms 21 (I could not refuse a man seeking knowledge to read) Stop press! Classic example: the guy I had the tête a tête with has just this minute come to the cell gate to scream at me about giving him my old batteries.

Once again while I write; Kenny walks in telling me about someone playing dominoes, of course I can ignore him, but the distraction has already taken place.

I sleep well at night (nowadays) but only for 4 hours, so while reading, sometimes I doze off. Today I got woken by Kenny, who asks me to do something for him later (hell! I am awake now!), only to find that what he wants doing has been put off for 3 or 4years! So I am agitated.

Ciggs were on the block, they are few and far between.

This morning I had a slight run in with my cell mate: Just after our morning roll, an inmate from the cell that had been slagging us off came here, to my cell and started to shout something at Chi Chi, something about him knowing Chi Chi has cocaine and he knows his guards and people just talk to him because he has blah, blah, blah. Chich did not offer much resistance, so when the guy left, the other cell mate (Kenny) comes in and I tell him what happened and that I thought Chi should keep his business more low key, especially with those guys. Chi walks in and I tell him the same thing, then he gets angry with me, telling me, how I and the other cell mates were talking about him and his business. I was merely trying to tell him to be careful, but he fails to understand that if his arguments progress with these guys from the other cell, I would also consider that, his business, therefore I would not raise a hand to help him. Anyway, Australia is better. *When I landed Christian had met me with a car she had bought me, we called it the 'Fresh mobile.' I stayed with her, her mum and sister (lovely people) in Darlinhurst. My experience down under was good and I did have a nice time. I worked in two different restaurants and met some really nice people. I saw many great sights that you would have to see for yourselves to appreciate, like the Blue Mountains, driving up and looking down across a vast green valley of forest as far as the eye can see, even if I were a writer I could not do it justice, so I'll leave it at that. I used to wake up at six in the morning and drive about 10/15 mins to the world famous 'Bondi' beach and jog along the sea front were the waves reach the shore, with the fresh sea breeze blowing though my hair. At night, I could go to Bondi and eat scampi and chips (the done thing) at midnight, and if possible, there were more people on the beach at that time than during the day. I went to support Christian with her horse 'Bear', in competition dressage, (she always won a ribbon of some sort) somewhere miles from Sydney and I would help to clean the stables. When Chris would work late, I would pick her up in the Fresh mobile, but not before I bought Kentucky fried chicken and drove by the beautiful botanical gardens to a point called Macquarie's chair (I think). A place where young lovers drive to and get all romantic, not surprising. You have the serene Botanical gardens behind you and in front you are over looking the Sydney bay, in full view of the famous harbour bridge and the wonderfully lit Opera house.*

I arrived at carnival time, the gay parade (the gay community second only to L.A,). Christians' home was on route so I was in the heart of it all. There were some sites that I did not like seeing but overall the atmosphere was second to none. I had to admire the acceptance of the gay community on behalf of all the Aussies. Some may not agree with homosexuals, but all seemed to agree with human rights, this, and many other issues made for me, Sydney a great place to live; a 24 hour town with a vibrant night life, nice beaches, great culture and wonderful people. I met this gorgeous girl who raised serious money for different charities (she actually reminded me of Allison)and we got on well , we went to a few champagne parties and met more lovely people , once again although it was on, I was never with anyone but Christian. Chris took more photos of me at locations and I built a separate folio, then she introduced me to Mark, a really cool gay man, at the front management for Chadwick's, the number one agency in Australia. I was told they were breaking into commercial and film at the time and it would be good if I came on board. So everything was once again going grand. The standard of living was easily better than London and every thing else just seemed to fit. I took Stanislavsky drop in sessions, where I met other budding actors and actresses, I found myself in the newspaper with Christian at a Bob Marley exhibition, and another photographer wanted me to pose for an exhibition. Time was good, I also met a colour guy, American, bald but cool, he was also a model. I was parked up outside his home one day, in front of a park that was kitted for an annual kids' sports day. We were leaning on the car, just shooting the breeze when suddenly from around the corner like, a whole school of children came rushing towards us shouting, Lenny! Lenny!

"Lenny?" it took a moment but then I realised I was being mistaken for Mr Kravitz. I tried to tell them I was not he, but they would not have it, so what could I do. After a nod of knowing approval from the teacher I preceded signing autographs and explained how important it was to be good in school. It was not the first time I was mistaken for him, it was alright. Meanwhile I was having a problem getting a work permit; I believe I was thirty three at the time. I had to be a resident or citizen and that was hard. Ash, (Christians mum) wrote a letter for me, Mark wrote an official letter from Chadwick's stating that my 'unusual' looks would be an asset to the company, I considered marrying Chris to get residency but the ruling was to do with my age, if I had gone three years earlier it would have been different. With all the promise of Chadwick's I could not act because of equity card (basically the permit that I needed for work). I was put forward by Mark for a part in a movie with Kylie Minogue and Van Dame, it was all above board and for this I was turned down, which reminds me I had met Kylie in the Dome, on Kings road, in Chelsea months earlier and we chatted away for about two hours, nice girl, I wonder if she remembers me. Anyway, my

extended visa was running out and I had to make a decision. I explained my predicament to the Visa Office but after some time of trying to find a route, I was told by the woman in the office, that nothing could be done, but if (of the record) I wanted to stay illegally, I could take my chances, the consequences being if I got caught I could not return for ten years. In five years time Sydney was to host the Olympics and maybe Christian would take part, I did not want to miss it so I considered, no alternative. While in Auss, as I stated, 'I really would have liked to stay' I had my mini vision of the future, which had Nicky and Junior included, Chris and I would remain good friends but I am sure she knew as well as I that we would have gone our separate ways. Now, based on all that was happening at the time, even though I would not have classed myself as an alcoholic, in the six or so months I was there I was only drunk once. I did drink however but only socially and in those days I could stop after only one or two (okay maybe three or four) but the environment and the state of the people made Australia a pleasant place for me, it was a place where I could truly leave my troubles behind. But it was not to be. I came back to England disappointed but I still had the energy and self confidence that I believe are important attributes for success in any field, so on reaching London, everything centred on my acting, which this time around I found easier by claiming benefits. I was available to make all auditions and even help out young budding directors and collage groups who could pay nothing but a video, a cup of tea, and sandwiches, in return for my skills. But most of all I would gain experience and be involved in the trade. At the time I had a new agent who was very nice, and I was getting calls frequently, many of them successful. I accepted the occasional job for cooking, only if it was someway connected with acting e.g. I was a canteen chef at the National Theatre, where the lovely Dame Judy Dench and I shared a lift together, I remember patiently wanting to ask her advice but fought it back after thinking how tired she must be of people like me bothering her about her trade, so I did not. We did talk however and I found her warm and pleasant and unusually proper. I had a prescribed copy of PLC (for auditions), I received the stage& TV weekly (the N.T gets copies one day earlier so I was among the first for auditions). It was going okay again. I had no doubt in my mind that I was going to be a very successful actor. As actors know they get paid (maybe not the big guns)maybe up to six months after the work is done and so when I saw an add in a news paper for a chef in a restaurant two miles from me, evenings only, I jumped at the opportunity. Good fortunes continued, the owner, Rocky, was a mild mannered Aussie and this was his first restaurant (with his co partner Lee with whom I did outside catering jobs for. One namely: a private BBQ for some well off women in Hampstead, where I was to wear only shorts and a bow tie and yes, it was fun) so I basically knew more about the floor and kitchen than he. Without a rise in pay he began to take more time off and I began to run the place. He also had connection with the film industry, so I would go on sets sometimes after my shift finished at 11.15pm. I recall a review for the restaurant in the Guardian or Times making more of a deal out of me, than the establishment (I was their waiter at the time). This only added to my self confidence. Imagine that, I am getting good reviews from the Times or Guardian and I am not even acting, how could I not succeed? I will try to explain: During the time at the restaurant I became barman manager, waiter or chef, which ever was necessary, sometimes all three if someone was late or so. I met an Italian girl who kept popping in for an evening drink, or so I thought at first. It became clear later that she had designs on me which was no problem because I was single at the time, Once again I became involved. This woman had a single agenda and that was to obtain a PhD in philosophy, which was good for her. I tried to do what I could to accommodate her way of life, to help her achieve her purpose. Now, this girl was living in a small room on top of a pub when I met her (no problem, she was getting on with her life, she studied at a rate I have never witnessed, she literally had no friends and was on the computer day and night). We got together and I said it would be a good idea for her to move in with me, more space, freedom, a garden, our own toilet and kitchen ect, and she did not have to work, I seriously did not mind the role I played, although I must admit her continuous studies took a lot of my time away from her, which I did not convict her for, I simply found other things to do. I was now getting luckier with auditions, as far as films go I was a glorified extra in baby mother (with Don Warrington from Rising Damp and famed singer rapper Tippa Irie, I also met and signed up with the Assist Director of Family Affairs, on which I appeared on a couple of times. My biggest role in film to date was as Mad Frank Frasier's body guard in 'Hard men', fair enough, it was not a large part and I had no lines but my name is on the credits at the end of the movie and that what's important. Being apart of that set was good and important for me in all aspects; I was pampered by make up girls and hair stylists, looked up to(and envied) by extras and was a proper part of the team. Whether it be hanging out with Tippa and the crew or being spoken to by the watching public after a certain scene. I recall warmly, Mr Frasier's introduction to me; The director (lovely man J. K Amoulou) calls me over and says "Stuart, I would like you to meet Mr Frasier", now, I thought that this man was an experienced old school actor of some reasonable fame that I should know, so not wanting to let myself feel out of touch with the acting world, I reach for his hand and say "Stuart J Cole, pleased to meet you, love your work." Now, it so happens that I have to drive Frank about with his wife, in this really cool BMW around London's East End. While I'm driving, he is pointing out certain places, like, "you see there Stuart?, there was a race course, they gave us money," or "you see that pub?, we had a blinding shoot out over there, I got one of them as well" this went on for a while until I said to him "wait a minute Frank, if I am your bodyguard, where was I when all this was happening?" "No Stuart" he said "all this happened when I was about your age (he was 74 at the time).I was like, what! Then his wife (one of the great train robbers' daughter) filled me in on who 'Mad Frank Frasier' was. And for those who don't know, he was a very big underworld enforcer who I believe was at the right hand of the Cray twins and had run ins with the Richardson's maybe(visa versa), the crime lords of the East End of London, if not more. So after feeling as small as I was when my eyes were where my knees are now, we got on fine, he was in fact one of the nicest old men I've met, there was one time however I remember coming on the set to test different characters with myself and he turned to me and said "Stuart, something wrong mate". I told him that some guy and I had a situation the night before but, no worries, and he leaned with one arm on the chair he was sitting in, looked me right in the eye, and said, with his raspy voice "is there anything I can do to help" I was like "No!,no,no, Frank, it's all right, no big deal." I must admit around that time in my journey, I thought if any one messed with me, I had some one serious who I could call on (of course this was not the case but the feeling was good). When the movie was finished I took the Italian to the Rap Party and also went to watch the movie in the West End. This was it! I was in a movie being screened in the heart of London's West End. The movie did not go down all that well at the box office, but I was there, I did it. I had proved that I could do anything I really wanted. Now all I needed to do was progress.

Still hammering away at auditions and keeping up with my portfolio, the Italian girl took me to Italy to meet her family (well, strictly speaking, her mum had problems and I just tagged along). At the station in Rome while the girl was making a phone call, a well dressed business type man approached me asking if I had ever done modelling before "yes" I said, and showed him some pics, (in those days, even if it was my photo business card, I would have something on me always). He told me he worked for one of the 'big designers' and how would I like to meet people who could possibly get me on to the cat walk. Well, you can imagine, my first few hours in Italy, I was in range of every models dream (the Rome fashion show was to be held in two weeks). "Yes, of course" then quite matter of factually he asked me "do you like men?" I thought to my self: if I was ever gay, I would have been there done that and worn the T. Shirt already. I said "no" "a pity" he told me "lots of money" and then he was gone as quickly as he came.

Italy was okay I showed of my portfolio, did the site seeing thing, the ruins, the Coliseum etc, and went to Calabria, where her family owned a nice gym. The problem I think was with her brother, and the gym was getting run down, so I offered my help (I had previously taken a health and fitness course so I was qualified to run a gym and instruct patrons). It was however seasonal (which is the norm in this part of Italy) and I ended up having the gym to work out in, for myself. There are other memories of Italy but I do not believe have any consequence to the story, except for one; Her father was dying of cancer, I went to see him a few times to assure him he need not worry about his daughter, now this statement, true at the time as it was, was not meant in the way that it was to come back at me, I believe until today it was true of me and its cause, being effectively, to rest in peace. Nothing more, nothing less. Anyway he passed away and we came back to England. We both resumed what we were doing although she got a job as a secretary for a very eccentric professor of philosophy, which she needed as part of the coursework. I had made it clear to her that she did not have to work until she was a Doctor of Philosophy, it was agreeable. Okay, now I'm looking through adverts, I spot what has to be me. A part in a stage production of a modern day Chaucer work, share income of ticket sales (the latter not important) written, directed and produced by a now good friend Lawrence Audini. Needless to say I got the part. After numerous meetings and six weeks rehearsals we were on stage, my first full professional part in a production, at the renowned 'River Side' studios in Hammersmith. It was an, 'Off West End' Production which, for all budding actors is like a stepping stone, second only to the West End. I was the single main character that pieced together six acts, with a wonderful young actress called Sophie; we were the back bone of the show. This is not to distract from the other talent in the show, it's just how it was. We had some full houses and averaged over half. I could go on about the show but only one night is of any real significance to this story.

FRIDAY 22ND

Tuc shop day, it was late again because of a holiday in the week. The week passed by rather uneventfully. I had a nice talk with 'Aguard' during break today, about her inspirations from politicians, basically I told her I thought she had what it takes to be a successful one, but the talk was cut short by 'Roll Check!'

SAT 23RD

I felt like being outside this morning (the rec yard) but the constant trafficking and football drove me back in.

The English man keeps coming to me with his problems and I am running out of patience, simply because the advice I am giving him, he does not take and then he comes and tells me that what I said would happen has happened. He now owes someone for washing his clothes. I told him to wash them himself or send them to the laundry, but nooo, so he comes to me for ciggs to pay him. I told him no, I will give him a cigg when he needs a smoke but I am not paying for his laundry or food. Now I am in my cell, he comes to return an old newspaper and decides to reminisce to me about his two year old who can barely walk, but she switches off the TV and tries to run away. I listen because I understand what he is going through, but it won't be too long before I tell him to shut up, because I have two daughters of my own, and I start to think about them prematurely. For example; I remember when Nicky was crawling, she kept finding herself behind the TV. I put my finger up and said 'stop!' she looked at me and then at the wire, as if it was some kind of challenge. She went for the wire and I accepted her challenge, I stood up and told her she should listen to me and spanked her quite firmly on the bottom (she was wearing diapers) and she started to cry. I instantly felt so bad I picked her up and put her on my knee and told her to stop crying, she did, but she was shaking to stop. I never spanked her again from that day on, but she never disobeyed me either. Funny thing about being a parent: I doubt she will ever remember that, while I will never forget it. If that thought had just appeared in my head, while I was just reminiscing about my children on my own accord, I would probably have smiled, but having it put into my head (however unintentional) when I am not prepared, well, I don't need it, but enough of that let's get back to some occasion that had a more damaging effect on me.

Once again, quite unintentional I'm sure; my Mother was visiting England for the first time that I know of since I left Jamaica. I am really not sure for what purpose or for how long. She had my phone number and I had no problem with seeing her, in fact I quite looked forward to it. After all, everything had worked out for me; it was all going so well. I made it on my own. So we made contact, she was staying with friends or family, I don't remember, but they were alright. I think I got them comp tickets, so they all came to the show, it was another good house. During the play, I ad-libbed a lot, because there was room in the structure of the text. Besides, in those days I was Lawrence's key man, I could do no wrong. Now, when acting, you assume the mind, body and thought of someone else, this forms a character, this is your job and when done well, no matter what the review says you feel great (some actors have said its better than sex , all I can say to that is "I know what you mean"). But if you slip out of character on stage, it can be oppositely devastating. Well, this particular evening I was on form and even though I was ad-libbing, ad-libbing has a structure to follow (let's just say that one subconsciously or consciously prepares for an ad-lib), so I had a subject in mind and pertaining to the action of the audience I could "dig in" and come up with something. I had a line which went "my mother said you must always drink soup, soup is good for you, that's why mother told me" (it was done with an Indian accent) as soon as I said it my mind drifted, not to say I did not carry on, but anything can distract an actor's mind, even a cough, but if you have done your prep properly, you dismiss it until the show has finished. Well, what was in my mind, was that my *mother never told me about soup and I wondered how she felt about me saying that, and did she think that I said it to have a pop at her? Did she think I put it in on purpose? Or was it just the script? Did she even hear it? As you might well know, these thoughts last for a split second or so and then, they go. Now, after the play, when the rest of the audience had gone, I introduced her to Lawrence and his beautiful, now wife, Carmel, and gave her a newspaper with a good review and picture of me in it and she said to me "I am so proud of you". Now as I am writing this, I can see no reason for me not to take those words at face value, which is the way I am sure she intended it, and once again I doubt if she actually remembers even saying it, let alone know, that this was the time in my life, that I really started to drink. You see what was going through my mind, weather rightly or wrongly at the time (looking back defiantly wrongly), was 'how dare you say you're proud of me!? Especially in front of others. I did this by myself and you, have nothing to be proud of, you have never given me dietary advice or any advice, let alone a bowl of soup I must reinstate, I honestly believe and accept that she did nothing wrong that night , this was all me , fair to say it was what I had become because of her, which would emphasise my point on her having nothing to be proud of, but that was my point and it would be cruel on my behalf to blame her for that particular incident, but as I said before, I am just stating the path my journey took and what effect it had on me from my point of view. I said nothing of this to my Mother and the group of us went to a restaurant where I met Tom Jones (actually all I said was "good evening"). I was going to politely ask if it was no trouble to him and if he was leaving before us, would he come to the table and just say hi (something I would have done in those days had she not have said those words). When I got back to the table, they were disappointed especially a young cousin (I think) who was with us. I drank a bit at the table but controlled it until we parted. I think I walked home drinking along the way. By the time it was bed time, I think I just passed out. I did not tell the Italian girl and that is because, well, to be honest, looking back from today there is only one girl I could have told that story and I guess by now you know who that is, but we will get to that later. Now, my home scene was as norm, the Italian studied and worked. I carried on until the show had ended it's run, then , not all at once but over a long short in between time sort of thing, I began not to care. No, that's not true. I began to lose the passion for acting. I was not buying the stage, I did not renew the subscription for PLC and I stopped answering messages. If agents got me I would take it and do whatever, but if they left a message, I would rarely answer. The Italian did not realise until very late in our relationship and in the mean time my addiction was only known to me. I went to Turkey on a seminar thing, something to do with philosophy, and she had to talk, that was fun; I went into the hills of Asmier where some militia where supposed to be hiding but did not find any. I also saw the mosques' and heard them chanting from the roof tops. The people were good to us and we were treated well. I am at the time, in good behaviour. Some of the Turks would come and ask to touch my hair, which was no problem, but when I got to the hotel, I had a drink from the mini bar and then wanting more persuaded another lad, who went with us, to have a drink with me, under the assumption that we were just having a celebratory drink. We drank the two mini bars empty. So now I am socialising when I can, but I need a drink available to me about within an hour or so of the time me being there. At home, sometimes I might not drink for a day, maybe two. If I had to do something important, sometimes I lasted the day and ended the night with a drink, but I was not getting drunk, drunk. It so happens, around this time Anton's Mum who still had problems in Italy, under my suggestion, came to stay with us (I figured it would take a lot off her mind as it was beginning to affect her work and studies).*

Sun. 24ᵀᴴ

Just phoned Junior to wish him Merry Christmas and ask him to text a message to his sisters. Kayana is in France now. I wonder what Emilies' parents think about me now; such a wonderful couple but now is not the time to think about that. I had enough credit and time to phone cousin Ange that was a good move. The one person in the world (Junior is in a different bracket) that could say what I needed to hear with such heart felt gloriousness, but as I said earlier, we spent good times together. It must be like that when a parent tells you that they love you and the thought that they are being truly honest or they are just saying it, never enters your mind. When all around you seems to be against you and things, no matter how hard you try, just don't go your way. It's nice to have someone like Angela in your corner. Money cannot buy that. Timing was right; she was on the phone to her Sis, good ole Val, at the time. Oh, there was some girl I could have told something to, Angela.

WED. 27TH

Decided to take some sun this morning.

Chi Chi and I were talking about getting English into the cell. I don't mind, but as I told him, he should check himself. He is doing things that I would not want transferred into my cell and at present, his level of conversation does not appeal to me. Everything I told him will happen has happened and he comes to me with a surprised expression on his face, to tell me it has happened. His toilet paper has gone missing, his phone cards gone missing. And he wants to get a portion of weed in his cell and trusts these guys enough to think the weed will not go missing. He has been moaning all morning about not having a spliff on Christmas day and he has a habit that reminds me of a former inmate; he wants me to look at him when he is telling me this tripe. I told him what I did not tell Mrs Bond all those years ago "I do not like people touching me to get continuous attention and I don't like to gaze into peoples eyes when they are saying things I honestly do not care about." So I explained to him, if he wants to come into the cell, he has to sort himself out because, "I left all my luggage at the front gate and have no intention of picking up more inside here".

So her mum came to stay; very tiny person, 5 feet if that, very typically Italian. She did not speak a word of English and my Italian was still very limited, but we managed. She was a very busy woman always cooking, cleaning, or washing. She found things to do around the flat that I did not know needed doing. Only two things got on my nerves; one I got used to, which was the Italian in them: It seemed to me, that even if the mother asked the daughter what she would like for breakfast, it would entail a drawn out argumentative, physically descriptive shouting match; One morning I was woken up by this noise and thought that it was a serious argument, it so happens that the mum was ironing some clothes that the daughter did not want ironing. When I intervened they were embarrassed and assured me it was not serious, it's 'Italian.' I can relate to that, have you ever seen a bunch of Jamaicans playing dominoes? The second thing, I could not get over, and will not have in my own surrounding: when the girl and I argued, she would go to her mother and talk about it, without me being able to give my side of the story. She would not translate anything we were saying which inevitably led to more arguments, and I, accordingly, would leave the house and go and have a drink. I was still doing agency work but now I found that having the odd glass at work turned into the odd bottle, I was still very capable of doing my job though and it seemed, with a drink in my system I enjoyed work more, it's just that when I got home, if I was not talking to the girl for some reason ,i.e. she and her mother were conversing , or she was stabbing away at the computer, I would simply hang out on the streets with a beer and now, familiar crowd. This is how it went for months; I was still at the time, conscious of and helping her to achieve, what to her was the most important thing in her life, her PhD. I still drove her to work, even though the walk to and from each bus stop was less than a mile, her computer crashed, I bought her another , I made her mum as comfortable as I could have, and she never saw me really drunk. All these things remained important to me but as the evenings grew longer and her final days in university were drawing closer, I began staying out later at night (Mostly weekends). I used to hang out with some neighbours and we used to drink, smoke, go to the pub, and play cards, etc. The girl began to think I was having an affair, "not true" I rallied. She had my phone number and I told her where I was, so she knew where I was and who I was with all the time. I did feel a bit uncomfortable with this but figured I would meet her halfway. After all, when I was in the house of an evening we did nothing, she was either with her mum or on the computer, and I understood that, so she should understand me. It got to a time when she actually came looking for me to see if I was really there, so things were not brilliant, but I still did not let it affect her course. One morning (we were friends this particular morning) I left the house to go to work and as usual I forgot my keys, on returning, I ask her to phone my boss and explain my being late. The part of the conversation I heard was "yes, he has always been like that he will never change". I smiled at her and told her that I would see her later, and left. (Oh! I must mention something else about this girl; she wanted no children and tried to talk me into getting a vasectomy). On returning home that evening, I went to the bedroom just to relax for a while. Just as the norm, I dozed of for an hour or so. I thought there was something wrong with the flat but I could not pinpoint it. Then I realised the computer was missing, the table, printer and books belonging to her and me. I thought we had been robbed. When it occurred to me the mum and girl had gone. I thought they had gone for an evening walk. I went outside to look for them and saw my good neighbour, Grand Ma (I wonder if that's ironic or just peculiar) and she told me that after seeing the 'big white truck' this afternoon, she thought I had moved out and not told her ('you're such a lovely person, I could not believe you would do something like that'). After hearing this I ran back down stairs into my flat, and it dawned on me they had left, gone back to Italy I suppose, no goodbye, no warning, no explanation, they just left and took all including some of my belongings, not that I really cared about possessions but there was however, an

196

introductory book to Muslim I received from a good friend at the BBC that I never got around to reading, and that pissed me off. Now, of course you have your own opinion about me, but these are the facts, what I would really like to know is, forget my childhood, my parents, Jamaica, just based on our lives together alone (and of course her mum being there), did I really not deserve a goodbye, or a warning, maybe even a thank you, maybe even from her mum, an explanation? Maybe all the girls who left before, you could say I deserved it less, but they, all had the common decency to tell me they were going. Three days later I received an invitation for her to come to her graduation. I had served the purpose, she had obtained her PhD. Strange, it pisses me off more now than it did then. That night I simply got plastered (for anyone who may ask, I did what I did for her like I would have done for anyone I could, from the heart. I truly hope the PhD served her well and helped to make her life what she sought). Looking back, what pissed me off the most was that we slept together the night before as if nothing was wrong, and all the time she was planning this. She could have done a lot worse. The relationship lasted 5 years and not even her mum let me have a clue what was going on or even thank me for putting her up in her time of need.(have just remembered that this was the girl I was with at Mrs Bond's dinner).

WED 3ᴿᴰ 2007

Well, well, well, I have reached the beginning of the 44th year of my journey and if not interrupted by man or illness, I guess I have reached about half way.

The old and the new came and went, as any other day in here, although I did smoke a joint, more to have a memory of the day rather than anything else. There was lots of rum and wine, some home made, some not, which I found incredibly easy to avoid (excellent signs of recovery). In the cell; Kenny is leaving next month. He is holding well but you can tell his anxiety & happiness as his 5 years draws in. Chi Chi has begun to change slightly and I put it down to the people he

mixes with. Non stop abusive swearing, for everything, good
or bad "wa di muda cunt"is in his every sentence and he is
very confrontational now. I.e. we were playing dominoes New
Years Eve. He was losing. At the end of the game I pick up the
remainder of his dominoes that he had put on the table (floor).
He asks "why you look?" I tell him I want to see if I was correct
"no but you look" getting more and more aggressive, so I said
to him "if you don't want me to see your dominoes mix them
into the pack when the game is over.

"No, you don't look".

"Okay" I said, "if you don't mix them up I am going to
look".

"Okay you will see something".

"Okay". Now, the 23 year old from Venezuela is
challenging, me. No problem as far as I am concerned. I give
him one more warning "Chi if you don't want me to see your
dominoes push them into the pack"

"We will see" he says. The game starts, the game finishes,
he puts his two dominoes down, I pick them up "what the
fuck you gonna do now?" I say. Nothing happened so I told
him he should change his attitude or stop playing, but I don't
think he realised I was in defence mode to oppose a challenge.
I was very confident of being able to over power him. Now
he was either not aware or he was testing me, but I think that
because his English is not all that, he is picking up more and
more of the Kweyol speech and mannerisms than English.
He is becoming more like the lower class of Lucians in here,
which is quite understandable, but no harm done, yet, he is
still young.

The English is getting on my nerves still. He refuses to
tell people 'No!' Okay, prime example. Chi Chi has just this
minute walked into the cell waving a piece of cigarette, trying
to explain to me someone gave it to English and he could
not get to his cell, because a guy wanted to take it from him.
But it's only because he won't say no. I mean, if he is going to
give, give. But do not come to me almost in tears because they

won't let you smoke in piece. I thought I would have more difficulty with my drink so I have no pity for people in here with cigarettes. He is gonna have problems this week, because there is no Tuc Shop, and the holydays have been extended until the 3rd., Oh, yea, and there was a Boa Constrictor inside the perimeter so that gave him something else to moan about through the Christmas.

I was expecting a card from Nicky, it would be nice, but I was not holding my breath. However I hoped Emilie would have helped Ky with something. I try to look at things from her side but I still can't see how she can be justified by cutting us off. My feelings for her now come and go but still things creep into mind, like; what would I do if she thinks she can just take Ky away, how would I react? Of course, I cannot physically harm her but the mere act of taking her would cause pain to flow in all different directions, because I could not let it rest.

THURS 4TH.

Just got a pen from my Rasta brethren in cell nine so I am in a better mood today. It did not even bother me this morning when English repeatedly asked me how to get goods from the embassy. "You pick up the phone, dial the number and tell them what you want".

"Yes, I know, but suppose I want boxer shorts?"

"You're not aloud boxers so don't order them". We have had this convo 3 or 4 times and it is very irritating. Well, I hope he is not really like that and it's just the shock of being here. Anyway, it's raining now and I am hungry, so let's see what happened in the next stage of my journey. *Ah, yes; I was alone but okayish. I was staying out more often and drinking now became an even more serious part of my life. I took time out to do nothing, my trips to the off licence were more frequent and I had stopped working for a while. Amazing enough people around me did not seem to notice, or so it seemed. Looking back, it's more likely that they did notice but I did not really care and although I was nearly always under the influence I could still manage to work and or take care of important issues; I would wake up in the morning, have a beer, sign on, and look for a job (or so I would tell myself). To be honest I was happy just drinking and if I kept the drink flowing at a steady pace I did not see a problem at all, which was, of course, the problem. How could I even attempt to find something I could not see; A few months passed like this, I figured I had to get a job, I should really straighten myself out. So, I phoned the agency for temp chef's and got a job at the BBC, on the Strand. They had a gym there and I became a member and had a key, so I could use it 24, 7. The job was okay, the customers were okay, but they complained a lot about the food they received for the price that they payed. They did not understand you could not possibly cover the expenses even subsidised. Our catering company was losing money from their account and they wanted 5 star cuisine. Anyway, we did our best and it was not as bad as Morecombe & Wise would sometimes suggest. I was beginning to get back to my former self; I signed a contract, was in the gym and had a fling with a cute little Spanish girl. The Beep (BBC) was a nice place to work and had lots of opportunities for their staff. You could quite easily build your social life around your work, mountain climes in Europe, biking in Africa, for charity (not that I attended these) there was even subsidised flying lessons that I had my mind on but never pursued and there was a disco in the staff club/bar every Saturday which I frequently attended. Being as it was a full time job though, I had no thought for acting and although I did miss it I did not yearn for it. By now I am in the job for about six months and have managed through work and gym to cut down on the booze, at least until the end of the shift when I would find myself outside the off licence chilling with the rest of the lads in my home area, who had also just finished working. My days off; I would get up at five in the morning and go to the gym just to get a good start to the day, but I would eventually end up drinking by evening and it would last until late, then I would be at work and not have enough time to drink, things were getting brighter as I said. I was actually happy with the drink. I did not know what it was washing away but something was going and something was returning. I was only with the Spanish girl for a matter of weeks and did not see female company for sometime although I flirted quite a lot. I did however see another girl for a week or two, Turkish, very strange, a mini story in her own right. Other than that I was not really bothered. Until one afternoon, off from work, probably about a year after the Italian job. I was outside my flat on a nice sunny summer day, probably drinking a beer.* Stop press!; it has just dawned on me that I have probably not mentioned J, or Nicky in these past few years, and after all, this story is profoundly about and for them. I have not been the best father as you have probably gathered. Access was never denied, true , maybe I should have called more, or text more, or visited more, although I did go to Jamaica twice and I did ask Deidre if I could come and visit Nicky in Ireland but I was politely refused. Nicky did however visit London on the odd occasion, and that's when I got the chance to spend a day with her. I did want to see her more often but it was not to be, my ups and downs did not allow me to focus 100% and I also thought that growing up in her part of Ireland, would be much better than London, which is the way I felt about Junior also. I had told him, I would bring him to London, but I really wanted to have the full blown Jamaican in him and then come to England, learn the English way and then use both in conjunction to help him through his journey. I still think the choice was right. Nicky, I know, feels I abandoned her and, probably (like me), does not remember the times when I was there or did call or send a card or gift. But I shall not let it last a lifetime; this story will bear my witness. Green light. *I saw a very attractive girl, rather small but very attractive. She was standing by the phone booth looking rather lost, so as any gentleman would do, I approached her and asked her if I could be of any assistance, she was French. Now, I have to explain, about the French accent; it has been driving me crazy since my second school in England. I was eleven, the Lady's name was Mademoiselle Clemet and she was our French teacher (I did quite well in French but the trip to Jamaica whipped that out of my brain), however I have always been a sucker for the French accent (only from a woman). I gladly helped her find her way, she was going on an interview so I gave her my number and pointed to where I lived and we said our goodbyes. I did think about her for a while but not too strong. I live 15 min walk from the West End and pretty women, especially on sunny days, tend to come out of the wood work, but my mind did linger on her for a while. Then one day out of the blue I received a message on the answering machine; she was back in town and wanted to meet up for a drink, 'no problem'. The only problem was, I could not understand the name of the road she was staying on, I had the full address but for the love of God she could not pronounce the name 'Cromwell' as in Cromwell Road. It took me two days of playing it back and forth until I finally sussed it and we met. I showed her around London, took her out on top of the BBC roof to show her a special night view of the town and we had a really lovely time, I did make a pass at her but regretted it instantly, and I was graciously turned down which was good, because our friendship blossomed. I asked if she wanted to stay with me while she was here because where she was staying was not fit enough for her. I believe she had a spot on the floor amongst 5 or 6 other French guys. She did I remember have a friend over and all three of us spent the night in my king size bed, just as friends, we had a laugh until about 2.30am. I went to sleep leaving them giggling at an English teaching French program. I had to be at work at six and went to work with a smile on my face. I had a job from the agency that morning and the receptionist come security, was an obnoxious bastard; I was 5 minutes early and he had me waiting while he, it seemed, was talking to his girlfriend on the phone. Every time I beckoned to him he would give me a look, as though he owned the company and I was a mere unimportant worker simply because I came in through the staff entrance and the others could use the main entrance (here is one for you A.. holes who think you are better than other people who are also just trying to earn a living).*

Okay, I understand we must not interfere with your precious work during your hours, but we don't want you in the kitchen while we work either, but what is it that you find so offensive about us that we have to be relegated to a small obscured side street entrance that most who worked in the building not only have never seen but do not even know exists. It becomes even worse if its your first day on the job and you get through the main entrance, a so called proper receptionist excuses you from the reception and directs you out of the building; 'Turn right, 50 yards turn right again 20, 30, yards down a ramp, passed the rubbish bins, thru the underground car park, to the staff entrance where you can get a lift to the kitchen. Okay, you're in the lift, you press number 3 for the kitchen but someone is getting of on the first floor, the doors open... and it's that bloody reception, now that can only set you up for a bad day. Remember guys, we cook for you, you really should try to make us feel human, after all a piece of meat dropped on a dirty kitchen floor and put back on plate only saves money. Think about it. But I digress once again. So this jerk on the phone, thinks I really need this job, so I lean over the counter, place my hand on the phone to cut him off, and tell him quite calmly, that I have just left two beautiful French girls in my bed at home and I would rather be there than here and if the staff of this establishment would like food today I suggest he phone the appropriate people to come and get me, the Chef, and take me to the G.. D... kitchen! I really enjoyed that speech, it was like I was back on stage but I liked it more so because I let the 'A hole' know, who he thought was nobody, could speak to him like that and he could do nothing but comply, and the reason I felt that way was, because what I told him was true and at the slightest hesitation on his behalf I would have turned around and headed home. Alas he did not; I did the job and then rushed home to be with my French friends.

FRIDAY 5TH NOVEMBER

I have to figure out coincidences, for the first time, yesterday, I actually dedicated hours of thought to my French friend, of course I have wondered how she is but in my normal manner have not written , phoned, or sent regards, but yesterday I smiled as I remembered some of the fun times we had . After writing the above yesterday, we played dominoes and I smoked a spliff and thought about her some more- basically trying to get my thoughts together for writing- and having a pleasant time doing so. When for the first time since being here an officer brings mail after ten pm (lights out) and among a paper and a Christmas card from P.A was a letter, hand written. At first I thought it was from Junior but we agreed he should not waste time writing. Nicole? the "vibe" was not there (no I don't know her hand writing) it did not fit anyone's hand writing, but then I remembered they read every ones mail, so I sneaked a look inside, and to my wounderful surprise my little French friend is holding, I readily assume, her new born child. "Congratulations V.J, chatton" I have tried not to delve into peoples' lives that have not been caused by a direct confrontation with me but on this account ..., no, I'll stick to the rules, "All the best girl!" I am waiting for the right time for me to read the letter. These moments have to be savoured and drawn out in here. You know, nurtured proper, to get the full benefits of the good news.

Midday; English has been in the cell talking, but Chatton's photos and the prospects of reading it has held me in good stead, so I did a good turn and put in a word to Octave for him. Octave seemed in a good mood, he told me English could grab his stuff and move in, so to his delight he is now here (I hope I won't regret it). I also enquired about my package from J; he said to give him two weeks. Wow! I have jumped ahead to the future of the baby, who will be welcome in my home, because I know (I think 'she') will grow to be good friends with Ky. Alas yet again, I can delve no further into her life for it is her journey and I just crossed the path, but you will see how she has a special part in my story; *She stayed with me for a little while and then had to go back to France for some reason. She asked if she could bring her best friend back with her, "of course you can". Things looked brighter again; I was happy again and eased of the drink and as usual things started to work themselves out. You know something, when I look back* (Stephen Mongroo (the 'Ras') just walked in).

SAT 6TH

Rastaman walked in on me yesterday and we got talking. I asked his name so I could send him some books to read.

This lunch time, I was woken from a dream, by an inmate (my worker) from the cell next door, to inform me that the man, who previously shared the cell with me, when I first moved into this cell, has died. He had children with the Big Bulls sister and is the one that looked like a warrior. So, in this ever changing world a new life has come and another has gone and for us still here? well, life still goes on. Speaking of which; I was looking back a few sentences, which I do occasionally to see where I am. I really find it hard to believe I almost lost touch with reality; I can't blame the people who knew me late in my journey for thinking as they did about me, hell! I can't even blame folk who knew me for a long time. I hardly gave anyone a clue as to what was happening inside, but now, looking back on the whole picture, I can hardly see how I could have avoided some kind of personal psychological disturbance. But once again I digress, let's see what happen next.

I was looking forward to meeting her friend and even decided to redecorate. Work was fine and summer was here, once again my mental state returned to stable. I could drink, but it was not over the top. In fact, to a new comer in my life, it would have passed for and was, social, meaning I was not gone yet and I never got into embarrassing situations, yet. Anyway, the two girls are on the way back (this may read like I was expecting a relationship but it was not the case I simply enjoyed Vj's company and her friends were like her, so it was time for happiness in my life); I was patiently at home waiting for their arrival; the door knocked and I opened it and there was VJ with Emilie (I wish I was a writer). How do I explain? She radiated, she beamed, she glowed, and it was all from within, she had this smile on her face and she wore braces that looked funny, like some American teenager. She had, I was told later, been in a motor cycle accident delivering pizzas, which I could really imagine, her doing. She was quite slim and kind of narrow at the shoulders with short hair(and I have always been a fan of long hair) if you were out of reach with what she transmitted anyone who knew me then would have laid odds against us being a couple, just that smile, braces and all, she was beautiful. So, they come into the flat and my life was how it should be. The girls made the house theirs; they even finished my pathetic attempt on decorating. Subtle drawings, embroidered mirror framed pictures, they were always doing something. But she had a boy friend back in France. We all got on well and Em and I were obviously becoming more than just friends, although she would not commit herself to anything unfaithful "before", she said , she had returned to France and told her boy friend she had someone else. Excellent, a person with all this energy and zest for life and living, also had good natural morals. I did not press it, we slept together, but only in each others arms and it was beautiful. I looked forward for her going to France, so she could come back. While she was gone I had this job in a private ward of a hospital, where I had 4 hours break in the afternoon. I was getting ready to settle down for the first time (with no disrespect to the other girls) in my life I had found the woman I wanted to spend the rest of my life with. I was even getting in touch with old friends from theatre world and coming back out of my shell. When she came back from France we were a couple and her parents had been informed. They had no problem but they wanted her, quite rightly so, to finish some courses she was doing. It would have taken two years and I would have visits, the parents even said I could stay in their future retirement home that her dad had built with his own hands. She did try and I did visit, a nice home but literally in the middle of nowhere. Emilie was doing work experience in a 5 star health resort The few years ahead were beautiful, I did run over my past life with her, but how intense could I have been. I had been told I could be a time bomb, but when things are going so well one tends to forget the bad times and what really caused them, or at least one has put it all behind, 'there is no need to drag up the past into the future' so I just got on with life, as so many people advised me to do. (If I ever did hint that I had a psychotic problem, memo to anyone in that boat, seek a second opinion.) I would go with her to her job where she worked and wait in the car until she had finished, then one day she asked her boss if I could use the spa and I did, it was great. Amongst all the other things they had a really cool Jacuzzi that was situated on the side of the building looking out towards the sea. One half inside, where Em and I moved around being massaged by bubbles, then as we moved on through the plastic flaps, bubbles bubbling away we were outside in the Jacuzzi over looking the sea to a beautiful sunset, then it started to drizzle and a squad of F16's flew overhead as if in a salute to us.

There was a lot of travelling between us. Em would always be popping back and forth from France to England. The first time I went to visit her, for she had agreed to give it a shot, we both missed each other and were on the phone all the time. I took the Euro Star to France to where she would pick me up. I had actually noticed police following me as we got further away from Paris and when I had reached my destination was immediately accosted by 4or5 of them who were questioning and searching me when Em arrived. She bore her way straight through the police ignoring all of them, flung her arms around me and, well , how can I describe it , she is French and she kissed me, voila! She said something to the police and they went away red faced. More points for my love. When I got to the house I finally met the family; her little bro and sis her mom and later her father. To be honest I thought there would be some kind of "thing" against me. None of them spoke much English but we could get by, I thought at the very least, I would have to win them over. Although I was confident if given the chance I could do just that, it was not necessary, the family was naturally nice to me. I felt like a welcomed visiting cousin, even their little dog liked me. I bought a few things over for them, *as you do. Me and her little Bro got on well, her younger Sis had boyfriend issues which we spoke about, her mum, I guess a typical mum, in control as much as she could be with a house full of kids and a part time job. Her Father's job kept him away a lot but I could still tell he was a proud family man. I went out with him a few times, and it was a real pleasure to have met their family. After I cooked them a nice dinner, on my second visit, (which is actually when I met the father for the first time) the rest of the family kind of drifted into their own world of dishes, video games, and phone calls and left us quite expertly alone with the dog, some wine, and rum, but I am totally fine these times with the drink, (or let's say I could handle it) and he began to give me the father to boyfriend of his daughter talk. I felt so comfortable talking to him; it was all so proper and felt so right. We joked laughed and drank. The more we drank the better, the opposite languages got. Then he turned to me, looked me straight in the eyes and said "Do you love my daughter?"*

"Yes" I replied without thinking, I did not have to think I had fallen properly in love for the first time in my life. You may well ask; how could I mess this up now? This surly was the path I should stay on, but read on.

My biggest crime was not for drugs, my biggest crime was for letting Emilie and her family down; Now that I am guilty of, and deserve to be here, locked up in a prison on a small island in the middle of the Atlantic. An explanation, but please bare in mind I have no excuse for what happened, I merely offer an explanation to what happened and hope in their hearts, they understand. Her father, when I was leaving gave me some special bottles of wine from his cellar and six special bottles of champagne. A few of the wines I drank months later but one bottle I have kept through out my worst alcoholic days. I did not drink a certain bottle-something to do with Emilie's birthday relating to Kayana-. When Em and I got back to London he sent packages, he would remember little things, songs that I liked from certain artists. I would receive CDs of said songs, he sent a jig saw puzzle in pieces and when I and Em put it together it was a wounderful picture of the both of us on the bridge in St. James Park with Buckingham Palace in the background. All the gifts were real, not expensive, and from the heart, the type of gift I treasure most. He popped over to England and I gave him my 'special' tour of London. I could see he enjoyed himself and approved of my being boyfriend to his daughter. I was very stable for some years. Plans were being made; I was back to my 'other self' I could drink socially and privately, no problem (meaning I did not touch my limit then).

New Years, the Millennium; Not being one for the crowds Em and I were invited to a boat house, by friends from theatre land, (I took along someone who had nowhere to go that night also, but he like many others, tend to forget how good I have been to them). Anyway, there was a young woman who I was introduced to; who had heard about or seen me on stage prior, and thought I would be ideal for the leading man in her new play. Well, the champagne was flowing and it was, the millennium eve. So what happen was kind of understandable; we were all having a good time and I got the intro, she proceeded to tell me about the play "it's going to be quite passionate" she told me,

"no problem" I said with a glass of champagne in my hand

"Can you be convincingly passionate?"

"No problem"

"Show me." Now I am a man of impulse, but I also have serious moral convictions. What I did was not to offend Emilie, but merely an audition. People were watching, and it appears now, probably waiting. Emilie, was a few feet away and I put one arm around the girl, tilted her head back and kissed her properly and very convincingly. When I stopped she could hardly speak for a while, so she got some champers from someone and I went out on the deck with a bottle, alone, wondering if I got the part. While I was in a chair, taking in the whole atmosphere, someone runs up to me; "your girlfriend wants to fight", whatever her name is, I was genuinely surprised. She could not have known. I would not risk what we had for another woman. I really had put all I had into an audition and that alone. So now I have a little wicked grin on my face, if you saw the picture, the stand off, Emilie in

one corner; fist clenched by her side and the more furious she got the broader my smile got and the producer who quite clearly was not expecting this almost frozen in half shock, possibly trying to explain it was only an audition. She was twice the size of Emilie in all ways. One could really only laugh. After the situation returned to normal and we went home, I told her how good she made me feel and for what reasons, also that she should never worry about losing me to another woman, even if I became a Hollywood star, I would be like a Roger Moore kinda person. The rest of the first day of the millennium, I will leave to your imagination.

There was a lot of travelling between us. Em would always be popping back and forth from France to England. I had to go to Trinidad and bought her a ticket but at the last minute decided not to come. I had non refundable tickets and went alone. I did not do much and the highlight was watching Dwight York play for his country. There were lots of nice girls where I was staying but I explained I had a girl friend I called 'Madness' and she was waiting for me at home and even though she would not know, I would. They thought I was mad, I knew I was in love. When I got back Lawrence had phoned, apparently he had been trying to get me for some weeks. The script was written the cast was assembled, and we were to do the Edinburgh festival in three weeks time, good venue. Even if you are not in the field I'm sure most of you have heard of the Festival. It is, the Fringe place, to produce and show off your talent. If, as an entertainer up and coming, you have not done 'Edinburgh' you're not serious about your profession. People do, come from around the world to see and be seen. I saw the irrepressible Stephen Bercoff in arm with a beautiful girl, and to my surprise did not invite him to our show. Once again, I thought too many people must bother him; he deserves to be able to enjoy the buzz without being bugged. He gave me pleasure when I was in Sydney, with his own one man show, at a theatre Christian worked in from time to time. Anyway, I was very sober when Lawrence found me and he was quite taken back by my reluctance to jump at it, my lack of enthusiasm. He did not know how I felt after the last performance. Of course I wanted to do it, but could

I? was the problem. For the first time in my short career I doubted myself, the good thing was we were doing "The Canterbury Tales" I had done this already. So a few changes of the script should be no problem, I am with Emilie now, I can do anything, or so I expected.

Emilie came to some rehearsals in London and when the time came, a group of about nine of us trundled up to Scotland, Lawrence paid for a big house. This trip caught me by surprise so money was a bit scarce, although I ended up being resident chef and paid my way; Scotland is in the north and if you check the weather reports, it's always cold. Just coming from Trinidad I don't think I was acclimatised, either that or a bug of some sort, whatever it was, something was wrong with me, but the rehearsals were going good and I was 'green for go' the show must go on. I was playing three or four different characters and all seemed ready, the turn out was good, the lights went up and I made my entrance, the adrenaline subsided, the nerves were gone and all was going well, then suddenly for me, time stood still, I stood stage right, in what must have been utter stillness. I can vaguely remember being a part of something, but the stage, the people, the lights, I could not figure out what it was all there for, and with the suddenness that it appeared, it disappeared. I finished the play but at the time I was on stage I could not help thinking I, the leading man had screwed up. I had never done that before on stage (or had I?)I was in a state. I did not want to complete the venue but I knew I had to. I did not want to go back to the house because I could not face the cast, all I really wanted to do was phone mouse (her other pet name) just to hear her voice. Lawrence found me somewhere, feeling down in the dumps and sorry for myself. He started telling me how it happened to him, in his career, I should 'get over it' and it was not as bad as it seemed, to me. I forgot a golden rule of these types of plays; the audience does not know what's going to happen next. A few days later I received the best reviews in a local paper, but I was not to take the stage again bar once in the next four, five years. I was informed by L w some time later he and I had put on 74 performances of different shows. I got back to London and I was happy to be back with mouse. We spoke about my little happening and it was nice to talk to her about it, but I still did not crave for jobs as far as I was concerned at the time, it was a minor glitch, maybe I could do film a bit later, at least you get take one, take two, ect . No, for now I was happy working in a kitchen and coming home to Emilie of a night.

Emilie, meanwhile was working, always doing something. She had a job in a hotel just around the corner from us that she was not to happy with and when I could I would walk her to work, and on return, wait for her in a nearby park when she was not expecting me. I used to love to do things that made her beam or sometimes glow with happiness. Valentines Day 2002 she was not happy at work but would not leave until the time was right. I was coming home from work early and passed a shop with a lovely figure hugging soft black dress, and bought it, had it wrapped and got a bouquet of flowers, sprowsed myself up and while she was on duty, walked straight through the hotel lobby to the restaurant looking for 'my girl'. When my hair is down and I have purpose in the world, people do tend to stop and look. On this occasion I drew their attention on purpose without purposely doing so. I did it so Emilie would feel the special person she is and it worked. The smile that I saw when I first met her , I kissed her told her happy Valentines , to the ooss, rss, & sighs in the background, I smiled, turned around and went back the way I came (if you ever read this Em, I know you can't forget that moment).Em went through a period of finding what she wanted to do in life, she went through this bead making thing, which I had a feeling would not buy her lunch, but she was enthusiastic and happy, so I was happy, and even went to help her sell them. It did not work out but she tried and quit in her own time and I supported everything she wanted to do. Even if it was standing in the pouring rain, in Covent Garden, handing out promotional tickets for night clubs, when I could I would be there to keep her company. We watched Romeo and Juliet at the National Theatre and although she did not understand the language fully, she enjoyed it. We were a good couple with so much potential, things looked bright, the future

*was orange. To top it all Emilie wanted a baby, my first thoughts;
I could do it this time. Not part time, not if I can or when I can.
I can do the whole family thing (with no offence to anyone but
all the time people talk about trying to have a baby , I think '
preparing for a baby' is so much more an appropriate term. If you
can't have one, naturally seek an alternative. Adoption if it's you,
if not do insemination, your best mate ECT. but enough of the
trying, just prepare. My good friends on a visit to London some
years ago told me of there problem with trying to have a baby;
the amount of people they said they saw, tests they had, to find
out things and whose fault it was. I thought it was ridiculous.
Weather you agree or not, we are all connected somehow to
everything around us, i.e. the universe, we understand some, some
we do not, but we still seek answers.*

*Your body and mind are connected, your mind tells you to
exercise, you exercise and you see results right, ok. If you go into
parenthood in a big flutter of unnecessary complications of tryisms
that pressures the mind, do you not think it is plausible that the
body would react accordingly, a self defence mechanism (that we
may not understand) that switches on to self preserve the body
against what is causing unrest in the mind. I sat Andy down over
a spliff and some booze and reminded the two of them how they
felt about each other. If you are physically normal to have children,
go home and prepare for a baby, make love not pressure and your
body will respond accordingly. A few months later Andy phones
me; Chica is pregnant. I bring a present for him every time I go to
Spain and they were to have another later. With Emilie and me
it was amusing, so it has to be a woman thing. Is there a time in
your life when your body says it needs a baby? And nothing else
under the sun makes any sense any more? Now I have to take a
small very important detour from the story so bare with me; My
cousin Val had been dating a lad from Senegal and had saved
herself for Mister Right (the only person I have met to be able to
succeed in that feat), but she wanted when it happened the good
old fashion proper wedding, with family from both sides. They
knew it would be sacrilegious if I was not invited and of course*

I was with Emilie. Emilie's dream since she had been a little girl was to go to Jamaica (I guess and I her prince charming, well back to front but still okay). When I told her she was over the moon, the buzz going around could have lit a room for a week and some. Thing is, Chatton had the same dream, how could I let one dream come true and not the other, would that not be in some strange way like finding out you are not the same Father as your Bro and Sis. So I invited her and her boyfriend along as well. This was all going great, I let the girls do the planning (I don't plan, I do), and I went about life just fine, the two sisters with the help of their parents , one in J A the other in England planed the wedding. Nicole was to be bridesmaid and my son sat at the table of honour with her. The wedding was a success. I was busy driving people to and fro and it may have seemed like I was neglecting Nikki. But she was with the family, which I was happy to see. She stayed in the big house with them. I heard that the mosquitoes took to her in a very uninvited manner, and her legs were so sore that J had to carry her up the hill (which is no mean feat, even for someone like him).

The wedding ceremony was held on a hotel private beach where I had worked some 20 years prior and still knew the management, so I got a nice discount on the booze (I think they call that ironic). People were late but that was down to BPT (Black People Timing). You see, it doesn't matter what the occasion is, a black person will always be late. Emilie got around this with me, simply by telling me the time was 10.30 instead of the actual 11.30. To get to the beach, you had to drive or walk through the luscious hotel grounds over a small foot bridge with a cool running clear water stream passing underneath, through some mangroves, which shaded the 80 degree sun overhead, and then on to the golden sanded beach, which was a cove similar to Boston, but half the size. A line of dwarf coconut trees were strewn out in a line on the beach for shade for those who deemed it necessary. The pastor started the ceremony and I think if it was not for the subtle signs from the guests, and the fact that Nikki almost fainted from the heat, he would still be talking today. The reception was held in a _hotel close by in the hills (a lovely place). At the table of honour, with the bride and groom, sat Nikki and Junior and that made me feel really good. The both of them looked splendid. Dwight was also at the table. Em and I shared a table, but I was so into her and the kids, I really do not remember who else was sitting with us. When I greeted Dwight, we spoke for a while (he had now grown into a good looking, well mannered young man) and then he just came out with a question: "do you have a photo of my Dad?" Wow! He proceeded to tell me he had never even seen a picture of him. I took his hand and held it, I kind of controlled a fall onto one knee and told him how much he reminded me of him and that it was really a pleasure to have met such a truly loveable, generous, funny and kind man. But the only picture I saw of him was on his driver's license, which had to be around somewhere. After the dinner came the speeches which I had not even thought about- let alone scribbled one out- until I heard someone shout 'speech!', and immediately afterwards, Angela shouts 'Colin first!' Of course, the actor in me jumps up and proceeds towards the stage, not having a clue what I was going to say in front of the 150 strong audience, but I did a pretty good job with a few well timed jokes, and well wishes. But the part I was most proud of was when; somewhere through the speech, Mrs Ivy was making what she must have thought was an unseen late (I told you) entrance from the back of the hall. It all seemed so right, and I switched from the Bride and Groom and proceeded to thank Mrs Ivy for not only taking me in, but also her other grand children when it was needed (I told her on behalf of all of us that we thanked her and loved her dearly, and it was because of her that all of us in the room could be together at this fine moment). Then I led the entire room in a good minute or so of a saluted applause. I know she was slightly embarrassed, but her eyes showed appreciation. If nature takes its correct course and she leaves this world before I, we now know how we feel about each other._

Another great memory from the wedding was after dinner: people went away to change for the after dinner dance, also held at the same hotel. The guests who did not need to change were *straddled about in groups chatting away. The group I was in consisted of about 6 or 8 of us: Amru, very close friend of the family, Donna likewise, cousin Junior, and Em. I don't recall J, but we were all huddled in a little group outside on the lawn. A little way from the reception area on one side, and a private road on the other, all smoking Marijuana (I have already stated my views on this, so please don't take it as if we were breaking one of the 10 commandments), when all of a sudden, a car pulls up. Now, most of the people at the wedding know of us and would know we smoke, so being caught by them was not that bigger deal. We would simply stop smoking until whoever it was passed by, it was just like that. But just then, someone in the group whispered a shout 'Mrs Ivy!' Now, you really had to be there: from the giggling and idle smoke chatter, to the disappearance of all of us simultaneously in different directions in the time and appearance a top magician would be proud of, it was hysterical. No one knew where anyone went. Em followed me instinctively to cover behind some nearby bushes, and as we looked out to where we were, all you could see was this rising cloud of white smoke, and Mrs Ivy going towards the reception escorted by two people either side, as though she had appeared from the smoke. Afterwards we all had a good laugh about who went where and if we saw the smoke, etc. That was the kind of respect Mrs. Ivy commanded. Em and I danced the night away; we did have a great time.*

I did do something. The house on the hill had been finished and I had been there once before; 6 bedrooms 3 bathrooms a wash room 2 kitchens and two large dinning /living rooms, divided between two floors with stairs, inside and outside. Painted white with a red roof, it looked spectacular, by far the biggest house in Boston at the time I was upset later though to find out that there was some kind of family feud. I was not there so I cannot elaborate, but I must say I know Mrs. Ivy was the foundation of the house and the last thing she would have wanted was for it to upset the family, so, message to all involved "get over it!"

We stayed at a friend's guest house for the first few weeks or so. VJ had a room and I shared with Emilie and Nicole and Junior *when he was around (always). It was good to be back like this, I even started to call Mrs. Ivy, Mrs ivy and felt quite comfortable (what was all the fuss about?)I'm thirty 38 now, Boston had not changed much at all my old mates had children of their own, some went abroad, some stayed the same. I turned up one day before the wedding (my usual timing) with Em. V j and her boyfriend had to take a later flight. My mother was there along with her sisters, Donnia and I the only two of her children who was there. From the time we got on the plane Emilie was Jamaica struck. We flew Air Jamaica because I wanted her to have the feel before we landed, and she did, in true Jamaican style we were delayed for more than an hour. Once in the air the stewardess's took to her like flies to sugar, they even forgot to serve **me** dinner. I remember her getting up to go to the toilet and about half an hour later I got a bit concerned, so I went looking, only to find her happily chatting to four stewardesses, about only they know what. I smiled and returned to my seat. It was too late to travel the extent of the island that day so I phoned up Lee from Rockdale's, (whom through my advise packed up and made home in a most beautiful part of the island and became the executive chef of Sandals) and stayed the night with him. We rented a car and drove to Portland the next day. As we drove over I took the pleasure of showing her the beauty of the island, something she had only dreamed of. We stopped at a nice little hide away, J. A style, with a beautiful beach some 2 min walk from the gates. I took her to a stony part of the beach first, an alcove with one or two fishing boats (picture long rowing boats)moored towards the end of the beach gently bopping up and down to and fro at the waters edge, the sun was setting, I had a disposable camera and just watched her, as she was standing on the remains of a jetty facing the water with the sun behind her, even from behind she felt beautiful, in a second, she turned spread her arms and smiled, more beautiful than ever, that pose was captured , it came out as a semi silhouette. I do not have the picture but many nights I have closed my eyes thinking of her and I see the picture as if it was in the palm of my hand.*

The next morning I took her to the beach a minute further away; golden sand with clear water breaking up to the beach. When we were in England, I told her she would be on a beautiful beach with golden sand and water so clear that when the waves break by the shore you can see the little fish swimming as if in an aquarium and we would have that beach for ourselves, well, there we were. The first night after we met the family I took her to a hotel I once worked at, it was also where the wedding was to be held, and after that we kinda let Jamaica do its thing. Every body loved Emilie, some of the kids would not leave her alone, Junior got on great with her, she and Nicky were cool (Nicky had arrived earlier and was staying at the big house with angela and the crew she was bitten badly by mosquitoes and big bro looked after her, along with everyone else); the relationship with them was just as I had hoped for. I was told some time later by Emilie that I did not get involved with Nicky enough. However, I thought I did, although I did take a back seat most of the time because she was being pampered by J and the rest, and it was good to watch from a distance. Nicky had to leave earlier than me because of the flight, but she was looked after. When she left, J focused on us more. Emilie liked a smoke; J would appear with a handful for her and to her surprise she had to give most of it back because it was too much. I introduced them (Em and Chatton) to a nice Rasta friend of mine, Neville king, who lived opposite our guest house. You could not see the house because of the surrounding bush, just a wooden hut with two rooms, no electric or kitchen. There was a fire place outside and he grew his own food around his house. He could make the right tourist's dream come true and he did. I told Emilie and Chaton if I were busy and they needed something or had to go somewhere i.e. the beach, if I could not make it, he would accompany them and he did. He also had this thing about cable TV; We could leave him in the morning, spend a day out, come back and find him sitting in the same place watching the same channel, he would not even touch a button for fear of breaking something. We also took him with us, or should I say invited him out, with us, when ever we could. Many times if I

had been busy with the car I would come home to find Chaton
and Em happily talking to him while chewing a piece of sugar
Cane he had chopped from his garden. We went to dances which
Em and Chaton loved, but strangely enough Chaton's boyfriend,
at the time, a Sound System man, did not like the dances and
would not go. If asked, personally, I think he was just frightened
of what the foreign press had to say and attitudes of some so-called
Jamaicans who lived in England, but I will let Chaton's story
remain Chaton's, I am happy she came and hope she had a good
time. We went to Reach Water Falls in the Parish that I went to
school; it was beautiful; high up in the blue mountain range,
the home of the world's most expensive coffee. We played like kids
in the cool spring water and Neville took off deep into the bush
up the falls to where we drank fresh spring water. They loved it,
I took them to the famous Dunns River Falls, (just because it's
the place people go to, if they do leave the hotel in Jamaica, the
only Jamaicans you see there are the guards). Although we had a
good time I knew and confirmed Emilie preferred Reach, just as I
knew she would. There was of course Boston beach, where Emilie
could be found with Neville and a few of the local kids enjoying
the warm Caribbean Sea. A friend of mine (Fatty's daughter) did
her hair like Bo Derricks and that was it, Emilie was perfection
in my eyes. There was another local beach a bit further off the
beaten track where we snorkelled in the reefs, played lovers games
underwater and drank cool coconut water which the lads would
go and pick for us, and then just lie in the sun. Shaggy the rapper
appeared one day; at this time he was topping the charts, but
Jamaicans on the whole do not get excited if a famous person
passes through their midst, they might turn and say "see my man
de" but that's usually about it. Hence, a lot of famous people like
Jamaica & Jamaicans. But I know this is not the way of many
European countries, so not wanting her to 'miss out' on having
her picture taken with him or getting his autograph while she was
swimming at the other end of the beach. I approached her, telling
her that Shaggy was "just over there" she interrupted me "so what"
and carried on swimming. What can I say, more points scored on

my heart. Junior would take her away sometimes and she would always comeback with a smile on her face, she exhausted herself by day and slept well (when I let her) by night. We went in the bush with J and his friends, who were the children of my youth hood friends and "stole" Jelly Coconuts just like we used to do. Emilie loved Jamaica and in return Jamaica loved Emilie.

By this time we had moved into the big house; we were only supposed to go to the island for four weeks but her birthday was on the 28th sept so we took the extra week for the memory of that birthday. She loved it, but who would not? Other guests had gone and we had the ground floor of the big house to ourselves. We later took the car back with Junior to the other end of the island, so we had to take the hill up to the house by foot (small price to pay) but it was fun. Sometimes we would spend the day out, come home to fresh, to go back out. But we would be so shattered from the day, we just stayed at the house or perched on the very wall that I took apart in building, listening to the blasting of Reggae music below, while gazing out across the Caribbean Sea under the blanket of stars. It was like this. Well, writing this, as you can probably imagine, brings back so many memories of what was, but was not to be: If my subconscious was anything close to normal, what was to happen would not even be remembered let alone worth writing about. You see; when I first heard about the wedding I knew earlier on that Sis would not make it, but I was so looking forward to seeing my Brother, we could be back together, if what briefly and...be brothers. I had heard his garage was successful, he had built a shopping mall and I was also looking forward to seeing his house that it so happened every one else had seen, except me. He was well off, not surprising to me. After Lee's death I understood he buried himself in work, and if you work all the hours God sends you must have money, it's a pity though because money did change him, at least towards me. I must admit I often thought he blamed me for breaking up his family, it seemed at times I could do nothing right, his comments always niggled me, but when I saw him again, it would be forgotten. Well, one evening (I'm pretty sure Emilie was not there) Val, my Mom, blossom and

Grand Ma were upstairs on the veranda; it had been a good day and Val decided to phone him, I took over, I wanted to phone him to ask him why he did not show for the wedding and if I would see him before I left, I did have a few drinks but I was more elated than drunk. I dialled the number and a woman answered, I said "hello" and asked to speak to him, the woman hesitated for just a second and said he was not there. Now, I had called him before, years back, and he had a Jamaican maid who sometimes, I know for a fact, if it was too much trouble to call him she would simply say 'he is not here at the moment' or if he instructed her to do so. With this in mind I simply said, "if he is there can you get him to call his brother on this number", and she hung up. I had the time to tell the onlookers, he was, there and then the phone rang, I picked it up (I knew it was him) "yo bro"

"Don't call me at my #!@! # house again!"

"But, wait a minute" and the amount of abusive words hurled at me in that short space of time must have been a record in itself. It was not even what he said, it was how he said it; with pure hate. When he hung up I was totally lost, my head was spinning my heart was thumping I did not know whether I was coming or going, that cup I spoke of was riding on the brim and I did not know it, that 'Time Bomb' that could explode anytime, the one the counsellor told me about all those years ago. I understand now. In front of all of them I burst into tears of disbelief, anger, rejection, the lot; After all the crap I have been through, the promises he made to me when he offered me money, because I broke my holiday in the states to introduce him to a manager I knew, so he could get special parts for his stupid cars in his stupid garage sent cheap to him. I refused the money and told him just not to forget us when he got rich (Me and Sis, he never got to know Donni, his loss) he promised me he would not, I believed him thoroughly. I was on the veranda waving my hands around like a mad man, ranting and raving about how I new he hated me and just used me when he saw fit, I was not crying, I was bawling. How could this be happening to me? It's over, I don't think about things like that anymore and I am not this, emotional in front of anyone (even

Mrs Bond's dinner was light compared to this.) I was officially screwed up. When I calmed a little, people were talking to me but I was not listening. The next day Val told me he phoned and said his wife called him and said someone sounding drunk called her a liar and blah, blah, blah, this was fine for me because, one, I had four witnesses that could state I said no such thing and two, the time it took to phone back, technology and speech is not quick enough yet. To dial a number, relay the message and dial back in the space of time he achieved it, and all around agreed with me. So I pissed off, but I hear he is going to come to a dance that we all planned to go to previously. I thought, okay, I have acted silly, I embarrass him, he will explain, I will forgive him, all is well. The night came and I drove with Em to the party, Val was in a car in front of me and signalled; he had just passed and stopped on the opposite side of the road behind me. I got out of the car, Val got to him first and I was behind her waiting, just to say something, 'hello' or something like that. He totally ignored me and drove off. I was beginning to get upset again but this time I had control. That night must have been tense for Emilie, we got to the dance and in the parking lot I walked up to him with my hand stretched out introduced him to Em. He went up to her, shook her hand and in his old stylish self, greeted Emilee and walked right passed me, mumbling something. I think he said; he can't talk to me until he has had something to drink. He paid for every one and we all went in, the flock gathered around him, people who had only heard of him were treating him like he was God almighty. I waited for about two or three rounds of drink, he and the flock on one side of the dance floor and Em and I on the other. I wanted to stay the night for Em's sake but I could not, we left without telling anyone. I was not feeling great.

Tue 9th 4.30ish

I just received a Christmas card from Mrs Bond; it's not the time for me to read it.

Looking back at this particular time back in J.A has depressed me, but once again, although alcohol is all around in this unit I have not thought about having a drink, I just think about the state I would be in if I did and then this whole episode would have been for nothing. I will leave that path for someone else, and Mrs Bond can wait for better times.

I have not seen my little friend the 'Aguti' for some time, they say a snake must have got to the baby and she must have left for safer grounds, I guess that's what Emilie did.

WED 10TH

The following day *he came up to the house; he grunted something at me and I nodded; For about half an hour people spoke, he, me and Mother hardly said a word, then he left to get his machine washed. I stayed at the house for a little while contemplating my actions and moaning to Mother and Mrs. Ivy about why he would treat me like this. I think Mrs Ivy understood but could not find the words, I don't think my mother understood at all, in fact all she said to me was "Are you on drugs?" Well, for Mum, here is what happened "I was left by you and who ever is my father, and I could not deal with the thought of my brother doing the same, okay." I said I was going to sort this out now. Mrs Ivy said nothing, my mother said I "should leave him alone and forget it". Well, all that sentence meant to me was that that's how she deals with problems, 'leave them alone and forget them' (I will not elaborate). I got in the car, sped down the road after him and found him talking to Trevor, beside his ugly looking 4X4. I got out of the car, walked over to them and not wanting to interrupt, simply because it's bad manners; I stood 4, 5 feet away from them for about 4, 5 mins an then started to get impatient to the state of anger, so I rested my arm on the bonnet of his machine. No sooner had I done it, he looked up and gestured with his hand towards me, as if he was brushing aside a fly, you know, two flicks of the wrist. I was fuming but I had no energy to do anything in response but get in the car and drive. I found a bar and once again drunk for a purpose...*

6.00pm; just come in from Rec yard, the Aguti is back, I will think of it as a sign; Positive Thinking.

I woke this morning; exercised earlier than usual but I feel depressed. I guess at this moment it's because of Bro and the thought of why I believe I have lost Em (I guess I have not mastered positive thinking). It has occurred to me that even in this state of depression I still have a deep down feeling of love for my brother. I guess that has always been there, coupled by the fact that I have grown up, hearing, reading and watching stories about brothers and it seems to be the norm that all brothers argue and fight. I am afraid I can't honestly say that I have the same feeling for my parents though, for pretty much the same reason. I grew up with an outside notion that your parents would be there for you if the going got tough. Well, I would not expect any word from my father, simply because he does not know I am here (I think) but if I have this profound love for my Bro would it not stand to reason that my mother would have a similar feeling towards me, yet a year has nearly passed and there has been no word, and this time around, I cannot say time has made me forget that I may have received a word. I speak of this lightly in a way, because quite frankly, I don't give a dam. That love I should have for them was never there (or never got a chance to develop) so if we ever do meet again I do not think it could ever be on a level of parental love, which I think is very sad.

English is getting on my nerves but it's not his fault; when in the past I have been in my moods, like these people around me, I tend to do and say nothing right. On the other hand, he is still going on about these bloody cockroaches and he insists on having my full attention when he decides to tell me a story about him and his two and a half year old daughter, which, although I try to make out that I am interested , inside I still would love to, 'shut him up'. Actually, I told him a few days ago that he should not talk to me about his girlfriend, because my next six months should remain stress free and I could not take stories about his girlfriend and cockroaches for that period of time. But all these feeling are not in my head. I can process the feeling into words in my head but I actually feel the feeling inside my middle section i.e. in my throat, in between my rib cage and in the pit of my stomach, you will understand, the next time you have strong feelings analyze where you actually feel the hurt or the love, it's not in your head is it? Which is why you cannot consciously stop it? You can rationalise it, but you can't consciously make it go away, which I guess is where the mind steps in when it gets too much and shuts it out, which is good for a while, the problem with that is, what if someone or something brings those feelings back to you before your mind is ready to cope with them...? Here endeth my lesson for today.

The next part of my journey is really hard to put down because I am anticipating the mood swings already; Joy, pain, hurt, despair but if this book amongst other things is to serve as healing therapy to me and others like me, I must go on.

FRI 12TH

Evening 7.0clock, the lads are playing dominoes. I am/ was reading Sophie's World, (Joston Gaarder) (good book). I was still feeling a bit depressed and started to listen to the radio. Two songs; Guilty (Striesand), and Island in the Sun (Parton and Rogers). I may have said something about listening to love songs in prison, I was right, but times, circumstances and feelings change and now I contradict myself; I am sitting on my bunk with my feet on my keg, looking through the slit in the wall. All I can really see is a section of the fence in the Rec yard lit with spot lights. There's a few distant lights in the hills about 5 miles away and the darkness of the sky, and as the songs were playing, a soft cool breeze found itself through the slit, so I shifted closer to the gap in the wall and closed my eyes to attain the fullness of the breeze and what it bought. I began to think of how I would often have a female lie in my arms and fall asleep with such a look of contentment and security on their face, it was nice. I thought about certain women in particular and then remembered something from Shakespeare, that I would always debate with myself and never come up with a justifiable conclusion or one that, to me, could justify the statement he made; "tis better to have loved and lost than to never have loved at all". Now, I can say 'yes' I agree; The feeling I had before I caught the breeze, heard the song and looked across a lit dark plain has been replaced by the feelings of the memories of the love I once had. In my present situation, I am happy to disconnect myself from this present, and go back in time to a present where all was well (in love). I would not like to imagine what it would be like if I had to be in this same depressing situation, without even a past love of some sort to turn too in the hour of need.

SAT 13TH

I am somewhat more depressed today; it's probably the addition of the weekend.

Pork today and knowing there is no mail either, the feeling of anticipation has been replaced with something else, and then of course I think of how Nicky is feeling. I do not think she has sound reason not to drop me a line, and then there is Ky who, if she could, I think would have answered one of my letters. Its' probably because the way I feel at this moment but I am becoming increasingly anti Emilie. I expected her to be upset, pissed off and angry but after calming down I would have thought that a letter with even a scribble from Ky would have been in order. I want to write and I want to phone but I can't now. I have done and said all I can. What I do now is for my little girl, she appears not the person I fell in love with, so I guess it will not be that difficult to deal with the situation anymore. Pity though, but without being conceited, I really think she will regret it in time to come, just as I think Bro regretted his actions later after the last time I saw him.

I made every effort to think of Em and her time in J A, I could not ruin it, but to my weakness, I could not do it without. If I had it in my system, I could control myself, not enough to get drunk, but just enough to block things out. It worked, but I had seriously lost my appetite. We had a cook who prepared food for us and over the weeks I hardly ate a quarter of a plate, at a time, making up some dumb excuse. People probably sensed something wrong but my eating habits or lack of them is legendary so it could not have been all that obvious. 9/11 came and went; I caught it live on cable at the big house, some flights were delayed, which compared to what Manhattan suffered was minute to what us collation forces have and are doing to the middle east, in my opinion even more so, but that's politics so I will leave that there.

Emilie's birthday came and I never really made an issue out of it. Neither Miss Ivy or Blossom, because their religion do not celebrate birthdays, so I was very pleasantly surprised when I just mentioned it on the day and Mrs. Ivy came out in song with, Happy Birthday. Blossom, who was at her shop at the time, did the same thing when she got home. What felt so good was that Blossom had no idea that she followed suit (thanks guys)Em was over the moon , my guess, her most memorable birthday and all without presents, cakes or a party, see? Money is not everything, which reminds me how money can turn sour. Em and I had planned to bring junior back we had budgeted for this but the rental car, because of the wedding and other stuff went back late. The fee was also to be split which it was not (for reasons too silly to get into) with all the trouble of air traffic, flights took some time to get back to norm and when they did the prices were going up daily. Well, we could not leave early and he could not get a flight with us and the travel agent, who I am sure saw the necessity of the flight in our eyes, was not the most helpful in the world, but we booked a flight for the following month, thing is, we did not have enough money with us, so I had to ask my Mother. I did this with great thought, I could have got the money else where, but I thought she would like to help out. After asking her she told me she did not have it, but when she got back to the states 2 days later she would send it. Okay, I thought. Junior would be happy and I had fulfilled my promise to him. Then Mother did something again that disturbed me (probably me being too sensitive, but you can see there is a pattern here): she called Junior into the living room, and lounging back in a comfy chair with feet up on a cushion as if she was the queen of Sheba (she did look good must admit), she proceeded in telling Junior how she would help him get to England, and then began to lecture him about how he should not let her down. Well, to be honest, it did piss me off somewhat , but between the alcohol, Em having a nice time, Junior's smile and the steam I had let off prior, I guess my cup was not even half full, so I let it ride. I was to find out later I should not have. Anyway, we packed in a lot and the trip was good for all, it was time to go. We got our gifts, mine to her Father was Jamaican and Havana cigars and Blue Mountain coffee for mum. It was very sad when she had to leave and I had never seen her so emotional before or since in that way. She literally cried for four days after we got back to England.She was the first person I had taken to Jamaica over the tweny years I had been away. We even made plans for Jamaica, I cut down on the drink but she did not know what I was going through inside, so she would not have really noticed, I don't think she really got it all back together until Junior came from Jamaica. They really got on well together; playing in the snow at his first sight of it, we had Christmas together, got caught up with presents and trees ect. At first, J was impatient he had only got six months on his visa and was worried he would be sent home, I, however, knew he would not. People say he and I are more like Brothers than father and Son, which I thought was cool. We argued rarely, once some time later when I was drunk and he accused me of never having done anything for him, me in reply "how do you think you got here!?" His reply "Grandma did it!" I was upset, but not so much on top as deep down. So, on top of her having something to be proud of about my acting, she also took away me bringing my Son to England. Well, I explained it was I and Em and somewhere along

*the way, he threw a chain towards me that I had given him to pass
on to his Son. Well, in the heat of the argument, I guess we were
alike. I threw it away as well, but that was really all. We have a
good relationship and more important, so do his two sisters, with
him. Now back to Emilie and I.*

SUN 14TH

I am feeling not depressed today, and have thought; why?
The circumstances are the same, yet I feel different today, I
feel comfortable. Again, I have come to understand something
about myself and I think other humans also. I think I have
begun to realise more about feelings and the nature of them,
although this example is back to front I am sure you will
understand; While I was busy being depressed I forgot about
how 'comfortable' I am here, in this facility. The overall feeling
of depression had a hold of me, now, a few days later I am
feeling comfortable again, but looking back I can now say
that, although I was depressed, I was actually feeling quite
comfortable being so. What I am getting at is that the mind
suppressed my knowledge of being comfortable, so that I could
be free to be depressed (I am not exactly sure why) in the same
way my mind locked out certain happenings, so I could be free
to let other things happen. I believe a large part of my problem
is (and was) that I was at some point, in conflict with the past
and the present, not knowing which path to let go and which
to follow. I could not figure out the root cause of a problem I
did not know I had. But I could feel the effect of something
I was trying to understand , what I am getting at is that over
the last few days I was comfortable, I just did not realise it and
through my life's ups and downs however tragic or happy I felt,
I did have this overriding feeling, that I was "comfortable." I
have meaning and purpose. It's just that it was too many times
"blocked out", leaving me with the thought I often tried to
explain to Emilie: I feel as though I am two people within
one, fighting for the right to be me. In the eyes of Emilie

and many others, who 'I' called the 'bad me' (who appeared through alcohol) had won. Though, looking into myself right now, I have no doubt, who I call the 'Good Me' has won. I think I know now why I drank so much and it is so painfully clear; 1, because I wanted to forget and 2, even more simple, is that alcohol is truly physically addictive, if mistreated. It may sound so easy to say "Just stop drinking if you can't handle it" well, it's not that easy. Have a check on the number of alcoholics in the UK alone and make that statement to anyone of them... On second thoughts don't, for if you are not or have never been. To an alcoholic, it would probably be one of the most pretentiously ignorant statements you could possibly make. Since I have been here I have heard that Mel Gibson is having a serious problem with alcohol. If you, like me, are a fan of Mel, you, unlike me, might think, 'How could that be possible for Mel?' One of the most famous, popular, coolest, handsome, richest, nicest, sort after actors of this generation, how could he possibly be an alcoholic? Here is some advice if you would like an idea, go a bit further than money, looks, fame and try along the lines of 'suppressive feelings' and you might come close to realising that it's entirely possible for even Mad Max (that's a good one, huh) to be one of me(message to Mel , good luck pal).

Well, as I draw closer to the beginning, I am sure I will continue to have many mood swings and they will no doubt have me in a similar condition as the same moods prior, and I will let them take their course, only this time, it will happen with more understanding. At the moment you may think I should probably feel happy, but I don't, I feel "comfortably content" and I know why; 'The happiness is suppressed and will pop up when necessary'.

Well. I am almost ready to join the outside world again, but if being locked up here and dissecting my life has drawn me to this conclusion thus far, I must see it out (it is possible to get out sooner, with a little cash, but as I keep pointing out 'money cannot buy everything').

So here we are in England; J is at college and has moved out twice, for no other reason than to have his own space. Em has taken a massage course, J and I are keeping in touch with Nicky, J, I admit more so , and Nicky is doing finals in her exams in Ireland; me , I am working for the agency again in a nice stress free place in the city.

Emilie is getting more and more agitated about the baby, she is now beginning to conclude she has a problem (obviously it's not me). I try to give her the same advice I gave to Andy and it worked enough for her to 'relax the mind'. I remember she used to get the pregnancy test from the pharmacy and was quite upset when it was negative, which I found and showed it was funny, because, I knew, that beyond her immediate feeling of disappointment, she knew, she would have a child, and it was so (the only words I can think of is "beautiful trying", it really was). One day she came to me with the test, she said she could 'not look at it' so she gave it to me. Enter the actor, Stuart.J.Cole. I told her it was 'negative', and as she started to change mood, I showed the positive test. We were going to have a baby. We celebrated and I was good, we were happy and although I knew then, as I know now, I should have stopped drinking. But even though I still was, 'the bad me' had not introduced himself to Emilie, J or other people i.e. work mates etc. I carried on in what most thought was moderation. One does not become a fully fledged alcoholic over night, there is an art to it and it's based on excuses; first to yourself, and then to your loved ones. I worked every day and made Em feel as I believed she should. When she felt frightened of being a mum, I comforted, if she had bad days I was there, I made a deal with her; that no matter what happened, through argument or travel (her to France) or just being depressed, I could talk to the baby via her stomach, every day, and I did. Even when she went to France I spoke via phone through her stomach. Her parents were happy for us, my parents, well, just like the other two, they missed out. Mrs Bond however did not.

I went to the hospital and saw her for the first time on the scan that was good (Em has the pic), they stole a really nice bicycle from _me that day outside the hospital. Emilie wanted a water birth so she sought advice from the midwife and was getting lots of stuff through the post, (I should mention, the government health dept or whoever is responsible, do take good care of pregnant women , if you ask. I do believe those to thank are the people who care and "Maggie") Then the day came; I was at work, the time was two o'clock when I got the call from V,j, 'Emilie is on the way to the hospital,' I spoke to my boss (another lovely French girl) and she covered for me. The contractions were far apart. I had a drink at work to 'celebrate' and was at the hospital a few hours later. Now, I had lived in the vicinity for about twenty years now, so I knew St Thomas's quite well, but I had never been to this ward before. The midwives and nurses were so nice and the room was, well, it felt like we had booked into a private ward, it was spotless, but it did not feel like a hospital. The bed was in the centre of the room with the headboard against the wall and through the large super clean double glazed windows; Big Ben and the Houses of Parliament over look the river Thames and Westminster Bridge, and was beautifully lit up and reflected upon the river. Em was there looking like a part of nature, her two friends were also there Chaton, who you know about, and Morgane (our spirits do not seem to get on), camera in hand. When the time came the midwife and I walked her down the corridor to a waiting delivery room, once again better than I expected. Even though all I can recall is a stool or chair, which I sat on and a bath tub that looked more like a large Jacuzzi cut to fit. Em was in pain but we both knew she had to go through that, my job was easy; I sat on the stool, held her hand, and with the other hand I controlled the water temperature(which has to remain constant 38 degree I think)). Emilie was good, I shed a few tears, the girls were snapping away, Em was pushing and then the water turned red, I saw something appear but, it was not a baby; the midwife read my apprehension and immediately reassured me that all was well, our child was born without breaking water 'en sac', I was told it would give the child good fortune: Kayana had arrived. (Memo to expecting dads, watch the birth, another thing you can't buy). Em first had_ *her and then I cut the cord, now I could become a proper father, I know I can. Em deserves it, Ky deserves it and so do I. But I am here now so, well, let's get on with it.*

WED 17ᵀᴴ

Another month me in here; my overall feeling: still 'comfy'.

I was reading the book 'Sophie's world.' There was a section were the author lightly brushed on Sigmund Freud, I found it interesting. I had heard of him before and probably thought that his philosophy link to psychology was true, or at least it could apply to me, what I did not have at the time though was someone to interpret it to me. How I would have reacted to it then though, is another matter. I still think writing this and serving time has been so far the most successful remedy.

Aguard came to talk to me the other night; it felt quite strange speaking to her from behind the bars. For the first time, I did feel like a prisoner, although to everyone here that is how they perceive me. I feel like, I am in a 'get well' clinic. I have clothes, food, a place to sleep, a roof over my head and most important of all; the time to reflect.

The other day one of the close friends (a very select few of which I am one) of cell nine, came to me and asked if I would like to smoke with him outside. I was a bit hesitant at first because of a few reasons; 1, the ciggs were very low in the unit and it usually causes problems having the smoke in "public" and 2, because of a guard sitting on a rail at one end of the Rec yard. But I said yes anyway. He bought this big spliff out and he and I sat at the other end of the yard in full view of everyone, and smoked. I could tell what they were thinking, but no one said a word, so it seems to me, within reason, I am now one of the few untouchables. That's okay; I'll just go with the flow. Which reminds me of Chi Chi's behaviour; I believe I was correct in my assumptions; his verbal manner is not always suitable to the time and conditions of use. Two inmates have sternly warned him to be "careful how you talk and act because it's not every day that I joke!" I could see by the look on Chi Chi's face, he was not expecting such confrontation, but as I tried to explain to him, you can learn a language in no time at all but social isms and culture is a part of one's self and even if you do learn them, they take a considerably more amount of time to master.

The English lad is still getting on my nerves, although now I have conditioned or customised myself to his idiosyncratic ways. Here's one just to let you know again, what it is like being locked up with someone's habits. If you don't know someone who habitually repeats themselves, well, I hope you never do; last night we were talking about nothing in particular and he was emphasising about himself being locked out of a house by a woman, it was something like this; "you know when you get locked out? you know, locked out, I mean locked out, you know locked out," then while explaining he gets up from his bunk and animates locking the door with a key "look, look, you know what I mean bro? Locked out bro, you go out with your friend or something and she locks you out, you can't get in, locked out" then he got back on his bunk and repeated 'locked out' three times. Now, if you knew this was his trait in every conversation, would you start one with him, if you were locked up in the same cell? Kenny and I have put it down to stir crazy (jail malfunction of the brain). There was another time he was late for Roll check because he was writing a letter for an inmate in another cell. Now, depending on the guard, or mood of, this is a two week lock up offence, but he is not a trouble maker and we new that this would not be likely so Chi was winding him up. So, English is outside the cell waiting for it to open again, it went as follows; Chi,

"Dat is two weeks lock up".

English "I was just downstairs writing a letter for a man, you know, a letter."

"Still two weeks".

"For a letter Bro, you know, not for pay or anything, just a letter, something neat, you know, a letter, writing it".

"Same ting, two weeks" then the guard lets him in , he thanks her, and turns to us.

"I was writing a letter for a guy in cell 5, you know, a letter! That's why I was late Bro, a letter, you know, look, look (more description) a letter mate, you know, writing."

It may be hard to believe but I have not exaggerated; in fact more so the opposite. Since I have become comfortable with my inner self, I have found it tolerable; also to be fair, I found out that his father died a few weeks ago, so it is more than likely an added contribution factor.

The prison has been tranquil. Have not phoned or received anything.

Mrs Bond just wanted to know how I was and to tell me she was in touch with Ky. My feelings at present for Em are that of resignation. I now, for some reason, imagine her walking around naked comfortably, in front of another man, with Ky present (hopefully he has the decency to stay dressed around Kayana). Somewhere deep down though, I still can't help thinking that she knows, although he might be a nice guy, he is still only second best. They cannot have what we had, even if she had a child for him, which I still hope she does not do while I am in here. What we did have was special, but I suppose that was then.

After the birth I got a job at the Imperial War Museum, it was kind of okay, it's just that I was not used to a routine and it's quite annoying having to arrange your life around a job; to me it's just a waste of a life. I thought and still do think I am the type of person who can only arrange my job around my life. Squeezing so much into the time you have off, it's really not reasonable to have humans conditioned this way, take the gym for example; when I am on form, I like to go to the gym 4, 5 times a week. Work starts at 8, finishes at 4. Gym opens at 6.30 a.m, closes at 10.30,pm. I have to, at sometime in a given day, get to the gym, and go to work, changing clothes 5 times a day. For that day, spend quality time with Em and Ky, do the odd things to keep the cycle going, i.e. pay bills keep in touch with the world, spend time helping J out, trying not to neglect him and the rest, there is no time to do what you really feel at ease with because you've been spending your time doing whatever, to make those trivial jobs seem worthwhile. But I was doing it so; I could be a family man. That is not my idea of a family man's job, I could not do it, but I tried. Emilie and I shared Ky's years equally. If ky cried in the night after feeding, I would give her a break and have her till she fell asleep. If she had to be somewhere, and Ky needed to be collected from the nursery or so, no problem. We went to France together to introduce her to the grandparents, they were very pleased. Monsieur took time from work to come and see his first Grand child and the whole family was as nice as before. Madam babysat while Em and I socialised (I do like the French). We toured Nantes and I went to watch them play football at their stadium. I almost got the ball for a souvenir and Chatton was with us that time. Things were still okay, but now I kept having binges, my system was beginning to tell me the alcohol had to stop, (this never happened in France but it was in the system). Back at home, the job was not so much getting to me; it's just that I was now drinking more than I should there. I noticed also I was getting highly emotional about pretty much everything and I began to worry about things way too much e.g. J was getting on his own way and handling himself well. He was now head security at a night club within walking distance. One day, during a period when I had stopped drinking (which happened often and lasted for no more than three weeks), I saw him preparing for work and for the first time, I saw him put on a bullet proof vest. Instead of being rational, it would be the start of another binge, only this time and each after, it would be worse (one thing I must state, throughout my life, I have never been violent, unless in an unavoidable situation. Through the whole time of my illness, I never laid a hand on anyone, unless it couldn't be helped). Another time Em took Ky to a house to stay over for the night so they and their friends could catch an early flight to Switzerland for a break. I was "resting" but as soon as I saw the house, it's state and the occupants. I told Emilie that Ky would not be staying here, "this is no place for our child". I remember her just handing me my jacket and giving me a sign to leave all in one gesture, I left because I did not want to cause a scene and I know, the first two or three drinks after a relapse, can make you seem more rational than you really are. I had my two cans of special brew on the way home, phoned her and through serious tears explained to her why she and Ky should come home and that she could get to the airport from my place. I also said something I regretted, but meant at the time; it was what I would do to a certain person if Em and Ky stayed at the house and something bad happened to our girl... The gods were looking out, she came, nothing happened I did not drink that night, but the next day I was so ashamed of my feelings I hit the can again. Emile had a good time in Switzerland and I pulled off my not drinking stunt again, but by this time I am on a trip of conflicting emotions. Everything in my head was strange. When I did not drink I had the 'good Colin', but by now the 'bad Colin' had began to introduce himself every time I binged. Cousin Ange let me know I was doing too much, Ossie had a word, Tanya (Trevor's daughter, just like him) had said things to me as blunt and to the point as always and Emilie, well, she told me if I could not stop she would leave. I thought I was at rock bottom. I started to seek help for the alcohol, not realising that the problem lay far deeper than that. First, I went to the AA and in my first session I did not say a word. I just sat listening to people tell their stories of who they were and how alcohol had ruined their lives. There were one or two drug addicts and their problem seemed to mirror image the alcoholics but they seemed to be having more fun, I enquired about this and one said "it's so different and nice to be high on life". I sat down after a break and listened to more heart broken stories, and tears just rolled down my cheeks. How could I have possibly got myself into this situation like them? After a few weeks, I stopped. I had already lost my job so I thought I had time to get it together, sign on for a while, get back in the gym etc. I did not drink for six weeks and then J had a problem and I just started again. Em decided she wanted a flat. I believe I actually suggested it. With plans to get away from my flat and start in a new environment, the idea was good but I had to fill in form, claiming I was throwing her and Ky out and although it seemed to make sense, I felt that I could not have that hanging over my head in writing, even if I and Em were the only ones that knew it was not true. However, I signed the form she got the flat, I drank more heavily. I don't actually know when she really left, but I am sure I was too much under the influence. I was now more seriously fighting myself. I knew I wanted Emilie back, for that I had to stop drinking, to do that I had to sort out the problem I knew I had but did not know what it was. In this state I could not do a contract job so I started to try certain businesses. Private dinner parties or birthdays ect, I could stop drinking long enough to do a good function but afterwards as with most functions, they end up inviting you to have a drink with them and that would be it. I could still get more jobs because I was good at what I did and I was 'fun' to be around when I was sober. I had good vision and spoke to the correct people but as something got of the ground I would start drinking again. There was one time I did a function for an art gallery across the road from me; the food was great, the money was fine, but I had access to free booze and took full advantage. By this time my state is such, my limit of alcohol never came gradually, it would just hit me! One minute I would be just fine, just thinking, 'one more', the next minute I would wake up at home in the early hours of the morning not knowing how or when I got there. This particular night, I can remember cleaning up in the gallery and walking across the road with a pot in my hand. I remember falling and I remember being cleaned up, then I remember waking up in bed, (it's amazing how you can find your way home no matter how pissed you are, if you are awake). The next day, I was in the off-licence and a friend stopped by to have a drink with me and he said he watched the whole thing; I came across the road with the pot in my hand and tripped over the pavement. I did not drop the pot but fell flat on my face apparently unconscious. he took me to his house and he and his lovely wife (Lisa & Mark 'cheers') cleaned me up and got me back home. Things like this keep happening to me, I was sober enough to get a job and then lost it.

If I had to look after Kayana for the week end, I would wean myself off to the state where two or three cans for the day and night would keep me level headed and if I had to see Emilie, I could stop for that duration, although as soon as I left I would start again.

Nicky came down from Ireland, I think they stayed by cousin Angela and I so desperately wanted all three of them to be together for the first time, so they could have that bond. Emilie even put off plans to go abroad but something happened at Deidre's end and she cancelled. Nicky came later but by then Ky had gone to France. I believe Emilie went to tell her mum we broke up it did not even enter my head to tell my people. Hell, they didn't even know them anyway. I was sober throughout Nicky's trip. By now she is growing into a fine young woman; it hit me hard that I missed out on all that. It all seemed to have happened so fast. So junior, I missed, Nicky, I missed and look at the state of me now at the two year stage in Kayana life. Nicky went back to Ireland with promises from me that I would call more often, which I did. She said she was into music, so I sent her my big key board and we texted each other.

I figured out now that I needed some kind of counsellor. I still knew I could honestly beat this thing but I just did not know how .I just needed some kind of direction. I saw my G.P, who was really good. He put me onto a counsellor to coincide with a drinking program, it was good, and she was good. They taught about what alcohol does, how it does it, and the staff were all ex alcoholics, they knew their job. We had acupuncture, lectures, and sports programs 6 weeks and I finished the program. Then I had the opportunity to go to drop in classes for moral support, I don't remember the name of the place, but it would defiantly work for some people. Me and the counsellor became friends, although I know now that was her unique approach to the job. I tried to sort my life out again ever fearful of the 'bad Colin' uprising again. I had a few close calls but I was good... for a while. Meanwhile, I enjoyed seeing Emilie and Ky when I could. I acquired another car and would drive to see them late at night and leave early the next morning, so the council officer would not catch me, some times we would spend a weekend together, and go for nice walks in the park, it felt so good. But I still knew all was not well, it could only take a drop and I would over flow again, I could feel him trying to surface. I tried telling Emilie what it was like in my head with these two people but alas, she could only sympathise. It now began to hurt me, because I was hurting her. How could I be doing this to the girl I love? It's got to stop.

One day by the off licence I saw a nice looking girl and in my semi sober state, started chatting, her name was Jana, she was to fill one of the gaps in my life.

FRI 19TH

English is still getting on my nerves; he witnessed his first fight Wednesday evening (it was over that phone), again between 'Short crop' (the one who threw the concrete cleaner in the eyes of another inmate), and 'Mr. Muscles'. The short one got the better of it and it was stopped by an early Roll Check; it was all very exiting for him. But for me... Roll check was at 6, we fell asleep around 11.30 and the amount of time I heard the word "fight" and the phrase "E dun im bad" was passed monotonous. The embassy will not see him for about two months so I am treating him as Jackson treated me; He gets weed almost every night, he smokes ciggs like a chimney, Chi gets him extra food and Kenny gave him ten ciggs this morn but through out the day and night, "oh, no not chicken, one piece of chicken bro, I cant believe, one piece". It's the same for roaches, bread, tea, water, sleeping space and lights out. Chi Chi and I have attempted a deal, no more complaining until our five months are up, and apart from that we're cool.

I'm trying to help Mrs Aguard with some advice about education in England; we will see how it turns out.

When Jana came aboard the ride, I was at a low, but true to form, I managed to stay in good stead for a few months. I wanted the company of a woman, but I also knew if I died prematurely, it was not a life long thing. She was a German and she is also a chef. She moved in after a while, and she was happy, as you are in the beginning of a relationship. Being semi sober in the first few weeks was okay, exploring the new person in my life, she was as good as a person can be, but I would rather we had remained good friends. Emilie had got her flat now and it was only 4, 5 miles from me. She insisted on doing all the painting and decorating by herself, I felt a bit left out, but it was her flat. When she needed to concentrate on stuff, I would take Kayana, who got on well with Jana. It was she who actually decorated Ky's room at my place and would often bring her presents. I showed my appreciation by taking her places sharing things with her that I would only share with Emilie. Don't misunderstand me; she met the cousins and they got on fine. J and her got on exceptionally well and we went to many places of interest I took her back to my childhood on a picnic with her Ky and J on the golf course at Oakfield. If you can imagine what two chefs could prepare for a family picnic, you will know it was a good day out. Oakfield had gone, which I had known before but my biggest disappointment was the' lightning tree' with the figuration of a cows head. I spoke to a golfer who was about to tee off, and after telling me about his memories of Oakfield and those days, he explained that the youth of today burnt the tree down in their idea of fun (memo to youth of today, don't go destroying things out of fun, they may mean a lot to someone today and tomorrow may mean a lot to you). I told of the good times I had (to keep the day on a level), but through out that whole day I could not help thinking, it should be Emilie here. Jana was good to me as my son pointed out one day when 'Mr bad' was about "what's up father, this girl would do anything for you, my reply "I don't know, and I know". She and Em met and to me seemed to get on well. Then, one day, Emilie told me she was seeing someone, to be honest that day I had resigned myself to losing her, although of course I had to go to her flat to pick up or drop off Ky, I always gave notice and when I turned up he was never there. That did not bother me, she and I had become friends although I could never look her directly in the eyes, because of that sinking feeling you get in the bottom of your stomach when ever you lose a lover and she is not coming back (I still get those feelings from time to time in here, but that is understandable, isn't it?). Anyway, I did something maybe I should not have done, glad I did it and happy the way things worked out. I shall explain; for her reason only, she had decided to keep me away from him, but I wanted to know about the type of guy who was spending more time in the presence of my daughter than I. So one day out of the blue, popped around in a van I had acquired from a new venture of mine (buying and selling lamps, good business with okay money, if only I could have stayed sober long enough to take care of it), the excuse being I had a delivery in the area, when I got there she told me I should not have come, but I could tell by the look in her eyes, she did not mean exactly what she said. He was in the kitchen and I told her to bring him out. Not to my surprise, he was a white dreadlock and a member of a band (two best friends I think grew up picturing the men in their lives would be dreadlocked and in a band). He seemed alright and I was as polite as I could be, and as Emilie and Ky deserved. I found out later that I went over the top though, when I gave him a new watch, for some reason I found it on my wrist. I don't know what I said but I wished them well and left. I was not jealous or anything then, why? I am not sure, once again that feeling was there but probably suppressed by another. Em felt comfy asking me to do little things for her, and one day she was showing me something in her bedroom, it would have not been a problem, for she would take a bath with the door ajar and I never invaded her privacy. But this particular day, I saw his trainers thrown down beside her unmade bed, now bearing in mind, when ever I was to see her the 'good Colin' turned up and when ever I got home, by the time it took me to drive the 4 miles, I was Hyde; and that was what Jana got, much more often than she deserved (memo to Jana, sorry girl).

FRIDAY

Just had lunch and saw that the phone was empty, so I used the opportunity to phone J. He was just stepping into

Angela's place so I had a quick word with her too (always a pleasure).I was trying not to, but I had to ask J If Em has a man, (I would expect it to be the same guy); he said he did not know. I am expecting a visit from the boys in blue, more on that later.

I would say and do silly things and one day against my better judgment, I borrowed money from Junior and took Jana to Jamiaca.I told Em the plan I was going to J.A with Jana, so I will be away for a few weeks, she said to me; she knows she has no right to say it, but she hoped that Jana and I would not be staying at the big house. She wanted it to be our memory; this did not send my trip of to a good start. I had been rather irritable from the airport and had a go at her for shouting at me, J called me aside and assured me she was not. The trip was nowhere as good as when Em was there. Nevertheless, Jana did not have a terrible time; after all, we were in Jamaica. Yana got rugged and liked the hills bush and beach but felt uncomfortable in town. I, on the other hand, basically drank the whole time, staying on a permanent level until I collapsed at the end of the day. I have no idea why, but I decided to rent a car and drive across the island to see Bro, probably just to get on his nerves, you know, "hello Bro you can't get rid of me". We met, he invited Jana and I into his office smiled his smile shook his head from side to side in slow motion and asked me what I want, I said 'lobster', he sent out and got the biggest plate of lobster I've seen, showed us around and we left, after him stating that "you can't say I never give you nothing now'. Back on the other side of the island people were telling me I was 'drinking too much' as I was in a bar, when ever we were doing nothing. Even Trevor said I should "cut down" and he is not one for idle talk. I took it in, but could not pay it any immediate attention. That had to be stored and used later, more slowly like. I had come to a point where he found it fit to give me advice. We got back to England and once again I was in a continuous semi sober state, only people close could know how much I was really drinking. Even Em, for when I was with her I made a serious effort to appear I was getting better. One day she called me up out of the blue (we were always in contact but I never gave her much chance to just phone me) saying that she should never have left me, she was babbling so I told her to calm down and we met by a coffee shop in Kennington. She burst into tears and was telling me she wanted us to get back together. I was over the moon, I had to get rid of Jana, (don't worry it's not that sinister). Jana was still living with me and for all that she did for me and even though I was the emotional antenna lackey in the relationship. She saw I had a problem and stuck buy me, so I could not just "get rid of her". So you see my dilemma; I need Em and Ky back together with me but I did not know how to go about it. First things first , I cut back on the booze gradually being able to do with a few days off completely here and there, getting prepared for the next few chapters in my journey with Emilie. We started sleeping together again even though Jana was still at the flat. If under different circumstances and I were younger I would probably have thought I was a right jack the lad, I was with Em because, we had to be together. I was with Jana because I could not find a way of expressing how truly sorry I was, although they never spoke to me about the two of them, they knew I was sleeping with the other. It was Em that finally bought it to me in a conversation leading to; when are you going to tell Jana? It took a few weeks for me to finally get the 'bottle'. I explained that it was because of my family and I had to do everything that I could to keep us together. Em came to the flat on the same evening; Angela had popped in on one of her famous flying visits and junior was present. Jana was in the bedroom and would not come out. Em with Ky in the front room with the rest and I was bouncing back and forth trying to make it all feel under control, I did not succeed. Emilee did. She gave me Ky and marched into the bedroom. I had a brief flash back to the encounter on the boat but then quickly shook it off. Emilee spoke to her for about fifteen minutes and they both came out together giggling (I don't know how you women do it, maybe a few more of you should be heads of government). Well, we were back together again AND NOW THE END IS NEAR...

It's just after lunch and I have just had a smoke in cell nine. Just me and the guys. We had a little reason and I have returned to my bunk. I have been running through my journey thus far, as I usually do before and after writing; one, to reflect on what really happened in this incredibly short space of time and the other, to have a rough imprint in my head as to what happened next. I have been on my bunk thinking about the latter and for the love of anything I cannot remember a very crucial part of my journey. _I know Em had left the other guy some time ago, it was almost like a game to decide who was going to tell the other first, and I know we got back together because I remember her telling me she had told her parents, but I cannot remember us splitting up again, I can just remember me knowing we were not together again and trying pathetically to get back together. I had acquired a flat for Jana which she decorated and did not have to pay rent because, well, just because. Junior's girl had pretty much moved in, so the place was now small for me and I lost the job with the lamps. I can remember having a seriously bad routine, I was out of a job now, and a woman, and I had even more time to drink. I was still trying what was my perceivable best but it was no good. The bad me was closing in on the finishing line and I was spending most of my days outside the off licence and evening out and about just drinking and smoking. It got to a stage were I was going to sleep in the afternoon for a nap so I would wake up about 3, 4 and have to go to a all night off licence for a couple of cans so I could get back to sleep, then wake up at 8, 9 another beer "special brew" (it should be banned),watch TV and start the process over again. I found out now that the first thing I did when I woke in the morning and had a beer, was to throw up as soon as I put it to my head to drink. I rarely made it back home. I was still trying to be rational but with no luck. I invested quite a bit of money in an invention along with J (which I thought was a good idea then and still do now) and was to get some firm or individual interest and get it on the market. We got it patented and got off to quite a good start, but I could no longer stay sober for one complete day. J and his girl could not leave any alcohol_ *around the house or I would surely drink it. The only drink that remained untouched in the house was Kayana's bottle of wine from her Granddad, even though there were times when I wanted to. So somewhere inside of me, something had not given up. But now what? I made some other investments which ended up similar, only this time ended up with me getting into debt. Now, I had never really been that great with the money concept but I had also never really been in debt, not to banks, to people who once trusted me. I was sure I would be able to pay back but, well, you know the story. It seemed that everybody wanted their money back at the same time, letters, phone calls, visits, with everything else going on, not to mention a van I had bought second hand and loaded with near £2000 worth of goods (which could have covered the trivial debts) was parked illegally and the council took it. By the time I could retrieve it, it had been crushed, so that was it. (No, I did not decide to smuggle drugs, as I have told all who I thought would believe, I could not do this just for the reason of money). What little money I was getting now was for booze. I had pretty much stopped eating and even had my fair share of crack cocaine (memo to young people DON'T GO THERE) and knew this was not looking good. I had to make one of the two decisions in my life I never wanted to make. First, I had to get some money so I could answer the phone and not be pissed off every time the door knocks, so I started to make calls to who I knew had the money, and who would not miss it. I got excuses (I guess that's why they have money). Finally and with a heavy heart, after trying my mother, whom I knew would not have it but I asked anyway, through a bit of research, I found my father's number.*

I remember Dell's stories about him, all good and caring and blah, blah, blah. Dell had also told me he doesn't like liars. In my right frame of mind that would not bother me, but I contacted him and found myself acting so... Not me. 'I' was calling him 'Sir'. Can you imagine that? Me? Calling someone, anyone 'Sir'. I do in here but it's my private joke. Anyway, I asked, I told him the problem first so there was no room to question me. If he did, I would have just hung up. To my half surprise he asked "how

much?" and I just blurted out a figure. He said he would take care
of it A.S.A.P.; That was weird, all I had to do was ask, so I must
have been on his mind sometimes, so why did he not make an
effort? If I had never been in this state I never would have called.
Anyway, I did. It took time but the cheque arrived in another
name. As I said, I changed my name before but in one of my states
of mind changed it again, so now I have three different names. But
I did not know if any of them matched. Anyway, all went well. I
paid my debts and tried to get on with life. The next thing I had
to do was find a way to start going forward, I had a spring board
and now I had to use it. I went back to the doctor, there was a new
one on duty and after looking through my records we had a little
chat; he could obviously see from the computer what I was like;
from blood tests, liver count, alcohol level and counselling, etc. He
had an idea what kind of state I was in. We got talking a bit and
I explained that I had just lost my driver's licence and was away so
did not pay the fine (this would not usually be a second thought for
me), so there was a warrant out for my arrest. Now, bare with me
this is important; the police in my area knew me quite well, but
not for breaking the law. I have my own set of laws and they go for
both sides. I have never been what people call a 'grass' although in
my way of thinking, if you are an innocent victim, I believe you
should call the police. It's amazing how many people don't do that,
and that's what they are there for. Anyway, one evening about five
years ago from this date, I was going for a Chinese take away, just
a few doors down from the off licence, when an argument began
to develop. A small Chinese woman was waving a chopper on her
side of the counter and on the other side a big West Indian, mama
type woman was hurling obscenities at her and seemed to be going
into some sort of a fit. A crowd began to form, and not physically
but verbally, taking the West Indians' side (probably because they
could get no more credit, which in that area would not surprise
me). Anyway, police were on the scene; two cars, about four officers
with a WPC. I managed to get the chopper and calm the woman
down (I was a good customer) and I took the West Indian outside
through a small crowd, most of who I knew, and sat her on the

side walk; the crowd were still getting warmed up for trouble but had now turned their attention to the police and while the WPC entertained me and the woman, one police man inside the shop, one at the door and the other idiot single handily starting to orchestrate a riot- some of the crowd were taunting him and he was retaliating in a way that a sensible officer would not. The crowd started getting rowdy and the other two officers came from the shop to 'assess' the situation. The WPC, I could tell, was getting scared but she was a pro and held well. I saw the crowd was going to make a move so I stood up and walked over to the officer who could not do his job properly, and started calmly to tell him that he was going about this all wrong and he should calm down. I heard shouts of 'yeah, dread you tell him!' that grew while I was talking then it grew to laughter. Then all was calm and the crowd began to disperse, which somehow left me with the West Indian woman and the WPC, who was thanking me and saying 'it was getting a bit rough wasn't it?' A bit later an ambulance took the West Indian to the hospital. The WPC was still talking to me, about something to do with me joining the police force. I said I could not put on a uniform and arrest these guys; I knew them and anyway, I was too old for that (35 which means it was nine years ago, oh my how time flies) She said I would not have to wear a uniform and not arrest anyone. I said I would think about it; I did, but I didn't. Anyway, my point being, from that time on, all the police from that station would give me a subtle nod and smile when passing. Two years later the WPC and I bumped into each other at a gas station, she recognised me and asked how I was doing and stuff. But while I am on the subject; some time had passed since that incident. On the way home from the off licence one day, I noticed some police cars a few hundred feet away from my flat, so I with my nosy self popped over to see what was happening. As I am getting closer, I am witnessing a couple of kids on bikes and two or three standing by, none of them more that fourteen years old. Now, there was a police van, two cars with police in it, other police were out of the vehicles stretching their legs then paying attention to the pathetic situation taking place before me, police were terrifying one of the youth, he had a hold of his arm and was saying things to him like "Do you know what it's like in jail? Do you know what the big boys will do to you in prison?" I could not believe it. I stormed passed the leg stretchers shouting "what's going on!?" I walked up to the boy and pulled him away from the sergeant (he had a flat hat on, can you believe it!?) I put him behind me and asked him, the sergeant, "what's going on!?" He, for some stupid reason, was upset and started on about arresting me, for interfering with something, and signalling two police to come towards me, I was like, "you think I'm thirteen or fourteen years old!?, you gatta be kidding, I've already got your number" Then I turned to the one WPC (a bit unfair you might think but I needed an ally) and shouting "what's wrong with you!?, you're a woman, how would you like to see your son like this?" (the kid was holding my hand, still shaking and shivering), then I turned to all of them and said "you have a woman here and you won't let her natural abilities be the one in charge in taking care of a twelve year old boy for one moment?". They all calmed down and when they left I asked what had happened. He told me that he and his friends always play jokes on each other but he doesn't like them any more, because they threw a petrol bomb at a garage (a council garage with nothing in it), called the police and blamed him. The police believed them and they were going to arrest him. I asked him-in a way that he would feel free and obliged to tell the truth- if he did it. He said "no". I believed him. I watched him grow into a full teenager, still on a bike but always calling to me with a respectful smile and wave, "Alright, Dread?" That was a nice story wasn't it? It's funny looking back over my life, no matter what condition I have been in, I've always helped people, and to be honest I don't think I ever will change, it's another one of those feelings related to money. But once again I digress.

TUES 23

𝒴esterday; while I was reading in my cell, Chi chi burst in with five or so other inmates behind him, ranting about something I could not understand. I was not really bothered because the first were two big guys that Chi had been close to since before I came here. Anyway, I soon came to understand that, out of the blue, someone had paid for his release (which goes down as the months pass). He was going home. I put my book aside and lay on the bed taking in the excitement. It was very... unbecoming. While he was trying to pack his pillow case the five lads, including his two 'best mates', were almost fighting for his belongings; ciggs, shampoo, biscuits, books, pens, etc, not a lot of anything. I cry came over thinking something was wrong, Kenny was barricading the gate so no one else could get in and only one person quietly asked me for a pen and paper and wrote, I assume his number, passed it to Chi, and left as he had come. I found it quite shameful that no one was wishing him well. He turned to me and threw me some grease, a pair of head phones, vitamins and a new pair of designer flip-flops. I nodded to him and when "Roll Check!" came, the officer moved all out of the cell and I got up, wished him well, shook his hand and asked him to write his number and address. Three armed Venezuelan police picked him up. So the cell is back to three. I put English on the top bunk and told him straight up, that I could not have him across the way from me because of his constant complaining. I moved Monero from top to bottom (yes, I am running things in here now). As soon as English got up on his bed he started complaining about the four bar ladder being to tough and his feet were killing him. I let him rave for about five minutes and then told him he had to "Shut the fuck up with the complaining and grow up, mom and dad are not here and everyone in the cell has far bigger problems than small roaches and soft feet!"

27TH

Well, things have had a swing for me now. I guess it's about time, for as usual, when I have felt better in the past, another one of those curved balls is thrown at me, although this time it's different. I feel quite nonchalant about the whole thing; let me explain; I thought that the police were coming here to interview me about a search that took place at my flat just after I got arrested here but in fact it was two of J's lawyers; an Aussie and a quite likeable English woman, rather large arresting eyes, very pleasing to look at. They had come for a statement that could possibly be used against me but could help Junior immensely. I told the truth and signed the papers and now await the effect (at the moment it's Junior's story, so as a rule of this book I cannot go any further). I was however warned that the statement could be incriminating and I may also be extradited to testify and face trial, if found guilty, face four to five years in England. Isn't that something? I am on the verge of finding the solution to my life long problem. I was getting ready to challenge life with all the zest I once had, but without the baggage, and now this. Well, I have just looked through the cell bars and I see directly across from me into another cell. They are shaking a one gallon container of the 'stuff' they distil. I have not seen any or thought about it for ages, what timing huh? But have no fear; I think if I want to kill myself I would rather put a bullet through my head now. These circumstances having not changed what happened and may or may not have an effect on the story so far; so I am going to rush along and hope I can finish without a diversion or interruption, wish me luck. One thing before I sign off from Bordelais; I am already regretting having English in my cell. Now, where was I? *Ah, yes, the warrant. I was paranoid about being arrested (actually, around this time I was paranoid about everything). I asked the doctor if I had to spend six months inside could I receive psycho treatment and tablets. I don't know if his answer was off the cuff or what, but he said "to tell you the truth, I think you would be better off in prison". For a while, I took that statement very seriously but did not act straight away. I was going through another 'Mister nice guy' period and really trying as always, to hang on. Gemma and J would leave food for me and I would eat this time around. I began to look better, not much, but I did. I had the craving and I thought I could beat it. Emilie was smiling more with me now and things were looking up. I began to drop hints (maybe too heavy) about how much I loved her and how I truly wanted us to be a family again. She stated something to me that I also took very seriously; she told me that it would take at least 'Two years' before she could consider coming back with me and within those two years I would have to prove worthy. Now, as things were going when 'Mr nice' was in town, I was always optimistic about everything and I thought; I could do this. However, one night at home while watching a movie, the door knocks. I have never had problems with the local lads, even though some of them are... undesirable. Over the years I have helped many of them out of awkward situations so I was quite respected in the area (that was of course until they noted my steady decline, and saw an advantage point). Anyway, upon opening the door, one of the locals was standing there with a 'demo tape' (he is a gifted singer and I promised to listen to it and pass it on to a studio boss I know), so I let him in. He was with another lad who I did not want in the house so I closed the door on him. Inside the flat all was well, then he started talking about how he had just come from my son's club and my son refused to let him in. He actually told J he was going to the flat to rob him. J did not take him seriously and did not phone me, so there I am quite unprepared. On a good day and being prepared, I would have felt up for the challenge -even though this guy has a history of fire arms and knife violence. As it goes; I found myself cornered in my own flat. I was defeated before anything happened and although I would not let him touch J's jewellery, which was on the side, he picked up his work vest. The probability of him having a weapon and knowing he was high, drunk or both, helped me make the decision for him to take it. I did see him a few days later and confronted him. He apologised and told me what state he was in when he did it, but during those few days in-between I had hit the bottle again and just as before, it was worse than the last time. What got me into this state this time around, was the way I looked at it; It was the first time since I left Portland I found myself in a probable position where I could not, if they were there, protect my family. When I did find the lad again physical anger had been suppressed, so I let it ride, but the real damage was already done. Now I had reached the bottom and often thought that I would not get back on track. My appearance deteriorated rapidly. I started taking drugs a bit more often even though I did not like it, because it took away the effect that I needed when I drank. I started borrowing money again for ventures which when sober could not remember I had done. J's patience had run out. His girl friend now spoke to me (quite rightly so) as if I was nobody, even Kayana recognised and did not like my behaviour, although the very few times I had her for a day my drink was minimum. I had to drink to stop the shaking and the constant nausea feeling but that left me short fused, and in case you're wondering, no, I was never violent around her, I could not be, but my controlled temperament is not worth writing about and I will always be ashamed. Somewhere along the line, I got talking to Jana who often visited. We would go for walks on which I would practically beg her to buy me a drink, just to get through a stroll along the embankment. On one of these walks she stopped me and with a tear in her eye she told me she could no longer go on seeing me like this (we were just friends now) and she compared me to watching the beached whale dying in the River Thames, that we both saw and watched helplessly earlier that year. That also registered painfully, I knew I was going out now, I fought and I lost; I tried my last card, I had asked Jana to drive me four hundred miles, close to Scotland, to see the Bonds. If anyone could help, she could. Stupidly enough I carried no booze for the ride, although my tank was full and I had four hours plus reserve, it took one and a half hours just to get out of London, and you cannot get alcohol on the motorway. After a terrible journey and me shaking like a leaf, we got to the small town, thankfully they served Special Brew. I had one, threw up and had another. I was 'fine' we got to the house and over the course of two weeks I poured my heart out but still drank, although not on a very detectible level. I got back to London semi okay and Emilie trusted me to take Ky back to Bina's* _a few weeks later (by train), we had a good time. I thought I was just on the road to recovery when Bina asked if I would 'house sit' for her while she was away. No problem, I thought. Although I was drinking heavily in London, I slowed considerably in Siloth, a very quiet & boring town in Cumbria._

Mrs Bond makes her own wine and often travels to Europe, to see friends and also brings back cheap but good booze, she had everything there, cases of beer, a ten gallon keg of distilling wine, bottles already distilled, Rum, Whisky, Sherry, Port, the lot. I do not know how or why I did, but in the space of two weeks I drank it all. When she came back she showed her disappointment, but she was very understanding (let's put it this way: she was how I needed her to be). I got back to London ashamed of my life and myself. I took a few trips to Amsterdam, I had a friend over there and it was cheap, besides, the red light district was fun. During my last visit I was picked up by someone I had met on a previous visit and rather than take the train we drove to Amsterdam where he was conducting some business. We were in his car and on reaching the circular motorway going round the Dam he kept missing the exit. By this time he had noticed I had been shaking and then he started questioning me on my appearance. I told him it was a 24 hour bug (huh, more like a 24hour dinosaur). The man smoked cigarettes continuously and it did not help my cause. I needed a drink but he would not get off the motorway until he found the correct exit. When he finally did stop to get something, I ran to the nearest shop and bought three bottles of the strongest beer, guzzled one down, threw up and took to the next. He came back and I hid the other two in my coat pockets, we drove off and the next thing I can remember is waking up in hospital with tubes in my arms and a pleasant doctor welcoming me back to the land of the living. I dozed off again and woke two days later. Someone told me the story; apparently an off duty nurse was passing by in her car on the motorway and happened to notice me shaking, and my eyes buldging as if they were 'going to pop out of your head' and it looked as though I 'had burst'. Stuff flew out of every orifice. She called the ambulance and there I was. The doctor said I was lucky _she had noticed and called the hospital, before she acted (message to stranger, "Many Thanks"). In the hospital the doctor confirmed what I already knew; in my state of alcoholism you must not just simply 'stop drinking', the effect can be life threatening and lead to an epileptic fit. After two more days and no sign of my driver, I was told I was fit to leave. I got dressed, packed up some tablets from the doc and then realised my passport, return ticket and money were gone. Still light headed from the medication, I begged the Doc to let me stay an extra night, but to no avail. I could not even afford a phone call or a bus ride, both of which require pre paid cards/ tickets, and to add salt to the wound... It started to rain. I walked the streets of Amsterdam with my suitcase until after dark then went back into the hospital grounds and made my bed in the open air, half sheltered by an over lap of roofing and on top of a warm air vent. I slept... okay. The next day I went to the embassy who phoned (guess who) Jana, the only friend I had at the time. She sent me some money and I was back home within 24 hours. My memory by now was very patchy. I spoke to my doctor here and the police who knew me prior. I got a call from someone who was to take part in something that was not going to work out as planed, then after some arrangements had been made, I went to Emilie and Kayana. I was semi sober but determined. I did not tell Em everything because... well, just because. But I told her I was going away for 'Two years' otherwise my life would be over very soon. I reminded her about her 'Two Year' thing. I remembered the "Beached Whale" and I remembered the doctor's advice. Somewhere deep down, I knew if I could get away from everyone I knew and alcohol, I could find and cope or be rid of my problem once and for all. At the time, I had had Emilie and Ky on my mind as a reward. All was in place, and of all the places in the Caribbean, this location fitted all my needs, including the sentence. The ticket was paid for and things were arranged. I said my final goodbyes to Emilie and Ky and promised I would come back a new man. I know Em did not know the truth, but she was happy that I was trying everything in my power. I had a tearful goodbye and have not seen them since. A lawyer who_ *interrupted me on the grounds that I was 'digging a deeper whole for yourself' (I was a real mess at the time, the police had taken me to the hospital and I was on some kind of tablets) gave a nice speech, and I was charged with illegal possession of Cocaine on the 12.2.2006. I was remanded until 14th Feb and transferred to here. The Bordelais Correctional Facility.*

2ND FEB. 2007,

Twelve days until my year is up, four months to go. I cannot look back in my mind as to what it was really all like, for that, I myself would have to read the book, and that, I will not do until I am at a computer back home. What I can say though, is I have had good times and bad times, I have met good folk and bad, I have laughed but not cried and lived and not died.

I believe I have cured myself of what could, in this country be described as a 'Generational Curse', and in England as a very serious disease. Which ever way you look at it, I was a mess, and I, and I alone, got myself out of it. It may be extreme to you who read this but extreme actions demand extreme reactions.

I got myself here for a reason; I was facing death from alcohol, I could feel that. It was not that people did not want to help; it was just that they could not. But the honesty amongst a certain few did help to promote my decision.

I spoke of feeling comfortable, and I am now, I have this tremendous spiritual like feeling that says I will remain this way for a long, long time. No matter what is to happen to my future I am ready at last to bear it. For my cup is now empty.

I look into the four months left and predict more fights, noise and arguments, laughter, happiness, jealousy, and malice, same as on the outside. I will leave behind some good folk; 'I cry' the little boxing champ, he came out fighting and remains so, like a true champ. Mongroo, my little Rasta brethren, Aza (head bull) the guardian of the block, who assured me after coming to my cell one day and offering me to smoke with him, that; "I am not a bad man English. I just speak with great ortority" then there are others who I have not mentioned or cared to think about, because (one in particular) some are the most cowardly pitiful, poorest excuse for a man that I have had the displeasure of meeting. English, who I do now regret having him in the same cell, has let down himself and his country; I know he will be my Achilles heel. Then there's Kenny; who leaves in four days time and I have to say, maybe baring the Ras is the one person I could say "it's been a pleasure doing time with you."

My status now? I am up there, nobody harasses me, the few enemies stay away, and I get what ever I want in here, without moving from my bunk.

Nicky has not written, but I understand, I just hope she does (I will always love you Nicole... Dad). I have still not heard from Emilie and will not call until I reach England where at the very least I shall print a format of this and send them to the people I have loved in my own way. I wish you all the best in your respective journeys' through this time and space and I hope I have not caused any of you too much pain along the way.

Goodbye.

May 5TH 2008

The Beginning.

We finished this book together, thank you Emilie.

Lightning Source UK Ltd.
Milton Keynes UK
06 October 2010

160838UK00002B/3/P